WITHDRAWN

Miracles on the Hardwood

THE HOPE-AND-A-PRAYER STORY OF A WINNING TRADITION IN CATHOLIC COLLEGE BASKETBALL

JOHN GASAWAY

TWELVE

New York Boston

Copyright © 2021 by John Gasaway
Cover design by Jarrod Taylor. Cover illustration by MUTI. Cover copyright © 2021 by Hachette Book Group, Inc.

Hachette Book Group supports the right to free expression and the value of copyright. The purpose of copyright is to encourage writers and artists to produce the creative works that enrich our culture.

The scanning, uploading, and distribution of this book without permission is a theft of the author's intellectual property. If you would like permission to use material from the book (other than for review purposes), please contact permissions@hbgusa.com. Thank you for your support of the author's rights.

Twelve
Hachette Book Group
1290 Avenue of the Americas, New York, NY 10104
twelvebooks.com
twitter.com/twelvebooks

First Edition: March 2021

Twelve is an imprint of Grand Central Publishing. The Twelve name and logo are trademarks of Hachette Book Group, Inc.

The publisher is not responsible for websites (or their content) that are not owned by the publisher.

The Hachette Speakers Bureau provides a wide range of authors for speaking events. To find out more, go to www.hachettespeakersbureau.com or call (866) 376-6591.

Library of Congress Cataloging-in-Publication Data

Names: Gasaway, John G., 1964- author.
Title: Miracles on the hardwood : the hope-and-a-prayer story of a winning
    tradition in Catholic college basketball / John Gasaway.
Description: First Edition. | New York : Twelve, 2021. | Includes index. |
    Summary: "In MIRACLES ON THE HARDWOOD, author John Gasaway traces the
    rise of Catholic college basketball - from its early days (Villanova
    made an appearance in the Final Four in the first NCAA tournament in
    1939) to the dominance of the San Francisco Dons in the 1950s and the
    ascendance of powerhouses Georgetown, Villanova, and Gonzaga-through
    their decades-long rivalries and championship games. Featuring
    interviews with notable coaches, players, alums, and fans -- including
    Loyola Chicago's most famous and dedicated fan, 99-year-old Sister Jean
    -- to get at the heart of what makes these universities excel at this
    sport. Small in number but devout in the game's spirit, these teams have
    made the miraculous a matter of ritual, and their greatest works may be
    yet to come"-- Provided by publisher.
Identifiers: LCCN 2020042928 | ISBN 9781538717103 (Hardcover) | ISBN
    9781538717127 (eBook)
Subjects: LCSH: Basketball--United States--History. | College
    sports--United States--History. | Jesuit universities and
    colleges--United States--History. | Small colleges--United States. |
    Basketball teams--United States--History. | NCAA Basketball
    Tournament--History. | National Association of Intercollegiate
    Athletics--History. | National Collegiate Athletic Association--History.
Classification: LCC GV885.7 .G38 2021 | DDC 796.323/630973--dc23
LC record available at https://lccn.loc.gov/2020042928
ISBNs: 978-1-5387-1710-3 (hardcover), 978-1-5387-1712-7 (ebook)

Printed in the United States of America

LSC-C

Printing 1, 2021

For Jerri Gasaway

Contents

Contents

Author's Note

It is a truth universally acknowledged that Catholic schools are good at college basketball. When such programs do well over the first weekend or, especially, the first two weekends of an NCAA tournament, feature stories are duly written up explaining how this proficiency came to be. So far, the overarching run of success from Tom Gola and Bill Russell through Dave Gavitt and John Thompson all the way down to Mark Few and Jay Wright would seem to support such an interpretation.

Coach Wright once said that basketball in the Big East, a conference inextricably though not exclusively associated with the Catholic religion, is "like a religion."

My hope is that this book might shed a bit of light on the American paths of both faiths.

It takes an army of players, coaches, scouts, doctors, trainers, and bottleholders to make up a football team. Two or three good players, plus a few spares, and a coach who doesn't drink on the job can make up a winning basketball team, and that can happen to a small school as well as a large one.

—*San Francisco Examiner*, 1956

Introduction

Parish and Plains

O n the day after her 100th birthday in 2019, Sister Jean Dolores Schmidt received a visitor in her office and talked about college basketball. Sister Jean had become a household name as chaplain for a Loyola Chicago team that made a surprise run to the 2018 Final Four. When she was asked by a reporter at that year's NCAA tournament what it was like to wake up and find oneself a national celebrity, she edited the question before answering it: "*Inter*national celebrity."

In her office that day, Sister Jean shifted effortlessly between discussing the X's and O's of the 2018 Ramblers and dissecting Loyola's national champions from 1963. She had observed both teams at close range and, as a basketball addict, her knowledge extended well beyond the Ramblers. Sister Jean spoke perceptively of Bill Russell at San Francisco, as well as of the St. John's teams of the 1950s. She could cite chapter and verse from all of the above, based not on research conducted decades after the fact but on the real-time observations of an enthralled fan.

Speaking with Sister Jean about any 20th-century event leads to a quick mental calculation of her age at the time in question. When

Pearl Harbor was attacked, she was already teaching at a parochial school in Southern California. She was born less than 30 years after James Naismith invented the game of basketball, and her spectating predated the creation of both the National Invitation and the National Collegiate Athletic Association tournaments. The joy that Sister Jean found in watching basketball and the contentment in her voice when noting that Loyola is the only team from Illinois ever to win the NCAA tournament ("We're very proud of that") were both unmistakable. She's also been impressed by what she's seen from Catholic programs more recently and from Villanova in particular.

Consider one pocket history of 21st-century Catholic college basketball: Villanova won two NCAA titles, Gonzaga reached the national championship game, Loyola Chicago made its run to the Final Four, and Marquette and Georgetown appeared in national semifinals in their own rights. During this same span, Xavier earned a No. 1 seed and reached no fewer than three Elite Eights, while Saint Joseph's also received a top seed and entered the tournament with a 27–1 record. Wooden Awards have been won this century by players from St. Joe's (Jameer Nelson), Creighton (Doug McDermott), Villanova (Jalen Brunson), and Dayton (Obi Toppin). Nor will we ever know what might have transpired in a 2020 NCAA tournament that was never played, one in which Gonzaga and, potentially, Dayton might have earned top seeds.

Perhaps the first element to note in such a thumbnail is that so many of the programs named—all of them, actually, except Villanova and Dayton—represent Jesuit institutions. This prominence is a feature not only of Catholic basketball but perhaps additionally of Catholic higher education as it's commonly perceived. While they are a populous and visible presence, Jesuit institutions, or indeed those of any one order, do not constitute a majority of Catholic colleges and universities in the United States. Nevertheless, the frequent conflation of "Catholic" with "Jesuit" persists among the general public, and college basketball is likely one significant contributing factor.

There are nearly 250 Catholic institutions of higher learning in the

United States, of which less than 20 percent play Division I basketball. For Jesuit colleges and universities, conversely, that figure is closer to 80 percent. With but a few exceptions, like Rockhurst in Kansas City, Regis in Denver, and John Carroll near Cleveland, a "Jesuit campus" tends to be synonymous with "men's team that plays D-I basketball." The 11-member Big East conference alone includes no fewer than four Jesuit programs. Jesuits are far less ubiquitous in the halls of the Association of Catholic Colleges and Universities than they are on ESPN. When Loyola faces DePaul or when Fordham plays Manhattan, there are priestly bragging rights on the line in these clashes between different Catholic orders.

Today's successful Catholic programs might fairly be said to stand on the shoulders of 20th-century giants: Mikan, Cousy, Gola, Russell, and Baylor, not to mention Gavitt, Thompson, Massimino, Ewing, Mullin, Gathers, and Kimble. The story of that success is by turns inspiring, surprising, troubling, and illuminating. It is, above all, a story that is both American and Catholic, despite its setting within a sport invented as a means of proselytizing by a Presbyterian from Canada. Catholic colleges embraced Naismith's game in its infancy and never looked back.

Hundreds of colleges of all types, sizes, and affiliations did the same, of course. It's a mark of Naismith's genius that he created a sport whose numerous and dissimilar adherents competed so avidly to be seen as its foremost disciples. In this rivalry dating to the sport's earliest years, we can glimpse the emergence of two distinct traditions of college basketball that have proven to be remarkably durable. These differing variants within the game may be termed the "parish" and "plains" varieties of the sport. They are far from the only such traditions within college basketball, and these nominal opposites are in fact alike and ultimately constricted by the fact that both were uniformly white in their origins. The two traditions are the direct result of a creation story that is itself dichotomous. Naismith invented what is, among its many perfections, the perfect city sport. He was inspired in part by a game he played in the great outdoors as a child on a farm. Parish and plains.

At first glance, the two traditions may appear to have reversed their respective "real-world" roles. The Catholic Church dates back two millennia. Yet within the confines of a mere game invented just 100-some years ago, it is the plains tradition that holds pride of place. In basketball terms, it beat the parish tradition to the spot. The sport itself was created under the auspices and, indeed, at the specific behest of the Young Men's Christian Association. No less a plains giant than Kansas head coach Phog Allen himself took the lead in establishing the National Association of Basketball Coaches in 1927. No less a college basketball landmark than the NCAA tournament itself was proposed by Ohio State coach Harold Olsen, with Allen's enthusiastic and crucial backing, as a response to the parish tradition's inaugural National Invitation Tournament. It is the plains tradition that can claim the closest thing college basketball has to a recognized apostolic succession dating back to the creation: Naismith, Allen, Adolph Rupp.

The plains tradition embraced baroque administrative hierarchies and *ex cathedra* dictates to an extent befitting Rome in the time of Pope Leo XIII. In place of bishops, cardinals, and a pontiff, the plains school of thought installed athletic directors, conference commissioners, and, at the pinnacle of the edifice, NCAA executive director Walter Byers. All the while, in the bounded earthly sphere of college athletics, Catholic programs were displaying as much iconoclasm and independence as any 17th-century Puritan. For years, Catholic programs eschewed membership in the NCAA, and for even longer, they held off on joining conferences.

Notre Dame still fights that second battle in football, of course, but even the proud acolytes of Fighting Irish exceptionalism were brought to heel eventually in basketball. The NCAA rather quickly mopped up all resistance with what became its irresistible tournament. As late as 1970, Al McGuire and Marquette famously loosed one last elegiac blast of rebellion by turning down a bid and choosing the NIT instead. It was a doomed gesture of defiance. Within seven years, McGuire would secure his place in the coaching pantheon by winning the tournament he once spurned. In college basketball terms, all souls now profess fealty to the church of the NCAA.

Naturally, the distinction between the "parish" and "plains" traditions isn't always tidy. Early NIT champions included Colorado, West Virginia, Kentucky, and Utah. Georgetown and Holy Cross both reached the national title game in the NCAA tournament's first decade, with the latter winning it all. In this same vein of stubborn facts, there is Saint Louis University. As early as 1937, the Billikens were members of the Missouri Valley Conference. With SLU's 1948 NIT title, the Jesuits had forged a winner west of the Mississippi, with a coach who was a native of Reynolds, Nebraska.

Nevertheless, a cognizance that college basketball was in large part built on plains foundations endures to this day. That recognition may nourish the persistent differences in styles and emphases between the traditions. Plains coaches pontificate and wax infallible on occasion. Parish coaches are regarded as being more prone to quips and tall tales. The plains school of thought was the first to avail itself of what would much later be termed "analytics," with a former player of Allen's, Dean Smith, leading the way as early as the 1950s. At the opposite extreme at that same moment was the *New York Times* sports section, comfortably situated within the parish tradition and a faithful chronicler of the NIT from that event's inception. Well into the 1950s, the *Times* would print box scores that still listed guards and forwards as "lg," "rg," "lf," and "rf." These were hieroglyphics from a lost age, cryptic markings that referred to left and right guards, and left and right forwards, as though it were still the 1920s. Basketball-obsessed house organs of the plains tradition, like the *Indianapolis Star*, had put away such childish things decades before.

Additionally, the plains tradition has long been fond of portraying opposing coaches as being engaged in chess matches, a descriptive proclivity that at first glance would seem related to this same analytic impulse. Certainly, it's true that, for whatever reason, parish coaches like McGuire and John Thompson would seldom be limned as masterfully shuttling pawns and rooks this way and that. Motivators, recruiters, leaders, inspirations, legends, yes. Chess masters, the conventional wisdom ran, not so much. Be that as it may, both coaches won national titles. The chess metaphor itself can be limiting, and a more catholic definition of coaching excellence may serve us well, particularly if said definition extends beyond the habits and reflexes of both traditions. As Thompson pointed out with his usual acerbic accuracy, the style of play pioneered by Tennessee State coaching legend John McLendon "was considered to be undisciplined—until white coaches started doing it." Amen.

Coaching excellence spans traditions and assumes many forms. In the 1970s, one admiring sum-up of McGuire held that the head coach was a fearless competitor and an exceptionally charismatic gym rat whose X's and O's at Marquette came from his longtime right-hand man, Hank Raymonds, and from his brilliant assistant, Rick Majerus. Among the more cerebral figures produced by the parish tradition, Majerus would be named Saint Louis head coach exactly 30 years after the 1977 national title with MU. At the press conference introducing the new coach, SLU's president, the Rev. Lawrence Biondi, noted that the name Majerus was doubtless derived from the Latin "Magnus, meaning great." To which Majerus, that rotund and perpetually besweatered Sheboygan native, beloved in basketball circles, broke in without missing a beat: "The name is really from Luxembourg, and I think it means 'sausage eater.'"

The parish tradition also produced its own version of the Naismith-Allen-Rupp line of succession. This particular line of descent is more recent in its establishment and unmistakably humble in its origins, yet it has been extraordinarily influential in its own fashion.

Alvin "Doggie" Julian was born in 1901, the same year as Rupp. Julian coached basketball and football at Muhlenberg College before landing at Holy Cross, in Worcester, at the close of the Second World War. His 1947 national championship team included not only celebrated figures like Bob Cousy and George Kaftan, but also a war veteran named Joe Mullaney. Julian coached the Boston Celtics briefly before being replaced by Red Auerbach, whereupon the ex–Holy Cross coach returned to the college game at Dartmouth. What his tenure in Hanover lacked in affiliation to the mother church, it more than made up for in repercussions for Catholic college basketball. Julian gave Al McGuire his first coaching job, tasking the then 26-year-old with overseeing the Dartmouth freshmen. One of the players McGuire had for a year before sending him along to Julian's varsity was Dave Gavitt, who in turn got his start in coaching as an assistant to Mullaney at Providence when the Friars' best player was Thompson. Gavitt then coached under and eventually succeeded Julian at Dartmouth. When Mullaney repeated Julian's sequence and left the college game to coach Wilt Chamberlain and the Los Angeles Lakers, Gavitt became the head coach at PC. The innovations he rolled out as a combination coach and athletic director to build media exposure for Providence in the early 1970s are emulated to this day, including by the major conference that Gavitt, almost Naismith-like, brought into being *ex nihilo*.

All who adore the sport happily pick and choose from both traditions, like the cafeteria basketball fans we all are. Sister Jean, for one, eagerly related that she loved watching Kentucky. Fans of the Wildcats earned points in her book by sticking around in Atlanta after their team lost in the 2018 Sweet 16 and supporting Loyola Chicago against Kansas State in the regional final. She also had a soft spot for a certain Indiana legend. "Of course, when Bobby Knight was still coaching, I loved watching him, even though he was rough-and-tumble. He knew how to coach." There is no need or wish to define one true church of college basketball. Everyone goes their own happy way, enjoying Kansas one day and Villanova the next. The traditions consist of tendencies, not border walls.

On occasion, even the blurriest and most tentative boundary lines between the traditions fail completely. The state of North Carolina is where the parish and plains traditions either joined forces or fought to a draw. Tobacco Road's excellence in college basketball was enriched not only by North Carolina State's hiring of peerless Indiana high school coach Everett Case in 1946, but also by North Carolina's success in prying head coach Frank McGuire away from St. John's in 1952. A Greenwich Village native, McGuire famously built his 1957 national championship team at UNC with players from the New York City area. When one recruit's parents voiced apprehension about their son attending college down south in "Baptist country," McGuire had to promise that he would convert the state of North Carolina to Catholicism in short order. After he had successfully brought his haul of New York talent to Chapel Hill, the coach found that several of his UNC players were making the sign of the cross before shooting, and too often missing, free throws. Finally, McGuire had to inform his players that he had heard from the bishop, "You guys have to stop doing the sign of the cross or improve your foul shooting."

Tracing the story of college basketball's parish tradition confronts today's reader with one wrinkle regarding the game itself. Over the last four decades, the sport has achieved consensus on a preferred set of rules, even as polemical trench warfare over the business model continues into its second century. This on-court status quo dates back to the catalytic moment when the shot clock, the three-point line, and an expanded 60-something-team NCAA tournament field all arrived more or less simultaneously. Call this the modern game.

Before that, the story of college basketball centered on a righting of a systemic wrong, as, quote/unquote, "major" programs at last opened their doors to African American players. That epoch might be termed the "early modern" form of the sport. Going back further still, the rise of intercollegiate revenue sports as a mass-spectator business took place against a backdrop of secularizing evolution, if not revolution, in the academy writ large. When basketball was invented, Catholic institutions of higher learning stood out because of their particular religious affiliation. Soon, the same schools would be seen as anomalous because they had preserved a religious affiliation, period. In this respect the parish tradition's present-day players and coaches carry at least one spark from the Naismith torch.

"Catholic college basketball" here refers to Division I men's teams situated within institutions of higher learning affiliated with the Church by name, by tradition, and, to a lesser extent as time passes, administratively. The players themselves, naturally, have always professed all manner of evolving beliefs, agnosticisms, skepticisms, and disbeliefs.

Asked in the 1970s why Marquette's Bo Ellis always seemed to play so well against the Catholic likes of Notre Dame, DePaul, and Detroit, Al McGuire hypothesized, "Maybe it's because Bo is Baptist." This same ecumenical spirit defines the population of coaches at Catholic programs, to say nothing of the students supporting the teams.

That leaves the Catholic institutions themselves. As of the late 1960s, and in response to the Second Vatican Council, many Catholic universities for the first time made provision for lay representation on their boards of trustees. As of 2001, even Georgetown itself, the nation's oldest Catholic university, had installed its first lay president, a move that would have been unthinkable to the prior 150 years' worth of Catholic educators and, no less, to their critics. Yet somehow, "Catholic college basketball" endures, coheres, and even flourishes as a meaningful signifier well into the 21st century. The mystery of the basketball faith, as it were.

What is it, exactly, that ties Catholic colleges and universities so indelibly to, of all things, basketball? When the question was put to Sister Jean, she admitted that the subject had received her contemplation.

"I've tried to think about that myself," she said, "and I only know what we do here. We have a good coach who teaches these young men not only basketball skills but life skills...I wouldn't even be able to tell you what religion some of the team members profess, because I don't say to them, 'Are you a Catholic?' We don't talk about that. We talk about God...We pray hard, and we pray before every game. Sometimes it's only a prayer. Sometimes I give the scouting report then."

1.

North American Originals

asketball was invented to save Protestant men's souls.

By the dawn of the 1890s, the Young Men's Christian Association had established what it somewhat grandiloquently termed "International Training Schools" in both Chicago and in Springfield, Massachusetts. James Naismith was drawn to Springfield because the novel and still somewhat heterodox vision of the YMCA meshed perfectly with his aspiration to, in effect, evangelize through sports. Naismith was a pious Presbyterian who never swore or touched alcohol yet had played football at McGill University in Montreal. Born and raised in Ontario, he was 30 years old in December of 1891, and his nominal supervisor at the Springfield training school, Luther Gulick, was 26. They were young iconoclasts in charitable yet determined revolt against a lingering remnant of puritanism: the idea that games, contests, and sports were a dangerous and, indeed, sinful diversion.

Gulick labored at length to find an activity specifically adapted for the gym that would go beyond calisthenics, something that would engage the clientele just like outdoor sports did. He asked his students in Springfield to develop such an activity, and Gulick's program statement specified what he was after with laudable concision:

We need a new game to exercise our students—a competitive game like football or lacrosse, but it must be a game that can be played indoors. It must be a game requiring skill and sportsmanship, providing exercise for the whole body and yet it must be one which can be played without extreme roughness or damage to players and equipment.

When the students failed to come up with anything suitable, Gulick turned to Naismith personally and assigned him to teach a class specifically charged with meeting this need.

The rest is history. Naismith's seminal innovation was to not only import the idea of a goal from lacrosse and from the then new sport of ice hockey but to elevate the target. Installing the goal at a height of 10 feet was a necessity born of the training school's particular gym (there happened to be a gallery at that height where baskets could be mounted), but the choice has stood the test of time. Naismith also realized that scoring would summon true skill—in shooting, as opposed to mere throwing—if the ball had to drop into the target instead of going through a vertically oriented goal. A soccer ball was drafted into service (it was, in the vernacular of the era, an "association football"), dribbling was neither allowed nor yet envisioned, peach baskets served as literal baskets, and the first game was played with nine men on the floor for each team in the gym at the corner of State and Sherman in December of 1891.

Naismith's invention was a relative latecomer to the intercollegiate scene, and by the time Iowa and the University of Chicago played a pioneering five-player game against each other in the mid-1890s, football and baseball were already well established as college sports. Educators tended to view this new and seemingly inexhaustible hunger for intercollegiate sports with a mixture of wonder and foreboding, a reaction that transcended religious affiliation. In 1899, for instance, a priest at Georgetown, apparently writing behind the back of his school president, sent an alarmed report on the baseball team's doings directly to his superiors in Rome:

The base-ball "Team" went forth in May on its long tour, to conquer the country. Every evening at 4 P.M., the long-looked for telegram arrived: "Beaten Princeton," "Beaten Yale," "Beaten Harvard." A Prefect had gone with the boys. While in New York they had the hospitality of our College, and were supposed to sleep there; in other places they lodged in hotels. One of the boys, while in New York, went to a…house, and himself related that there the woman drawing a pair of beads from his pocket, instead of money, exclaimed, "You are a Catholic." For the one simpleton who told on himself, how many others did not tell on themselves.

The mention of "our College" in New York coming from a Jesuit at Georgetown in the 1890s refers to either Fordham or, perhaps more likely, St. Francis Xavier on West 16th Street in Chelsea. (The latter would become Xavier High School.) The Hoyas' ecumenical itinerary, which included both games against nascent Ivies and fellow Jesuit institutions, highlights how early scheduling relied on a combination of proximity and familiarity. Eventually, this combination would be formalized by the birth of what today we recognize as conferences.

If early basketball was diffuse and even inchoate in its varieties, as well as global in its reach, it was also structured according to the racial discrimination of its time. There were occasional exceptions, and, indeed, no less a luminary than Paul Robeson played basketball for Rutgers in the World War I era, in addition to starring on the football field. Likewise, future Nobel Peace Prize winner Ralph Bunche played for UCLA in the 1920s. Robeson and Bunche were preceded in college basketball by at least two Black pioneers that we know of, Wilbur Wood at Nebraska (1908–10) and Cumberland Posey at Penn State (1910–11). Nevertheless, college basketball was, in its essentials, no different from the larger society in which it operated. As a result, the Colored Intercollegiate Athletic Association was formed in 1912, which included Howard, Shaw, Lincoln, Virginia Union, and Hampton. The

Southern Intercollegiate Athletic Conference, established in 1913, was also founded by and for African Americans, and took in Fisk, Talladega, Jackson, Morris Brown, Tuskegee, Clark, Alabama State, Morehouse, and Atlanta University.

The passion elicited by an entirely new sport and exhibited by college students irrespective of race, gender, religion, or geographic location constituted an American common denominator at a time of increasing peril for the Catholic form of the game. At the start of the 20th century, an observer could even be forgiven for assuming "Catholic college basketball" might soon be a thing of the past. Its existence was imperiled by the fact that the Catholic colleges themselves were suffering from declining enrollments.

This time of uncertainty in Catholic higher education marked a surprising turn of events for a tradition that traced its roots to 1789 with the establishment of the Jesuit academy that would become Georgetown University. The Society of Jesus, as the order was formally known, had been founding colleges across the globe since the time of Saint Ignatius in the 16th century, and the early establishment in the United States of Jesuit schools like Georgetown and Saint Louis did not go unnoticed by other Catholic orders. Mount St. Mary's in Maryland, founded by the Sulpicians, predated Saint Louis, while Jesuit institutions like Fordham and Holy Cross were established at the same historical moment in the 1840s as Villanova (Augustinian) and Notre Dame (Congregation of the Holy Cross). By the time of the American Civil War, Italian Jesuits had leapt all the way to the west edge of the continent and opened both Santa Clara and what would later become the University of San Francisco. Opportunities beckoned in a vast nation that lacked any national establishment of religion. Founders of Catholic colleges in the 19th century competed avidly against Protestant denominations and, to an extent, against rival Catholic orders, in what historian Kathleen Mahoney termed "the free market of religion."

The quandary facing many of these Catholic educators by the first decade of the 20th century was that they were failing in the free market. Catholic undergraduates voted with their feet in favor of Ivies and state schools at the expense of, among others, Fordham, Saint Joseph's, and Boston College, Jesuit colleges that had been purposefully and ambitiously established in some of the nation's most populous and most Catholic cities. Boston College saw its enrollment drop 29 percent in five years, and student populations at Holy Cross and Georgetown were also dwindling.

From the perspective of these Jesuit educators, outright anti-Catholic discrimination in admissions by their secular competitors might have, paradoxically, presented a less formidable challenge. Instead, their students were being poached by the likes of Harvard, Penn, Michigan, Wisconsin, and Yale, even as their educational methods and very existence as colleges were being dismissed as relics from a benighted past. When a few Jesuits resorted to making slight revisions to their venerable 300-year-old program of study, the *Ratio Studiorum*, an American cleric explained to Rome that it had to be done. "In our Province we were almost in the final crisis," he wrote. "Boston College and Holy Cross were at war with Harvard." This kind of adaptation *in extremis* was soon widely emulated, as Catholic colleges gradually but unmistakably adjusted their curriculum.

By the 1920s, students on many Catholic campuses could for the first time declare a major, fill at least a portion of their schedule with selections from a broadening range of electives, encounter Greek as an option instead of as a requirement, and even, in an increasing number of instances, continue their studies in Catholic graduate programs. In addition, Catholic educators took pains to update their campuses outside the classroom in terms of governance. Where Boston College students had once been forbidden to so much as receive mail, BC and other Catholic colleges now loosened strictures on curfews and off-campus travel, improved their facilities, and, not least, defended and even championed the presence of intercollegiate sports.

The birth of Catholic college basketball was therefore distinct from both the sport's religiously motivated invention and from its introduction as a novel bit of recreation on the rest of the nation's campuses. For the YMCA, basketball had been an attempt to mint virile and devout Protestant men in the heart of modern cities, which, it was widely held, tended to shrivel muscles and corrupt souls. Alternately, for elite colleges that were secular either in letter (Michigan, Wisconsin) or in newfound spirit (Harvard, Yale), the sport was an exceptionally popular winter activity, which soon became a moneymaker. But in the hands of Catholic educators, basketball was additionally an acknowledgment and even an affirmation of a particularly American strain of their faith.

This was a strain that, within a church famous for devotions paid to hierarchy and custom, went to some lengths to sustain an entirely student-led groundswell of passion for a new arena of campus life: Catholic intercollegiate sports. It was a bold stroke, which, to be sure, could have played out differently had early-20th-century technology allowed church leadership to realize its transoceanic wishes in real time. Authorities in Rome could be forgiven if they were bewildered by the reports they were receiving. The Catholic Church had been founding colleges all over the world for centuries. Now, suddenly, underlings in charge of a few precariously situated institutions in the United States were insisting that "basket ball" and other frivolities were somehow important. Educators at places like Georgetown and Notre Dame may have appeared to their superiors as though they'd "gone native." The phrase could be used with a certain bureaucratic correctness as late as 1908, for only then did the United States cease to be classified officially as "mission territory" by the Vatican.

As Philip Gleason put it in his history of American Catholic higher education, football in the 1920s "brought Notre Dame national recognition unprecedented for a Catholic institution of higher education." Catholic college basketball, like college basketball itself, would have to wait for its own breakthrough on the national stage. But not for long.

In 1920, when the Vatican warned American bishops about the danger supposedly presented by the YMCA, authorities in Rome encouraged their stateside brethren to create expressly Catholic youth organizations.

Holy Name Societies soon popped up in Chicago, an initiative that included a basketball league said by historian John McGreevy to have developed "fierce (and to outsiders incongruous) rivalries" between parishes with otherwise pacific names like Little Flower and Immaculate Conception. Uncannily echoing terminology used by Protestants like Naismith and Gulick three decades earlier, George Cardinal Mundelein of Chicago lauded Catholic sports in 1932 for "rescuing our boys from speakeasies, gangster hang-outs, street corners, and from the other temptations that lie in wait for discontented youth."

It has even been said that muscular Christianity had by this time gone Catholic, that what was largely a spent force within Protestant circles by 1930 was alive and well in the Archdiocese of Chicago. That was the year Bishop Bernard Sheil of Chicago founded the Catholic Youth Organization. The new CYO's creed captured perfectly the early-20th-century American Church's aspiration to be seen as both proudly Catholic and unquestionably patriotic. The creed cited four historical figures and one contemporary leader: Jesus, Thomas Jefferson, Abraham Lincoln, Leo XIII, and Pius XI.

Chicago's CYO was unusual at the time for its explicitly interfaith and, indeed, interracial character. YMCAs in the Windy City were segregated, but in theory the gleaming new CYO center in the Loop would open its doors to all young Chicagoans. Possibly, this reflected credit on the Church in general or on Bishop Sheil in particular, who in 1942 stated his conviction that "Jim Crowism in the Mystical Body of Christ is a disgraceful anomaly." Then again, the American Church, as we shall see, plainly contained multitudes on this front. So, too, did Chicago itself.

In 1930, the University of Chicago broke with precedent in its national high school basketball tournament and excluded Chicago Public League champion Wendell Phillips High School. The Phillips roster was made up entirely of African American players, and the university instead awarded the Public League's automatic bid to the all-white runner-up, Morgan Park. Nevertheless, events would prove that the basketball world stood to benefit immensely from the players Phillips produced. The school had already furnished Abe Saperstein with the nucleus of talent he needed to create the somewhat misleadingly named Harlem Globetrotters. In the late 1930s, Phillips would also contribute the entire starting five to one of college basketball's earliest Catholic dynasties, at Xavier University of Louisiana—then, as now, the nation's only Catholic historically black college or university.

College basketball had already experienced a building boom in the 1920s. Storied venues like the Palestra at the University of Pennsylvania, Hec Edmundson Pavilion at the University of Washington, Williams Arena at the University of Minnesota, and, on a somewhat more modest scale, Rose Hill Gymnasium at Fordham all date from this era. Also constructed at this same time was arguably the most important venue of all in the development of early college basketball: New York City's Madison Square Garden. As opposed to the arena that has carried the name since 1968, "old" Madison Square Garden opened in 1925 and was built by sports impresario Tex Rickard, primarily as a venue for the boxing matches he had long promoted. With a capacity of 18,000 and a location on the west side of Eighth Avenue, between 49th and 50th Streets, the Garden hosted professional basketball, hockey, and even rodeo, in addition to boxing.

When a 1931 college basketball tripleheader was staged at the Garden to raise funds for New York City mayor Jimmy Walker's Unemployment Relief Fund, Catholic programs were there at the creation, so to speak. Organizers bracketed area Catholic teams in all three games, with Fordham against Columbia in the opener, St. John's facing City College, and Manhattan playing NYU in the nightcap. Officials at the venue had to address the challenge of adapting their multipurpose space to basketball, and newspaper reports the following day gave the Garden good reviews in at least one crucial respect:

> The spectators who sat behind the baskets did not lose sight of the ball, for the back boards were of glass and the supporting structure was at a minimum. Wire struts from the upper reaches of the Garden and slender steel poles that

were cut away at a diagonal angle held the baskets firm and did not obstruct the visibility to even the slightest degree.

While Madison Square Garden had a large seating capacity and transparent backboards, one thing it did not have was a basketball court. The inaugural tripleheader was played instead on a surface described as "marble," one that, whatever its true composition, was characterized by a "slippery sheen" and "lack of resilience." One reporter noted that players "complained of the slippery going, which fairly mocked at all efforts to dribble and feint and use deception." A referee worried at halftime of one of the games that the sport was being denied the showcase it deserved. "Too bad that basketball's first big chance to prove its worth should be spoiled by the lack of a proper playing floor," the official was reported as saying.

One of the reporters in attendance that evening was Ned Irish. The 25-year-old sportswriter was on hand to cover this tripleheader, which would raise some $20,000 for the Unemployment Relief Fund. Irish looked past the issues caused by the playing surface and saw an opportunity for less charitable endeavors. He realized that, unlike the small on-campus gyms where New York–area teams played their home games, the Garden could comfortably seat a school's entire student body. Irish also envisioned all those paid admissions luring name-brand programs from all over the country to make the trek to New York, even if it was for just one game.

The young journalist was a keenly interested observer when Walker hosted a second fund-raiser at the Garden on February 22, 1933. This time spectators were presented, remarkably enough, with a one-day seven-game festival of college basketball. (Games did not take as long to play then as they do now.) The gate receipts from that event convinced Irish that even a less ambitious two-game program could be profitable.

The Garden had a true basketball floor by the end of 1934, when Irish tested his hunch by bringing Notre Dame to the city to face local favorite NYU as part of a doubleheader. It was a shrewd bit of programming. The team from South Bend, Indiana, boasted one of the biggest brands in college sports as well as a nationally celebrated two-sport star in Edward "Moose" Krause. The game was a commercial success if not an overwhelming display of offense (the host team prevailed 25–18), so much so that Notre Dame and NYU would henceforth play each other annually until the mid-1950s.

Irish never looked back. He quit journalism, and by 1936–37 he was drawing upwards of 140,000 fans for 12 games per season at the Garden. Other cities followed Irish's example, and college basketball extravaganzas became fixtures at large venues like Boston Garden, Convention Hall in Philadelphia, and Chicago Stadium. As Chad Carlson puts it in his invaluable history of early college basketball, the games at Madison Square Garden in the 1930s "began the process of creating a national basketball consciousness."

With college basketball firmly ensconced as a mass-spectator event in the Big Apple, Irish held his first National Invitation Tournament at the Garden in March of 1938. This inaugural NIT crowned Temple as its champion and stood out in retrospect for not having a single Catholic school in its field, a state of affairs that would not be replicated in the event's bracket for another 79 years. While the NIT was still getting off the ground, Kansas City had hosted the inaugural "National Intercollegiate basketball championship tournament" the previous year in its newly opened Municipal Auditorium. For the better part of the next 15 years, New York City and Kansas City would function as rival power centers in college basketball, a state of affairs that introduced new tensions within the National Association of Basketball Coaches.

The fact that Irish personally profited from the NIT was a point of contention with a number of coaches, and in particular with Phog Allen, NABC founder and longtime head coach at the University of Kansas. In the immediate aftermath of the first NIT, the NABC considered a proposal from Ohio State's Harold Olsen for a national basketball tournament that, like existing national championships in swimming and track and field, would be sponsored by the NCAA. In Olsen's model, this new tournament would be distinguished from

Kansas City's National Intercollegiate event by excluding smaller colleges and in welcoming only major programs. Crucially, Olsen proposed additionally that an NCAA tournament should direct its revenue to its participants and not to "outside promoters." The NCAA agreed to lend its name to a national basketball tournament while stipulating that the NABC would have to run the event and pay off any debts if gate receipts failed to cover expenses.

As the NCAA prepared to host its first national basketball tournament, the NIT held its second annual event. While the tournament at Madison Square Garden had already pulled in far-flung participants, NIT officials reserved two bids for "local" teams. On the whole, the resulting fields therefore tended to be both more eastern and more Catholic than early NCAA brackets. Indeed, programs like 1939 NIT runner-up Loyola Chicago were not yet even members of the NCAA. The Ramblers defeated St. John's in the semifinals, thanks in no small part to the nine blocks registered by 6-foot-9 Mike Novak. Though blocked shots were decades away from being tracked as an official statistic, sportswriters often kept their own counts. Goaltending was yet to be prohibited in 1939, and Novak positioned himself at the basket and methodically swatted shots away on their downward flights. When Loyola faced Long Island University in the title game, however, Blackbirds coach Clair Bee instructed his players to arc bank shots over Novak. Loyola's star recorded zero blocks, and LIU won the title 44–32.

Bee's roster made plain another characteristic that clearly distinguished the NIT from competing postseason events. In effect, the tournament at the Garden broke its own color line before it ever had one. LIU's African American standout Dolly King had already played in the first NIT in 1938, and he returned to lead his team to the championship in 1939. Players from both LIU and Loyola were given commemorative wristwatches by the NIT's organizers, and every team in the field received gold medals. Games at the Garden were played against a backdrop of large and rather visible amounts of cash, leading to questions that would persist for years regarding alleged violations of the sport's amateur mandate, and possibly even outright point shaving.

LIU was not the only team that could claim a national title that spring. Oregon won the first NCAA tournament in 1939, an eight-team affair that culminated in a championship game in Evanston, Illinois. Villanova that year nominally earned the distinction of being the first Catholic program to appear in a Final Four, inasmuch as the Wildcats defeated Brown and reached the semifinals before losing 53–36 to Ohio State. Then again, the term "Final Four" is an awkward fit both for an eight-team bracket and for a tournament that was over a decade away from advancing its four semifinalists to one site in a single-elimination bracket. Just as the NCAA had feared, the event in question did indeed lose money. The tournament might have been discontinued after just one year had it not been for two key backers: Phog Allen and, more surprisingly, the previously hesitant NCAA head office itself.

"It is entirely fitting," NCAA president W. B. Owens announced, "that the 'prestige' of college basketball should be supported, and demonstrated to the nation, by the colleges themselves rather than that this be left to private promotion and enterprise." Spurred by this new entrant in the field, all three competing postseason events made significant changes in their formats, business models, or both. Sponsors in Kansas City sought to make their National Intercollegiate event more purely collegiate and less "private" by enlisting coaches' participation in forming a National Association of Intercollegiate Basketball and rechristening their games as the NAIB tournament. Likewise, Irish's onetime sportswriting colleagues in the Metropolitan Basketball Writers Association ceded control of the NIT to a new Metropolitan Intercollegiate Basketball Committee more or less evenly divided between secular institutions (e.g., NYU, LIU, CCNY, and newly established Hofstra) and Catholic colleges (St. John's, Fordham, Manhattan, and St. Francis). Meanwhile, the NCAA negotiated for its second national championship game to be played in Kansas City's spacious Municipal Auditorium at a time that would not conflict with the NAIB event.

Timing was crucial for three tournaments vying for March dates in two venues. Teams in this new era of multiple postseasons benefited from a buyer's market, as the NCAA had yet to lock in exclusive agreements with its tournament participants. Coaches were still free to enter both the NCAA tournament and the NIT, and in 1940 that's precisely what Colorado and Duquesne did, becoming the first programs ever to appear in both events in the same year. The Buffaloes captured the NIT championship with an 11-point victory in the title game over the Dukes. A Spiritan institution founded in Pittsburgh in 1878, Duquesne was led by Moe Becker, Ed Milkovich, and Paul Widowitz in 1939–40. The trio was dubbed the "Iron Dukes," and head coach Chick Davies's group beat defending NIT champions LIU during the regular season before losing to eventual champion Indiana in the NCAA tournament semifinals.

If teams making appearances in both events was a taste of the new normal, backers of the new NCAA tournament wanted no part of it. Allen, in particular, was unhappy, writing to Olsen that the NCAA tournament was "an educational project and the [NIT] is nothing but a promotional venture which strikes at the heart of our tournament."

The "promotional venture" was triggering outrage in its own right and, specifically, incurring the wrath of Seton Hall. Passed over for membership on the NIT's new governing body, the MIBC, the Pirates occupied a somewhat anomalous position for a Catholic program located in New Jersey, less than 20 miles from Madison Square Garden. It often seemed Seton Hall was regarded as a New York team everywhere except in New York. During the entirety of the 1940s, the Pirates would play just two regular-season games at the Garden, both times as guests on LIU's home floor. The 1940 NIT extended "local" bids to LIU (19–3) and to St. John's (15–4) but not to the Hall (19–0). Weighing in on perhaps college basketball's first great selection committee controversy, the New York Times suggested that "tournament selectors will do well to avoid New Jersey for a while." Honey Russell's team did accept a bid the following year and ended the season 20–2 after reaching the 1941 NIT semifinals, but the injustice of an undefeated and unrewarded 1940 campaign would echo down through the ages in Jersey.

If the NCAA tournament and the NIT were competing so fretfully and even ferociously, this fact alone suggested postseason college basketball was, for the first time, thriving. When the second NCAA tournament turned a profit in excess of $9,000, Olsen stated that his brainchild had "unquestionably" demonstrated that it was "the outstanding basketball event in the country." The year 1940 therefore marked something of a turning point. Fordham and Pittsburgh had played college basketball's first-ever televised game that February at Madison Square Garden. The broadcast was carried on a precursor to what eventually became WNBC in New York, and the game itself was distinguished by an estimated 15-to-1 ratio in its on-site versus at-home viewership. Nevertheless, the NCAA began selling broadcast rights for its tournament. The exclusive authorization to carry the 1941 title game on radio brought $140 into the organization's coffers. Rights agreements netting the NCAA higher sums would follow.

On the eve of the Second World War, a wholly North American trinity of innovations had thus been established in the form of Catholic college basketball. First, there was the game itself. The true depth of James Naismith's genius, or possibly that of his sport, was by this time clear. Second, the Catholic Church's archipelago of stateside colleges and universities had survived its time of trial in the early 1900s. Third, college basketball was now a flourishing revenue sport.

BASKETBALL BOOMS, trumpeted the *New York Times Magazine* in 1939. "What is the secret? Primarily, basketball is a lot simpler to understand, and more continuously exciting, than either baseball or football."

2.

The Mikan Reformation

𝕴n the months following Pearl Harbor, no one knew if, or for how long, college basketball would continue to be played. The NCAA suspended national championship events in several sports. When the draft age for military service was lowered from 21 to 18 in November of 1942, many universities suspected restrictions to basketball could be next. A fair number of basketball programs simply disbanded, and a few colleges went so far as to eliminate athletics entirely. Nevertheless, life during wartime ended up providing enough space, barely, for a sport that required five players on each team.

The federal government's massive expansion of on-campus military training for specialized personnel was a clear benefit for athletic departments attempting to continue some or all of their sports. In particular, the US Navy's V-12 officer training program was something of a godsend for a Catholic school like Marquette, which purchased one hotel building outright and rented another just to house all of its enrolled officer candidates. The Navy's program even came to be studied by enterprising basketball minds as its own form of recruiting once the NCAA, in an act of wartime necessity, granted immediate athletic eligibility to V-12 transfers. This infusion of military trainees, along with the widespread adoption of freshman eligibility for varsity sports in 1943, helped supply enough players for both the NCAA tournament and its archrival, the NIT, to be held annually throughout the war.

Basketball in wartime even afforded opportunities for experimentation. Necessity was mothering more inventions than ever before on the home front, and what might be called a first great reformation of college basketball began in the mid-1940s. That reformation would continue into the early 1950s, and today we still live with many innovations and changes that occurred in the years spanning the arrivals of George Mikan and Bill Russell. Relative stability was achieved nationwide with regard to basketball's rules in this period, and, with the prohibition on goaltending, the game for the first time began to assume something approximating its modern form. The first "real" Final Four, with both semifinal games played at one site, would be held. By the end of this period, the NCAA tournament was solidifying its exclusive role as crowning the sport's single and, effectively, undisputed national champion. The AP poll was introduced. And, not least, the modern NCAA, led by Walter Byers, emerged as a sovereign regulatory entity in the wake of a major point-shaving scandal.

More urgent than all of the above was college basketball's most fundamental change. By the end of the 1940s, the sport was at last starting what would be a 25-year transition, one where major college men's basketball ceased to be, effectively, all-white and, instead, more closely resembled the population of the United States. Catholic programs have often been credited with playing a praiseworthy role in this midcentury movement, credit that nevertheless acknowledges that the coaches in question were interested primarily in winning games. To the extent that, famously, the University of San Francisco thrived in the 1950s in part by emphasizing Black players to a greater degree than was customary at the time, or insofar as Loyola Chicago won a national title in the 1960s while embracing the same dynamic, some measure of credit is deserved. That credit, however, does not belong to Catholic schools alone.

As noted in the previous chapter, Dolly King led Long Island

University to the 1939 NIT title. In addition, Jackie Robinson played basketball for UCLA starting in 1940, followed by Don Barksdale, immediately after the war. Toledo standout Davage Minor reached the finals of the 1943 NIT. Dick Culberson broke the Big Ten color line as a substitute at Iowa in 1944, and Bill Garrett was a starter and eventual All-American for Indiana as of 1948. At Catholic programs during this same moment in the late 1940s, Ben Bluitt averaged seven points a game across his junior and senior seasons at Loyola Chicago, and, more famously and fatefully, Chuck Cooper starred for Duquesne.

In short, credit for breaking down these barriers goes primarily to the players. Past that, any laurels are not so easily divided according to institution type. Geography was often just as weighty a factor, as demonstrated by what was required for one Jesuit institution to open its doors to Black students during the war. Taking such a step in the 1940s set off a bitter struggle and was played out in headlines across the country.

On February 11, 1944, the Rev. Claude Heithaus rose to deliver a homily at St. Francis Xavier College Church on the campus of Saint Louis University. He had given copies of his message the day before to SLU's student newspaper, the *University News*, and to the *St. Louis Post-Dispatch*. In fact, a *Post-Dispatch* editor was seated in the choir loft. The editor would call the newsroom with the go-ahead to run the story for the afternoon edition if and when the 45-year-old priest delivered the homily as written. It was 8:45 on a Friday morning, and in the pews sat 500 sleepy SLU undergraduates, who had been compelled to attend.

Heithaus began: "It is a surprising and rather bewildering fact that in what concerns justice for the Negro, the Mohammedans [Muslims] and the atheists are more Christ-like than many Christians."

Now the students were listening. Heithaus had been moved to action when he came across a copy of the *Pittsburgh Courier*, a prominent African American newspaper. The *Courier*'s February 5 issue was hard to miss, featuring as it did a headline that stretched across the entire front page: WHY JIM CROW WON AT WEBSTER COLLEGE. In an "open letter," the *Courier* lashed into the St. Louis archdiocese for refusing to admit an African American to Webster, its college for women. Behind the scenes, the nuns at Webster had wanted to enroll the young woman, but they had been, in effect, smiled off the idea by their archbishop. "Their Mother General went up to see the archbishop," Heithaus would recall decades later. "He gave them one of those wonderfully ambiguous answers, in which you couldn't positively say that he was opposed to it, but you would feel mighty afraid to do it."

In similar fashion, coeducational SLU was itself nominally considering whether to enroll African Americans. Heithaus went straight to the student body with his appeal:

> Listen to me. Saint Louis University admits Protestants and Jews, Mormons and [Muslims], Buddhists and Brahmins, pagans and atheists, without even looking at their complexions. Do you want us to slam our doors in the face of Catholics, because their complexion happens to be brown or black?

By noon, the *Post-Dispatch*'s write-up was on the streets: ST. LOUIS U. STUDENTS ASKED TO BACK ADMITTING NEGROES. The newspaper reported that Heithaus "asked the 500 students to rise if they shared his convictions. No one remained seated." Or, as one 21st-century article's title put it when recounting the events of that day, "Even the pews stood up."

SLU's president, however, was incensed that he had not been consulted by Heithaus. "It is unfortunate that, because Father Heithaus is a Jesuit, people will think his sermon reflects the opinion of the university," the Rev. Patrick Holloran told the *Post-Dispatch*. "I'm surprised that Father Heithaus spoke publicly on his personal opinion in the matter at this time. I told Father Heithaus so."

John J. Glennon, the archbishop of St. Louis, was equally unhappy. Archbishop Glennon had led the archdiocese since 1903, and in private correspondence he would characterize Heithaus as "a rather erratic person, an agitator and a trouble-maker." Holloran and Archbishop Glennon spoke and wrote as though they resented Heithaus for having forced their hand, which was precisely what had happened.

According to the subsequent account offered by Heithaus, the American assistant to the Society of Jesus "peremptorily ordered" Holloran to start admitting African Americans at SLU. Heithaus had succeeded rather spectacularly both in his stated objective and, no less, in ensuring that his days at Saint Louis University were numbered. When Holloran in effect banned Black students from any and all extracurricular activities, Heithaus again took up his pen and wrote "Why Not Christian Cannibalism?"—an article printed in the *University News*.

"Father Holloran was so furious that I was kicked out of here," Heithaus later said, where "out of here" meant he was exiled to Fort Riley, Kansas. In 1945, when the Rev. George H. Dunne voiced support for Heithaus, he too was speedily transferred off the campus. Within months of his ouster, Dunne had published "The Sin of Segregation" in *Commonweal*, resulting in the highest number of requests for reprints in the history of the Catholic journal of opinion to that time.

Holloran would soon turn his attention to finding a men's basketball coach who could win with all the local talent Saint Louis University had assembled by the late 1940s. As we shall see, the school president succeeded brilliantly on that score. In so doing, Holloran and SLU would put their names alongside an illustrious roster of successful Catholic programs of the period.

With no fewer than five NIT titles, four NCAA Final Four appearances, and one outright NCAA championship, Catholic college basketball established itself for the first time as an acknowledged feature of the American sports landscape in the heady years between 1943 and 1949.

The first Catholic program to win a national tournament title in the era of NCAA and National Invitation tournaments was St. John's. A commuter school that educated area students for 129 years before opening its first residence hall in 1999, St. John's was still located in

Brooklyn in the 1940s. The school's sports teams had been called the Redmen since the 1920s, because of their red uniforms. "Redmen" had an additional connotation at the time, however, and it wasn't long before St. John's warm-up jackets featured a large rendering of a Native American wearing a headdress. Joe Lapchick had arrived at the school as a 36-year-old first-time head coach in 1936 after a storied professional career as a player. He replaced the strikingly successful James "Buck" Freeman, who had been hired upon graduation from St. John's in 1927 and who then proceeded to win 85 percent of his games over nine seasons.

When Lapchick addressed his team of collegians, he was occasionally self-conscious about his own lack of formal education and the fact that, unlike his predecessor, he had left school after the eighth grade. Then again, he was a professional basketball legend who had played for the Original Celtics and who, at 6 foot 5, was visibly taller than all but one of his players. The exception to that rule was 6-foot-9 Harry Boykoff, who had scored 45 points against Saint Joseph's in February before delivering his team to the 1943 NIT's doorstep with an 18–2 regular-season record.

Despite 21 points from "Big Boy" Boykoff in a 51–49 win over Rice, it was Hy Gotkin who was the hero in the NIT quarterfinals. Gotkin was invariably referred to as "Little Hy" Gotkin and was, therefore, just as consistently photographed standing next to Boykoff. When the game against the Owls was tied at 49, St. John's held the ball for the final two minutes. After Gotkin missed a set shot with six seconds remaining, he achieved arguably the most remarkable feat of St. John's run to a title, by recording an offensive rebound at a listed height of 5 foot 8. His putback as time expired gave his team the win, and from that point St. John's coasted to the championship. Goaltending was still permitted, and Boykoff apparently recorded several blocks in that manner in his team's 26-point win in the semifinals over Fordham.

When St. John's defeated Toledo by 21 to win the title, Boykoff was named the tournament's outstanding player, with 56 points in the three wins. The season was not over for Lapchick's team, however, as the recap in the *New York Times* made clear: "St. John's will now sit back and await the outcome of tonight's NCAA final, but with more the casual interest, because in the Garden on Thursday night it will be the Redmen against the winner, with the Red Cross benefiting."

The NCAA tournament took on a different look in its fifth year, starting with the fact that both its eastern regional and its 1943 title game would be held in Madison Square Garden. The field looked different too. Teams like Kansas and Illinois turned down bids, due to players being drafted into the military. Notre Dame was offered the District 4 bid that would have gone to the Fighting Illini's "whiz kids," but on March 8, officials in South Bend notified the NCAA that the Fighting Irish would not be participating either. Just 19 days earlier, George Keogan had put on sweats at practice to demonstrate some new sets he wanted Notre Dame to use in an upcoming game against the Great Lakes naval training station. A sportswriter watching practice suspected that the next opponent was being overrated by the coach, who had won 77 percent of his games over the course of 20 years. The reporter called out to Keogan from across the gym, "Afraid of Great Lakes, George?" The 52-year-old coach answered, "You're darned right."

Within hours, Keogan was dead, having suffered a heart attack while reading the newspaper in his home on Portage Avenue. When *South Bend Tribune* reporters started working the phones to gather reactions and tributes, one of their first calls was to the head coach at Central High School. "We were together a few days ago," John Wooden said of Keogan. "He was in fine spirits and remarked how much more he was enjoying the game now than ever before." Under Keogan, the Irish had defeated Kentucky seven straight times between 1936 and 1942. Years later, after he had won several national titles, Kentucky coach Adolph Rupp would say, "Notre Dame taught me what should be done to improve my teams."

These abstentions by Illinois and Notre Dame in 1943 created an unprecedented opportunity for DePaul. In a "normal" season, the Blue Demons might not get a shot at a District 4 bid, which, already in the early years of the NCAA's event, had always gone to a member of the Big Ten. Now Ray Meyer's program was about to play in its first-ever NCAA tournament. Meyer's most promising player was George Mikan, a 6-foot-10 newcomer to the varsity who had personally enraged Rupp the previous month. Mikan's frequent goaltending had fueled the Blue Demons' nine-point win over the Wildcats at Chicago Stadium. Rupp vowed he would do whatever was required to legislate goaltending out of the game. While Mikan was clearly a talent, few could have guessed that in seven short years he would be named the greatest player of the first half of the 20th century by the Associated Press. In fact, in its coverage of the 1943 NCAA tournament, the very same AP would refer to him as "John Mikan."

Under any name, Mikan had to navigate a circuitous route to reach stardom. When he was cut from the freshman team at his high school, Joliet Catholic, Mikan transferred schools to forget about basketball and study for the priesthood. The priests at Quigley Prep had a keen grasp of basketball, however, and soon the young man was playing for the seminary's varsity in addition to making time to lead his parish CYO team. He was given a tryout by Keogan at Notre Dame, only to be rejected as too unskilled. But Meyer saw potential, and soon he had Mikan embarked on a regimen that included boxing workouts, as well as repetitions at the basket—banking the ball in with each hand (known henceforth as the Mikan drill). By 1943, the work was paying off.

DePaul reached what today would be called the Final Four by holding Dartmouth scoreless for 11 minutes and recording an 11-point win. Available evidence suggests that Mikan, like Boykoff in the NIT, was goaltending with relish in the NCAA tournament; for starters, he was called the "goal tender." The Blue Demons' win earned them a shot at Georgetown in the semifinals. Elmer Ripley's team had surprised the locals at the Garden by thrashing favored NYU by 19. Ripley had a dominant big man of his own, in 6-foot-8 John Mahnken, who had scored 18 in the first half on his way to a 20-point outing. While the highly anticipated showdown between Mikan and Mahnken didn't come off entirely as planned (the Hoyas' star fouled out with

10 minutes left, after having scored 17 points), Georgetown worked around Mikan's goaltending with bank shots and earned a 53–49 win. In a bow to Garden custom, which, one imagines, must have raised eyebrows in Kansas City, players from Georgetown, DePaul, NYU, and Dartmouth all received gold watches.

The newly accoutered Hoyas were no match for Wyoming in the title game, however, as Kenny Sailors and the Cowboys secured a 12-point victory at the Garden. When Everett Shelton's men from Laramie then defeated Boykoff and St. John's 52–47 in overtime in a benefit contest that raised $28,000 for the Red Cross, Wyoming could lay claim to a truly national championship. Boykoff left St. John's after his sophomore season, in 1943, to enlist in the armed forces. How he was cleared for service or, for that matter, how he was fitted with a standard-issue uniform in a military that set height limits is still unclear. One legend states that when Boykoff was measured at his physical he straddled the scale instead of standing on it. After two years in the service, he returned to St. John's and set a new Madison Square Garden record in 1947 by scoring 54 points against St. Francis. Following a short stint playing professionally, Boykoff apparently carved a niche for himself late in life as a very tall, elderly actor. He appeared in *Frasier* and in at least one *Star Trek* film, and is said to have been in at least one McDonald's commercial.

Boykoff wasn't the only player who would be absent in 1944 as St. John's defended its NIT title. Andrew "Fuzzy" Levane had been voted the top player in the metro area for 1943, and he, too, had departed. Lapchick would even be without the services of Dick McGuire, who, as a freshman, had succeeded Levane in earning the Haggerty Award as the top "Met" player. A master of the role that would later be referred to as "pass-first point guard," McGuire was something of a legend to his New York City contemporaries. "If somebody would have asked me of all the players who I competed against whose game I most admired," Bob Cousy would say in 2010, "Richard would have been the one I would have chosen."

After starring at St. John's for the balance of the 1943–44 season,

McGuire was drafted into the Navy in February and transferred to Dartmouth as a V-12 officer trainee. Demonstrating a scenario that coaches would vociferously oppose in the 21st century, McGuire was immediately eligible upon arrival in Hanover. With its sensational freshman from New York igniting the offense, Dartmouth reached overtime in the 1944 NCAA tournament title game before falling to Utah. As for McGuire's former team, even with all of its roster turnover, St. John's entered the 1944 NIT with a surprisingly respectable 15–5 record. Gotkin, previously a supporting player and the improbable hero of the Rice game in the 1943 NIT, was now Lapchick's leading scorer.

This time around, there was a chance St. John's would see its fellow Vincentians from DePaul. At 20–3, the Blue Demons were in the enviable position of fielding multiple postseason offers. In the end, however, technology fairly made Meyer's decision for him. DePaul announced that it would be playing in the NIT, but the *Chicago Tribune* explained what had really happened:

> Because of a 20-minute delay in receiving a telephone call yesterday morning, DePaul University's midwestern basketball champions chose to compete in the Madison Square Garden invitational tournament instead of representing the 4th NCAA district in the National Collegiate tournament...
>
> Coach Ray Meyer of DePaul told the [NCAA District 4] committee Friday night DePaul would accept an NCAA invitation but it must be received by 10 a.m. yesterday because of the previous invitation. When a telephone call was not received by 10 o'clock DePaul wired Ned Irish, director of the New York tournament, its acceptance. Twenty minutes later [a District 4 representative] called Meyer. When the Demons announced their selection of the Madison Square Garden offer, Ohio State was named to represent the 4th district.

In an era when coaches were decrying the increasing dominance of "giraffes" in the sport, George Mikan wasn't even the second-tallest player at the NIT. Bowling Green's Don Otten was 6-foot-11, and Oklahoma A&M's Bob Kurland, at an even 7-foot-0, was named the tallest player ever to have appeared at the Garden. This 1944 postseason was to be goaltending's last stand, and it went out with a flourish. If the tracking done by sportswriters was valid, the NIT's tallest defenders blocked six or seven shots at the rim while "playing goalie" in a typical game. Then again, in Bowling Green's four-point loss to St. John's in the quarterfinals, Otten demonstrated one danger of goaltending when he inadvertently deflected four of the opposing team's shots *into* the basket. As for Mikan, he would on occasion catch the incoming shot at the rim instead of swatting it away, thus combining a block and a rebound in one motion. Nevertheless, his eagerly awaited postseason showdown with an opposing big man was sabotaged by foul trouble for a second consecutive March. Mikan fouled out of the semifinal against Oklahoma A&M early in the second half. When the Aggies played the final 90 seconds with just four players due to foul issues of their own, however, the Blue Demons emerged victorious 41–38.

While the 1944 NIT reaffirmed the desire of the nation's coaches to move ahead with a prohibition on goaltending, the event also demonstrated the inadequacy of allowing each player just four personal fouls before disqualification. When DePaul faced St. John's in the title game, Mikan fouled out six minutes into the second half. His replacement, Jack Phelan, then lasted all of seven minutes before joining Meyer's star on the bench. With DePaul being devoured by fouls, St. John's had everything it required to record its eight-point victory. Lapchick's "war-riddled squad" had prevailed against its three opponents—Bowling Green, Kentucky (appearing in just its second NIT/NCAA-era postseason), and DePaul—by a combined total of 15 points. Each win was branded an upset, St. John's forward Bill Kotsores was named the NIT's most valuable player, and Lapchick's team became the first one ever to win two national tournaments in a row. Even a second consecutive loss in the Red Cross benefit game, this time to Cinderella NCAA champion Utah, did not alter the perception that St. John's was among college basketball's elite.

Much of New York City's 20th-century basketball history, both college and pro, would flow from these St. John's teams, as would a fair amount of basketball history, period. Lapchick and one of his star players, Levane, would each take a stab at coaching the New York Knicks. The most successful occupant of that position to this day, Red Holzman, was originally hired as a Knicks scout by Levane, whom he had known since high school. Lapchick's successor at St. John's was Frank McGuire, who had played under Buck Freeman in the 1930s and who would take the job at North Carolina in 1952. The coach famously won the 1957 national title in Chapel Hill with a roster of talent from greater New York, a group that Tar Heels fans adoringly, if somewhat bluntly, christened as "four Catholics and a Jew." And, of course, Lapchick's extraordinary point guard Dick McGuire had a younger brother, Al, who played at St. John's from 1947 to 1951. The two brothers even played alongside each other in college for one season, when Dick returned from military service. Al would become the unofficial patron saint of younger siblings when, in 1992, he was inducted into the Naismith Memorial Basketball Hall of Fame one year earlier than an older brother, who was the vastly superior basketball player.

The St. John's program of the 1940s also affords a glimpse into how a location in New York City, "the mecca" of college basketball, conferred incredible and, to modern eyes, almost inconceivable scheduling benefits. Over the course of Lapchick's tenure, St. John's effectively moved its home floor from tiny DeGray Gymnasium, on the corner of Lewis and Willoughby in Brooklyn, to the cavernous Garden. Access to the Garden was a tremendous programmatic advantage for local coaches, as potential opponents competed feverishly for a chance to play on Eighth Avenue. Particularly with the lifting of wartime travel restrictions after the 1944–45 season, the St. John's home schedule grew top-heavy, with quality opponents from all over the country.

In his last two seasons before leaving to coach the Knicks, Lapchick hosted Kentucky (twice), Georgia, Nevada, Utah, Loyola Chicago, Hawaii, Western Michigan, Rhode Island, Ohio, Saint Joseph's, Syracuse, Temple, and John Wooden's Indiana State team, all at the

Garden. Conversely, in Lapchick's first 11 years as head coach, St. John's played a total of two games outside the eastern time zone, at Loyola Chicago and at Bradley. That two-game road swing in 1940 notwithstanding, the longest distance St. John's traveled over the course of a decade was for an occasional road contest in Buffalo against Canisius. Claiming Madison Square Garden as home court in the 1940s gave a program possibly the best scheduling platform in the history of college basketball.

At the opposite extreme from the lofty perch occupied by St. John's in the mid-1940s was Loyola New Orleans. The Wolf Pack played in an on-campus gym so cramped that the court itself was smaller than standard size. When coach Jack Orsley brought his team to the vast Municipal Auditorium in Kansas City for the 1945 NAIB tournament, one imagines a scene straight out of *Hoosiers*, with Hickory High arriving at the field house. In that same David-and-Goliath vein, the local press didn't always see fit to capitalize Loyola's name. The players even heard through the grapevine that their return train tickets home had already been purchased for use after their first game. Through it all, the Wolf Pack persevered. After John Casteix drained the game-winner against Southern Illinois in the semifinals, Orsley unveiled a full-court press for the first time all season against a much taller Pepperdine team to record a 49–36 win and capture the championship.

If it was surprising that Loyola New Orleans won a national tournament title, it was no less remarkable that the team was able to make its way from New Orleans to Kansas City at all. Scheduling and travel became increasingly problematic both for teams and for postseason tournaments right up until the end of the war. These challenges reached a peak in February and March of 1945, when the NIT expressly sought to keep travel distances to a minimum as it created its bracket. Consequently, all eight teams in the 1945 National Invitation field were located east of the Mississippi.

Nor was the geographic look of the bracket the only aspect of the tournament that had changed since the previous year. The suite of rule changes rolled out nationally for the 1944–45 season was arguably the most sweeping to date. Goaltending was banned, players were now allowed five fouls instead of four before being disqualified, and, for the first time, unlimited player substitutions were permitted.

The modern game was taking shape, and Mikan, for one, was thriving. Contrary to predictions, the prohibition on goaltending was not a problem for the 6-foot-10 DePaul star, who led his Blue Demons to an 18–2 record in the regular season. By the end of the campaign, Mikan would average 23 points a game, thanks in part to the additional foul he was now allowed. True, five fouls were insufficient to prevent Mikan from exiting the contest with 5:02 remaining in DePaul's 24-point win over West Virginia in the 1945 NIT quarterfinals. By that point, however, the Blue Demons had the game well in hand and Mikan had scored 33 points. "The big, bespectacled ace of the Chicagoans was a one-man riot squad," in the estimation of the *New York Times*. That was tame compared to descriptions yet to come. DePaul's next opponent was fast-paced Rhode Island, which played its usual up-tempo style in a concerted attempt to fatigue DePaul's star. The attempt backfired.

Against the undersized Rams, Mikan set single-game Madison Square Garden records for made free throws (11), makes from the field (21), and points (53). The Demons' 97 points also qualified, easily, as a Garden record, as Meyer's team won by 44. Not even a leg injury suffered in practice the following day could stop Mikan, who went on to outscore the 6-foot-11 Otten by 27 in DePaul's 71–54 victory over Bowling Green in the title game. In leading his team to the 1945 NIT championship, Mikan had averaged 40 points a game. The stage was now set for what could have been college basketball's first true No. 1 versus No. 2 showdown. This postseason's Red Cross benefit game would match DePaul with the NCAA champion, Oklahoma A&M. It was going to be Mikan against the even-taller Kurland. The oddsmakers favored the former—DePaul was installed as a five- to seven-point favorite—but Mikan's performance, as well as that of the Blue Demons as a whole, was disappointing. Mikan fouled out in 14 minutes, and he was merely the first of four DePaul starters to exceed the foul limit. In the wake of Oklahoma A&M's 52–44 win, a few eyebrows were raised by the officiating and by the fact that the game had taken place at the Garden. One headline, from a United Press International story, called the speculation a RUMOR MONGERS' FIELD DAY.

Regardless, the Aggies were plainly the equal of DePaul. Indeed, Coach Hank Iba's team would repeat as NCAA champions the following season, the first program ever to do so. DePaul and Oklahoma A&M split a pair of games in 1945–46, with, interestingly, the road team winning both contests. The success that Mikan and the Blue Demons enjoyed in Stillwater, Oklahoma, however, was an outlier. A disastrous midseason road trip resulted in losses at Illinois, Minnesota, and Notre Dame. When Meyer's team reached the end of the regular season with a 19–5 record, there were no 1946 postseason invitations in the offing.

Still, Mikan would be there at the creation as professional basketball came of age. He transitioned through the National Basketball League (with the Chicago American Gears) and the Basketball Association of America before playing in the National Basketball Association's inaugural season in 1949–50 as a member of the Minneapolis Lakers. That was the year Mikan returned to Madison Square Garden, when, famously, the marquee on Eighth Avenue cemented his status as a legend with: GEO MIKAN V/S KNICKS.

Mikan's height defined his game, yet, even at DePaul in the 1940s, he faced taller opponents. He excelled in an era when the college game allowed just four fouls and didn't track rebounds. He flourished both during and after the reign of goaltending. College basketball and the Catholic affinity for the game came into their own together in the person of George Mikan.

3.

Cousy and the Era of the Veteran

On the evening of December 10, 1946, more than 6,000 fans celebrated the opening of the new college basketball season by turning out for a doubleheader at Boston Garden. All four teams in action that night represented institutions that had been founded purposefully and avowedly as religious colleges. Three still embraced that identity and pursued that mission in 1946. Two were from greater Boston. One would win the 1947 NCAA tournament.

Harvard faced Holy Cross in the opening game and, in the nightcap, Boston College played host to Georgetown. Since taking his team to the title game of the 1943 NCAA tournament, Hoyas head coach Elmer Ripley had, surprisingly enough, stayed put at Georgetown. The coach's years with the Hoyas marked a rare stretch of geographic consistency in a career that was remarkably peripatetic. Ripley was the head coach for one prep school (Englewood School for Boys, in New Jersey), two Catholic programs (Georgetown and Notre Dame), two Ivies (Yale and Columbia), one service academy (Army), two Olympic teams (Israel in 1956 and Canada in 1960), and even the Harlem Globetrotters. Future Miami Dolphins coach Don Shula would be just one of the players Ripley would tutor during his long and varied career.

That night at Boston Garden, Georgetown was facing a Boston College program that was still reconstituting itself after a two-decade hiatus. There had been no BC basketball from the mid-1920s until the end of the Second World War, and a 3–11 mark in 1945–46 indicated that bringing the program out of mothballs would be no easy task. Actually, the Eagles would go on to post a respectable 12–10 record in 1946–47, but in the first game of the season they were no match for the Hoyas. Georgetown was led by 15 points from "lanky" Andy Kostecka. Though no one in attendance could have imagined such a course of events, Kostecka was but 13 months away from being dismissed from the team by Ripley. By January 1948, he would stand accused of kicking an opposing player. Nonsense, Kostecka would reply. This was all about a hidden agenda that had long been nurtured by Ripley himself, he said. "Rip hates my guts and always has," a suddenly unmuzzled Kostecka told a no doubt delighted *Washington Times-Herald* reporter. "He has his pets and I'm not one of them."

Georgetown's ex-star was about to learn a lesson regarding the fickle editorial preferences of Cold War–era American sportswriters. The previously lionized Kostecka was promptly dubbed "the temperamental Russian." In his defense, he had seen more of life than the average college senior. Already 26 years old by the time he feuded with his coach, Kostecka quickly apologized for his newspaper outburst, but to no avail. He had played for the Hoya freshman team in 1941–42, and the following year the varsity made its run to the NCAA title game. Kostecka was drafted into the armed forces in February of that season, however, and by the time that Georgetown was playing for a national championship, its onetime leading scorer was en route to the Pacific. He served as an aide to General Douglas MacArthur, and, in August 1945, was one of the first Americans to enter Nagasaki after the dropping of the atomic bomb. Kostecka's biography and his run-in with his coach give one indication of the difficulties veterans faced in resuming their careers as athletes. His travails also illustrate how the war continued to have repercussions in the game long after 1945.

Kostecka wasn't the only ex-serviceman at Boston Garden that night. First-year students were still eligible to play, thanks to a ruling born of wartime necessity a few years earlier, and nominal Holy Cross freshmen like Frank Oftring and Andy Laska, 22 and 21 years old, respectively, were both fresh from the service. Oftring had served three years in the Navy, while Laska's tour of duty as a B-29 gunner in the Army Air Corps had taken him on several missions over Japan. One of their teammates, 21-year-old Joe Mullaney, had piloted a B-26 Marauder. Even Oftring, Laska, and Mullaney were youngsters compared to Bob Curran. The Holy Cross "junior" was 25, and his service in the Navy had spanned some three and a half years. These were veterans in both the demographic and military senses of the term. They were men who had been all over the world, yet in the eyes of history they would be eclipsed by an 18-year-old true freshman who had never set foot outside the northeastern United States.

In December 1946, Bob Cousy's sole claim to renown was that he'd been named All-City as a senior at Andrew Jackson High School in Queens. A 21-point win over Harvard would be the first of seven "home" dates at the Garden for a Holy Cross program that did indeed wear white uniforms in Boston that evening (against an opponent from Cambridge, no less) but that also, famously, did not have a home court. If nothing else, the alliance with the Garden brought money into the school's coffers. The Boston Garden front office allotted 25 percent of the gate receipts to Holy Cross each time it "hosted" one half of a doubleheader 45 miles away from its true home in Worcester.

Just the same, the lack of a home court was a sore spot. Cousy later told of touring the hilltop campus as a recruit up from New York City. "Coach, where do we play?" Cousy asked. "We're in the process of building a gymnasium," he was told confidently. It was a long process. Holy Cross wouldn't open its on-campus arena, the Hart Center, until 1975. During their 1946–47 national championship season, the Crusaders would play three home games at the nearby South High gym. Coach Alvin "Doggie" Julian held his practices in a cramped campus gym described by the *Boston Globe* as "a red barn atop cold Pakachoag Hill."

Though he was coaching without a true home venue, Julian had so much talent on his roster that he utilized a platoon system for much of the season. Cousy led the second unit and was the Crusaders' third-leading scorer, behind George Kaftan and Dermie O'Connell. Blessed with a deep rotation, Holy Cross roamed far and wide in search of quality opponents. Julian committed the Crusaders to playing a four-game stretch spanning December and January on a "western" road trip that would take them to Toledo, Indianapolis, Pittsburgh, and Cleveland. The journey turned out to be more demanding than the coach would have preferred. The opponents Holy Cross faced on its four-game odyssey would eventually win 82 percent of their games in 1946–47. A three-point victory in a true road game at Toledo proved to be the only win the Crusaders would record on their swing through three states. Next up was a neutral-floor match against North Carolina State in Indianapolis. Everett Case was in his first season at the helm of the Wolfpack, and the famed Indiana high school coach was already turning the program around in Raleigh. NC State hammered Holy Cross 58–42, and now Julian's men would face undefeated Duquesne in Pittsburgh.

The Dukes were making headlines of their own. A defining feature of the 1946–47 season nationally would be that it would both open and close with Black players breaking down barriers. Duquesne was at the center of that movement, now that Chick Davies had added 6-foot-5 freshman Chuck Cooper to his roster. When Davies's team traveled to Louisville to play Morehead State, for example, Cooper entered the game midway through the first half. The Louisville *Courier-Journal* hailed his appearance as marking a signal event in the city's history:

> The Morehead, Ky., Eagles lost to Duquesne 53-52 in the last minute of play last night at the Armory. But by living up to their nickname of Eagles, the American Eagle of democracy, they conquered an even more formidable foe—Prejudice.

"Never before had a Negro appeared in a college or high school game in Louisville against white boys," the *Courier-Journal* reported.

"The crowd of 2,500 responded democratically when Cooper entered the contest...There was one loud boo that faded out sickly. There was a patter of applause. Generally the crowd expressed no outward emotion."

Things went less smoothly for Duquesne three days later. The Dukes were scheduled to host Tennessee at the McKeesport Vocational High School, and some 2,600 fans gathered for a game that would never be played. Tennessee coach John Mauer gave reporters his account of why the Volunteers had traveled all the way to greater Pittsburgh only to refuse to take the floor:

> I heard the Dukes had a colored boy on the team two weeks ago and wrote a letter to Chick Davies, requesting him not to use this boy in our game. I never received an answer from Duquesne or Davies and therefore assumed when we arrived here the matter had been settled as we requested. Last year we played Long Island U. in New York and I asked Coach Clair Bee to withhold two Negro players. He did and we played the game.

Mauer had approached Davies before game time to thank him for accommodating Tennessee's request. Davies told the visiting coach that in fact no such agreement had been made. Mauer returned to the locker room, informed his players of what he'd just learned, and allowed them to decide whether or not to proceed with the game. Team captain Ted Cook later gave a statement on the players' behalf. "It's been the policy of the University of Tennessee not to compete against Negroes," he said, "and we players made the decision." When *Pittsburgh Sun-Telegraph* reporter Jack Henry showed Mauer a copy of the Louisville *Courier-Journal* article that had welcomed Cooper's arrival to that city, Coach Mauer replied, "That was in Louisville." Tennessee athletic director and head football coach Robert Neyland announced that he was "100 percent behind" his basketball coach, the team, and their decision to not play Duquesne.

The nongame went into the books as a 2–0 victory by forfeit for the home team, meaning that the Volunteers' refusal to take the floor likely cost the Dukes an actual win. Davies had an outstanding team, one that would remain undefeated all the way to March, when Duquesne would fall 57–39 to Kostecka and Georgetown in a game played at Catholic University in Washington, DC. The Dukes would go on to lose by a point to eventual champion Utah in the quarterfinals of the 1947 NIT, but their 19–0 start had included a convincing 10-point win over Holy Cross in Pittsburgh.

It never would have occurred to Julian to refuse to pit his all-white team against Davies's group, but, coincidentally, the Dukes were merely the first of two consecutive Crusaders opponents that were being threatened with boycotts. Julian was asked, after the loss in Pittsburgh, if he was still going through with the game scheduled for the following day against Wyoming in Cleveland. The Cowboys' head coach, Everett Shelton, had raised a storm of controversy, and for a moment it looked as though the end result might be some form of boycott by opponents against the coach and his team.

Wyoming's troubles had started just before New Year's. In the final minute of a game the Cowboys would lose by nine to CCNY at Madison Square Garden, Shelton and the Beavers' head coach, Nat Holman, were seen exchanging heated words. There was no postgame handshake, and Holman soon shared his version of events with the Garden press corps. "I heard Shelton uttering derogatory remarks and took exception," he explained. "In fact, I threatened to punch him if he repeated them." Two days later, when the Metropolitan Basketball Writers Association held its weekly lunch at Toots Shor's restaurant, Wyoming's coach dug an even deeper hole for himself, by giving what he apparently viewed as an apology.

"I am very sorry that my remarks caused such a disturbance," Shelton said. "However, what I said about Jews had nothing to do with religion or anything else. The word 'Jew' was merely descriptive. I did not swear. In our section of the country, when we play against Indians we call them 'Indians' and we call Swedes 'Swedes.' "

Later that week, the faculty athletic committee at City College enacted what amounted to a lifetime ban on Shelton personally. CCNY teams were henceforth forbidden to schedule a game against any team that had Shelton as its coach. Holman vowed to bring the matter before the NABC (only to learn that Shelton was not a member), while a New York state representative from Brooklyn pledged to sponsor legislation in Albany to "rid sports of religious antagonism."

Had Julian joined the protest and refused to play Wyoming, a controversy that was already national news would have received a new lease on life. Instead, the game was played as scheduled at the old Cleveland Arena, and Holy Cross lost 58–57.

When the road trip came to its merciful end in the first week of January, the Crusaders were 4–3 on the season. Within 80 days, this same team would win the NCAA tournament and finish with a 27–3 record. For observers who had spent the previous four years fretting that the towering likes of George Mikan and Bob Kurland were taking over the sport, Holy Cross represented a welcome change. At 6 foot 3, George Kaftan was known as a "rebound demon" who played a role that would later be referred to as "power forward." Kaftan, Bob Cousy, and Dermie O'Connell were all 18 at the beginning of the season, and Doggie Julian's combination of talented teenagers and war veterans improved as the season progressed. Many of the team's victories came by lopsided margins, and one headline captured both the newfound prowess being displayed by the Crusaders in road games and the boredom being exhibited by fans of vanquished home teams: H.C. DRUBS TUFTS, 71-29, AS COUPLE PLAYS CRIBBAGE.

The closest call for Julian's group came in February when Holy Cross recorded a 44–43 win at Seton Hall. The Pirates entered the game 19–1 and led the visitors for the first 36 minutes, only to fall short after team captain Bobby Wanzer left the contest with a sprained ankle. Julian accepted the NCAA's District 1 bid on February 26 with two games still remaining on the schedule. The tournament wouldn't begin for another three weeks, so to stay fresh in the interim, Julian scheduled a third upcoming game. That explains how a team that was about to win an NCAA title scheduled a road game against New Britain State Teachers College as its last regular-season contest.

New Britain's future teachers actually fared better against Holy Cross than would any of the Crusaders' upcoming NCAA tournament opponents. Julian's team had to rally to win 58–52. Playing in the NCAA tournament at Madison Square Garden, on the other hand, marked something of a homecoming for many Holy Cross players. In addition to New York City wunderkind Cousy, Kaftan was a graduate of Xavier High School in Chelsea, where his civics teacher had been future St. John's and North Carolina head coach Frank McGuire. O'Connell grew up on 133rd Street, and Mullaney was from Long Island.

Playing in front of family and friends, the Crusaders had the Naval Academy so out of sorts in the regional semifinal that the Midshipmen had to call time-out twice. That was notable coming from an opponent that had called just five time-outs over the course of 18 previous games. (Interruptions would become more frequent in the ensuing decades.) Holy Cross won 55–47 and faced CCNY in the regional final. Kaftan would more or less take command of his team over its next 80 minutes of basketball. His "30-point rampage" against the Beavers keyed the Crusaders' 60–45 victory, and the sophomore followed that up with 18 points in the 58–47 win over Oklahoma in the title game. Holy Cross had become the first Catholic program ever to win the NCAA tournament, and Kaftan was named the 1947 event's most outstanding player.

Julian was overcome with emotion after the game. "I never wanted to tell you during this season," he said to his players, "but, boys, you're the greatest team I ever coached." Nevertheless, emotion only went so far. Julian was fielding offers from both college and professional teams, and the coach was rumored to have an open mind. He doubled as assistant coach of the Holy Cross football team (the Crusaders had lost to the University of Miami in the 1946 Orange Bowl), and he reportedly wanted a situation where he could stick to basketball. With Joe Lapchick leaving St. John's that spring to coach the Knicks, many observers expected Julian to make the jump from possibly college basketball's worst facilities to its best, going from not having a home court at all to hosting teams at Madison Square Garden. Instead, the head coach surprised everyone by staying at Holy Cross and effectively opening the door for McGuire to take the St. John's job.

Cousy was coming off one of the rockiest individual NCAA tournaments ever recorded by a future legend. In his team's wins against CCNY and Oklahoma, the freshman had shot 2-of-22 from the floor. Then again, his talent was plain to see, and both Cousy and his team excelled in his sophomore year. The Crusaders again reached the national semifinals in 1948, lost to eventual champion Kentucky by eight, and posted a 26–4 record. It was another unqualified success in what was clearly the golden age of Holy Cross basketball.

At the same time, the team's 1947–48 season was suffused with odd moments. Julian took heat that February, for example, when his team played a particularly ugly game against Boston College. In an era before the shot clock, teams were known to hold the ball not just to protect a lead but also because they didn't like the zone defense being played by the opponent. This refusal to play basketball at a basketball game was carried to an extreme when the Crusaders faced the Eagles at Boston (later Matthews) Arena. With heavily favored Holy Cross holding on to a surprisingly slim lead midway through the second half, BC coach Al "General" McClellan had his team switch to a zone.

Andy Laska looked over at Julian, who motioned for him to hold the ball. No one moved on either team, and the minutes passed. Both coaches signaled from the sideline for their teams to stand firm. More time passed with no basketball. Kaftan ostentatiously took a seat on the floor and stayed there. Cousy removed his jersey and waved it to the crowd. Eventually, enough time elapsed to convince Julian that his lead was safe, and he instructed his team to run the offense. The Crusaders won 45–34, whereupon both Julian and McClellan were roundly criticized for days. Boston Celtics coach Honey Russell said the game had "smelled out the ball park all around." The *Boston Globe* approved of the Crusaders' strategy but deplored their theatrics: "For Holy Cross to hold the ball and protect a lead was plain common sense, but for George Kaftan to recline on the floor and Bob Cousy to take off and shake out his jersey was bad taste."

Amidst the talk that Holy Cross had perhaps become too showy, Julian supported, or at least indulged, his players' stylistic flourishes. After Adolph Rupp had seen one too many behind-the-back passes from the Crusaders at a coaching clinic he cohosted with Julian, the Kentucky coach was said to have shouted at his counterpart, "What are you teaching them?"

To all outward appearances it should have been a harmonious pairing in Worcester between Julian, "a players' coach," and Cousy, his flashy star. Harmony had grown scarce, however, by the star's sophomore year. The low point came after Cousy was benched for missing practice. When Julian called on him to enter the next game late in the first half, Cousy showed up his coach by refusing to budge from his spot on the bench.

By the beginning of March, well before the start of the NCAA tournament, Julian was reportedly ready to field offers again, college or professional. Such was not the customary attitude of a reigning national-championship coach who was in the middle of a 53–7 two-year run, not to mention a coach who would be bringing back Kaftan, Cousy, O'Connell, and Mullaney for a third year in 1948–49. That would be the season when Cousy, in a game against Loyola Chicago, would record what many believe to be major college basketball's first-ever behind-the-back dribble. But by then, his coach was Buster Sheary. Julian was long gone.

Like Brad Stevens in July 2013 and Rick Pitino in May 1997, Doggie Julian in April 1948 was a nationally celebrated college basketball savant who had just been hired as the next coach of the Boston Celtics. Sports cartoonist Gene Mack depicted Julian in a wizard's cap, and the Celtics were praised for having acted so promptly on the advice of Knicks president Ned Irish. "If you want Julian, you better get him quick," Irish was said to have told the Boston front office. "There's a long line forming at the door." The Celtics had been impressed when a

Boston Garden crowd stayed in its seats for most of the game as Holy Cross defeated Brown 90–35. "That's the kind of basketball people want," team founder Walter A. Brown marveled. "It is the kind we of the Celtics want to give them."

The team would in due course succeed in giving people exactly that, but not with Julian. He coached two sub-.500 seasons with the Celtics (with Kaftan on the roster the second year) before he was replaced by Red Auerbach. Julian promptly signed a deal worth a reported $7,500 annually at Dartmouth, where later in the 1950s he would coach Dave Gavitt. One month after Julian's departure from the Celtics organization, Cousy was drafted with the third overall pick by the Tri-Cities Blackhawks in the 1950 NBA draft. Boston was armed with the first pick that year, and it passed over Cousy, who was traded by Tri-Cities to the Chicago Stags. When that team folded before the season started, Cousy's name and those of two Stags teammates were put into a hat for a draft lottery of sorts. Boston chose last, and Cousy's name was still in the fedora after Philadelphia and New York had pulled out their slips of paper. Today, a statue at the entrance to the Hart Center honors the onetime Holy Cross recruit who was so puzzled during his campus visit that he had to ask where the basketball team played.

Nine picks after Cousy in that same 1950 draft, Duquesne's Chuck Cooper was selected by the Celtics—the first African American to be drafted by the NBA. His four-year career with the Dukes had ushered in an era of momentous change at the college level, and now he would have an impact on the professional level.

When Cooper and Cousy were freshmen, the NCAA tournament's de facto color line was at last broken at the 1947 event. The honor of breaking the line did not fall to Cooper, however. Instead, it fell to Joseph Galiber and Sonny Jameson when their CCNY team defeated Wisconsin 70–56, at Madison Square Garden in the regional semifinal. Galiber and Jameson merit a spot in the history books as the first African Americans to play in what has long since become college basketball's defining event.

4.

Pride Goeth Before Destruction

ollege basketball's postwar years were a time of expansion and abundance right up until the sport was consumed by the point-shaving scandal of 1951. There had, of course, been murmurs and an occasional outright statement in the press regarding illicit activities for years. There were even police actions. In January 1945, five Brooklyn College players were identified as having planned to throw a game against Akron. At the time, no applicable statute classified such behavior as a crime. That situation was remedied by the state legislature in Albany, and as of April 9, 1945, such activities were henceforth illegal in the state of New York. This fact would have significant repercussions six years later.

In the interim, Catholic college basketball would continue to enjoy success in the afterglow of the NCAA title won by Holy Cross in 1947. The successes would accumulate until, like all such victories at the turn of the 1950s, they became open to question. In this respect, 1947–48 would be perceived, correctly or not, as the calm before the storm. It was a season when, for the first time, a Catholic program would win one of the two major tournaments not as an independent but as a member of a conference. Presaging national titles won by Villanova in 1985 and

2018 (though not the one in 2016), this Catholic team would lose its conference race and then win the national tournament.

The season that culminated in the 1948 NIT championship for Saint Louis University possesses two further elements of foreshadowing for modern college basketball. First, the Billikens won a national title in the NIT/NCAA tournament era with a first-year coach brought in because of what today looks like a distinctly modern and performance-driven coaching change. The Jesuits were nothing if not practical when it came to their basketball. Second, Coach Ed Hickey's roster is one of the earliest for which we have some comprehensive statistics. Both of these qualities shed light on changes taking place in college basketball during the Mikan-to-Russell reformation of the 1940s and early 1950s.

SLU's president, the Rev. Patrick Holloran, plainly held high expectations for his men's basketball team. As the *St. Louis Post-Dispatch* put it in the days after the 1948 NIT title, "Father Patrick J. Holloran...has seen a quick fulfillment of his efforts to nationalize the standing of the Billikens in the field of sports." Holloran's basketball program was flourishing, with a roster made up almost entirely of players from the St. Louis area. HOME-GROWN! trumpeted a *Post-Dispatch* headline imbued with equal measures of brevity, accuracy, and pride. Coach Hickey's star player, Ed Macauley, had attended SLU High School. At 6 foot 8, he towered above all of his teammates and many, though by no means all, of his opponents. The much taller Bob Kurland had scored 58 points for Oklahoma A&M against Macauley in the latter's freshman year, and "Easy Ed" would long carry a newspaper clipping from that game in his wallet to, he said, stay "humble."

Now, at the conclusion of his junior season, he was a two-time All-American. In a burst of civic enthusiasm, the local paper went so far as to publish the young man's street address. "One of the few native St. Louis athletes to make All-America in any sport, Easy Ed lives with his parents at 5925A Page Boulevard."

The second-leading scorer in the 1948 NIT title game, D. C. Wilcutt, had graduated from Normandy High in nearby Wellston, Missouri.

Likewise, the balance of Hickey's rotation had been drawn from local programs, including McBride (Danny Miller), Soldan (Marvin Schatzman), Beaumont (Louis Lehman), Cleveland High School (brothers Joe and Bob Schmidt), and, from just across the Mississippi River, in Collinsville, Illinois (Joe Ossola).

Hickey won with this roster, but he didn't build it. John Flanigan did, only to resign as SLU coach after the 1946–47 season. "Because of the change in policy from part-time to full-time coaches on the part of the university," Flanigan said in a statement, "I deem it necessary to choose between my insurance business and basketball coaching." While everyone involved insisted that this was an amicable parting of ways, it appeared to many that Holloran didn't exactly strain himself trying to pry his coach away from the insurance industry. In fact, Flanigan had made it clear that he was open to staying on with the Billikens. He stipulated that a move to full-time coaching would require a raise in his annual SLU salary, from $2,000 to $3,500. Flanigan also wanted an assistant coach, full control over scheduling games, and zero interference with his in-game coaching. Holloran, in effect, said no. SLU's president explained that he didn't know what "Flanigan could do as a full-time coach, because basketball would not take all of his time and he would not be qualified for other duties."

Holloran may have additionally had playing style in mind when he permitted his coach to pursue other career opportunities. Under Flanigan in 1946–47, the Billikens averaged well under 50 points per outing. Convinced he had the makings of a great and, possibly, faster-paced team, Holloran brought in Hickey from SLU's Missouri Valley and Jesuit rival Creighton. The new coach was also asked to help out with football (the Billikens would continue to field a team through 1949), but basketball was plainly the main event on campus. In Hickey's first season, SLU's scoring jumped 22 percent, the equivalent of a modern-day team averaging 70 points one year and 85 the next. Saint Louis affords one of the earliest examples of a familiar basketball staffing set piece, one where grumbling about a slow pace ushers in hope that a new hire will make the team both successful and more pleasing to the eye.

Whatever Hickey was doing, it was working. The Billikens won their first six games, all of them at home except for one visit to the University of Missouri. The seventh contest would be a home game against reigning NCAA champion Holy Cross. Apparently, Doggie Julian had failed to learn any lessons from his team's ghastly 1–3 journey west the previous season. One year later, in January, he was coaxed to travel some 1,100 miles to face SLU in Kiel Auditorium. Those were tough miles in 1948. Research completed seven decades later would suggest few team sports have ever carried a larger home-venue advantage than did college basketball in the mid-20th century. Moreover, that advantage increased with each additional mile traveled by the visiting team. Naturally, the miles were just as punitive for the teams that kept making all those eager pilgrimages to Madison Square Garden in the 1940s.

The presence of the Crusaders on the banks of the Mississippi therefore constituted a rare opportunity for geographic payback, one SLU did not squander. Hickey's team easily brushed Holy Cross aside 61–46, despite Bob Cousy leading all scorers, with 16 points. The newspaper accounts in St. Louis that resulted illustrate how accusations of East Coast bias were part of the sport's original equipment:

> Back East, where the mentally myopic still consider St. Louis a French fur-trading post, the powerful basketball fathers read something today that must have opened their eyes. Holy Cross, the darlings of the North Atlantic seaboard, had been beaten by a Midwestern team—and, oh, so decisively.

By the time Hickey's group journeyed to Notre Dame for a crucial road game in February, SLU was 14–1. The Fighting Irish were the proud owners of a 38-game home win streak, with the most recent victory being a 64–55 triumph over No. 1–ranked Kentucky. A cottage industry had arisen in college basketball circles to explain why Notre Dame had not lost a home game since 1943. Perhaps it was the "physical peculiarities" of Notre Dame Fieldhouse, where one basket was affixed to a wall, and where the visiting team's bench was situated directly in front of the Notre Dame band. Depending on one's point of view, "physical peculiarities" could even apply to the makeup of the crowd. UK's Adolph Rupp was said to be unnerved by the presence of so many priests at Irish home games.

Having lost in South Bend just a few days earlier, Rupp offered a bit of public advice for the Billikens and placed particular emphasis on one tactic employed by the Irish. During the first time-out in Kentucky's game at the Fieldhouse, Rupp had looked over at the Notre Dame bench and was dumbfounded to see coach Moose Krause conferring with his players. Prior to this time, players had traditionally remained on the floor during time-outs. But, as was its custom, independent Notre Dame had adopted Big Ten rules for 1947–48. The Irish were therefore joining that conference's members in trying this experimental rule change, one which would be adopted nationally the following season.

Rupp stated afterward he had never seen coaches instructing players during a time-out. Even when he tried to follow suit during the game, it didn't go well. The UK coach claimed that his team was so unfamiliar with the idea that he used half the time-out just getting his players off the floor and huddled up by the bench. Hickey, on the other hand, indicated that he knew all about this in advance and was ready for it. Saint Louis won going away in South Bend, 68–51. The victory was so comfortable that Hickey was able to pull Macauley from the game after he had scored 21 points in the first 38 minutes. When Irish fans gave Macauley a "roar" in tribute to his performance, a Notre Dame official remarked that he had never seen a visiting player receive such an ovation at the Fieldhouse.

The Billikens played home games that season both at their on-campus gymnasium and in Kiel Auditorium. While university officials added seats to increase their gym's capacity to 4,200, they also moved as many upcoming games as they could to the larger downtown arena, just east of campus. Their game at Kiel against DePaul, for instance, was played as a benefit for Vincentian and Jesuit missionary societies.

The Blue Demons were now led by Ed Mikan, the 6-foot-8 younger brother of George, and SLU managed to escape with a two-point win in overtime. Ray Meyer's team won the return engagement at Chicago Stadium, however, becoming just the second opponent all year to beat the Billikens. Hickey's men had also dropped two games to Oklahoma A&M, giving the Aggies the Missouri Valley Conference title.

Nevertheless, the decision makers at the NIT saw a lot to like in a high-scoring offense led by an All-American like Macauley. Those evaluators had taken the measure of SLU in person when the team defeated LIU at Madison Square Garden in January 1948. By the time the Billikens lost to DePaul in Chicago, the team had already said yes to the NIT. Hickey had wired his reply to NIT chairman Asa Bushnell on February 25:

> Athletic Council unanimously approves our acceptance of your kind invitation to the NIT. Sincere thanks from the boys and myself.
>
> E. S. Hickey

SLU was seeded fourth in the eight-team field at Madison Square Garden, but after only one game, the *New York Times* declared flatly that the committee had underrated the Billikens. Hickey pulled his starters off the floor with 10 minutes left and the Billikens up by 24 over Bowling Green, in what would be a 16-point victory. Oddsmakers drew the same conclusion as the *Times*. The line on the semifinal between Saint Louis and nominal top seed Western Kentucky favored Hickey's team by two. The Billikens won by seven, and for their troubles, they would face second seed NYU on the Violets' home floor in the finals. Though that projected to be a significant challenge on paper, the game in fact turned out to be a replay of SLU's easy win in the quarterfinals. With Macauley alternately scoring or passing to teammates who were cutting to the basket, the Billikens attempted most of their shots from inside 15 feet. Again, Hickey cleared his bench, this time with five minutes left in the contest, and Saint Louis won the NIT title 65–52.

In the city of St. Louis, locals flocked to Union Station to welcome the team home. As chance would have it, the Billikens made their way there in a special car attached to a regularly scheduled train. Fellow passengers who had unwittingly booked travel to St. Louis for Sunday, March 21, were reportedly somewhat "startled and harried" upon arrival. The bewildered travelers had to gather their trunks on the narrow platform and elbow their way past Mayor Aloys P. Kaufmann, the police chief, the fire chief, the postmaster, and three separate bands before staggering out the 20th Street exit and taking their chances amid a jubilant crowd of thousands.

Saint Louis posted a 22–4 record in 1948–49 and lost to Bowling Green in the NIT quarterfinals. Ed Macauley was then drafted by and played one season for the hometown St. Louis Bombers before the franchise folded. When the players on the Bombers' roster were drafted by the rest of the league, Macauley arrived on the Boston Celtics' doorstep at more or less the same moment as his fellow Jesuit college basketball legend, Bob Cousy.

Among his many awards to that point, Macauley had been named the 1948 NIT's outstanding player. The verdict possessed far more statistical support than it would have had 10 or even five years earlier. Interesting developments were emerging with regard to measuring performance by the late 1940s. When SLU traveled to New York in January and defeated LIU, for example, a novel bit of tracking turned up, courtesy of a Madison Square Garden publicity staffer named George Sullivan. Back in St. Louis, the *Post-Dispatch* explained that in "an official box score, Sullivan pointed out [SLU's] number as 17 'assists'—passes resulting directly in scoring—and said it was the highest number of the year by any team in the Garden."

Later that same month, Macauley would be hailed for making 48 percent of his shots and thus ranking as the national leader in field goal percentage by the National Collegiate Athletic Bureau. The NCAB had been funded and established in New York after the war as a semiautonomous service by the NCAA. This ambitiously titled "national" bureau was largely the creation of one pioneering figure, Homer F. Cooke, who had been publishing his own college football statistics since 1937. The young NCAB did good work for postwar college basketball, tracking individual field goal percentages in a sport in which one of the few player statistics previously available had been total points scored in a season. Columnists accustomed to 154-game home run derbies applied this same horse-race template to a sport where individuals played wildly differing numbers of games. Cooke's influence was needed and, once felt, found to be highly beneficial.

Accurate statistics were in demand because in summer 1948, for the first time since 1936, the Olympic Games were going to be held. The United States needed a basketball team to represent the nation, and an Olympic qualifier was scheduled to take place at the Garden at the end of March. The eight-team field would consist of three Amateur Athletic Union teams, one YMCA club, the two finalists from the NCAA tournament, and the champions of both the NIT and the NAIB tournaments. Entrants would be bracketed to guarantee a final between one college team and one AAU or YMCA opponent. The final game was projected to be anticlimactic, however, since, in the US Olympic Committee's model, selected players from each finalist would be combined to form the national team that would compete in London. The only question answered by the final game's outcome would be the identity of Team USA's head coach.

The Olympic Committee's elevation of the NAIB to the same level as the NIT was a coup for the Kansas City event. Traditionally viewed as a "small school" tournament, the NAIB now had an incredible incentive to offer participants. Winning the title in the tournament would earn players a shot at representing their country in the Olympics. NAIB organizers capitalized on this status and, for the first time, sought to draw teams from what had traditionally been the NIT's footprint. Bids for the Kansas City tournament went out to NIT stalwart LIU, as well as to Catholic institutions in the East, like Manhattan and Siena. This was, in effect, a raid on the NIT's turf, but LIU and Manhattan both turned down their invitations when they learned that the NAIB expressly prohibited Black players.

To modern eyes, the stance taken by the two New York City–area schools is both laudable and, with regard to the Lasallians at Manhattan, a bit ironic. LIU had showcased Dolly King starting in the late 1930s, but in 1948 the Jaspers were still two years away from Junius Kellogg becoming the program's first African American player. Be that as it may, Manhattan was saying no to the NAIB while citing what the *New York Times* called "Catholic principles of racial equality." When the Jaspers made plain that they were in fact eager to participate if only this one rule were abolished, the NAIB replied by telegram on a Wednesday that it was too late to institute such a change for a tournament tipping off the following Monday.

The NAIB would backtrack literally overnight, but it would not be Manhattan's objections that would force a change of heart in Kansas City. Nor, most likely, would Indiana State coach John Wooden have been able to open the 1948 NAIB to all players by himself, had he attempted to do so. Though Black player Clarence Walker was a reserve for the "Scrappin' Sycamores," Wooden accepted the tournament's bid. When the local Terre Haute press then printed a roster of 10 Indiana State players who were cleared for postseason play, Walker's name was nowhere to be found. The NAIB would be forced to back down, but, rather than a Catholic school like Manhattan or a Protestant coach like Wooden, it was a Jewish executive of the Bulova watch company, named Harry D. Henshel, who earned the lion's share of this credit. As reported in the *Times*, Henshel had sent a telegram in his capacity as a US Olympic Committee member:

> Harry D. Henshel of New York said he had telegraphed Lou Wilke of Bartlesville, Okla., chairman of [USOC], suggesting the NAIB champion be dropped from the New York tourney in which the United States Olympic team will be determined.

Henshel said the ban on Black players was "not democratic," and that he never would have voted to include the NAIB winner in the Olympic trials had he known about its rule. His telegram hit a nerve. The same NAIB brass that had scoffed at Manhattan on Wednesday now leapt into action on Thursday. "At Kansas City," the *Times* reported, "tournament officials said reconsideration of the ruling against Negro participation would occur before the tourney." A "telegraphic poll was made to expedite matters" within the NAIB's executive committee, and, voting remotely, the group returned a 6–1 verdict in favor of allowing African Americans to play. While no record has come to light revealing each committee member's ballot, it's possible the lone negative vote was cast by Hamline head coach Joe Hutton. In published reports, Hutton termed Henshel's telegram "poppycock." "We do have a rule barring Negroes from competitions," he said. "But it has been in existence as long as [the] NAIB. So far as I can recall it has never been an issue."

Despite the single dissenting vote, the NAIB did overturn its ban on Black players. Indiana State's Wooden notified Walker that he would be playing after all, and Manhattan immediately accepted its previously declined invitation to participate.

Upon arrival in Kansas City, the Jaspers found themselves on the same side of the bracket with none other than Hutton and Hamline. In the resulting contest between what were said to be Catholic principles of racial equality and a coach who cried poppycock, the latter prevailed. No fewer than six Manhattan players fouled out, and the game ended with but three Jaspers on the floor. Indiana State and Walker fared far better, at one stroke breaking the NAIB color line and reaching the finals, before losing to Louisville.

The Cardinals proceeded to New York for the Olympic qualifying tournament, while NIT winner Saint Louis elected to stay home. Enough time had already been spent in New York and away from the classroom, the Billikens said. NCAA champion Kentucky advanced to the final of the Olympic trials, where it lost to the renowned Phillips 66 AAU team headlined by Bob Kurland. A combined roster drawn from both squads traveled to London, with Rupp serving as an assistant coach. Team USA eked out a two-point victory over Argentina in group stage before outscoring Uruguay, Mexico, and France by a combined total of 199–89 to win the gold medal.

With a rejuvenated NAIB and an Olympic qualifier joining the NIT and the NCAA tournaments, March 1948 had offered basketball in abundance. Never had so many games been covered so closely by the national press in such a short period of time. This expansionist impulse was not lost on the organizers of a new National Catholic Invitational Tournament, which made its debut in Denver at Regis University in 1949. Regis had been founded by the Jesuits in 1877, and Catholic programs were eager to travel to the Mile High City and face off against one another. The first 16-team field included Gonzaga, Dayton, St. Bonaventure, Siena, and Iona. Perhaps aided by altitude, home-court advantage, or both, the Rangers of Regis won the first NCIT title by four over the Terriers of St. Francis, after holding the ball for the closing three minutes of the championship final.

St. Francis would return to the NCIT and, in fact, would win it all in 1951. In its four-year run, the National Catholic Invitational would shrink to an eight-team field, move to upstate New York, and, not least, muddle through a controversy uncannily similar to what the NAIB had experienced in 1948. The second NCIT, in 1950, was originally scheduled to be hosted by Loyola Maryland, but organizers had to move the tournament to Albany at the 11th hour when it became apparent that Black participants would not be offered rooms in Baltimore hotels. Siena and Marquette would also win NCIT titles in the event's brief existence, but the NIT and Madison Square Garden still exerted a powerful hold on the Catholic basketball imagination.

Ordinarily, the 1949 NIT would loom large in those annals. That was the year San Francisco defeated Loyola Chicago by one to win the National Invitation title. USF's Don Lofgran was named the tournament's outstanding player, and his coach, 33-year-old Pete Newell, was clearly going places. Newell would win an NCAA tournament title at California in 1959 and serve as a key and recurrently cited coaching influence early in the career of Bob Knight. The 1949 NIT title game between the Dons and the Ramblers put the finishing touches on an extraordinary run of Jesuit basketball success. From Holy Cross at the 1947 NCAA tournament to Saint Louis at the 1948 NIT to the all-Jesuit final and San Francisco's win at the Garden in 1949, on paper it was quite the trifecta. But the 1949 NIT, among other events and teams, was not fated to be regarded that way down through the decades.

In 1950, CCNY became the first team ever to win the NIT and the NCAA tournament in the same year. New York had rejoiced in the success of Nat Holman's team. Then, 11 months later, pride turned to disbelief. On February 19, 1951, New York City district attorney Frank Hogan announced that his office had arrested five area players on bribery charges. CCNY's Ed Warner, Ed Roman, and Al Roth were taken into custody in front of their teammates and their coach at Penn Station as the Beavers were returning to New York after a road game against Temple. The district attorney's office also brought in NYU's Harvey "Connie" Schaff and former LIU player Eddie Gard. Hogan charged that Gard was the go-between who approached all of these players on behalf of a gambler named Salvatore Sollazzo. At his arraignment in felony court, Sollazzo was dressed down by the presiding judge as one who "appears to have corrupted these young men and brought disgrace on a great institution."

In the days that followed, Hogan's dragnet would take in more local players, including LIU's Sherman White and CCNY's Floyd Layne. White's arraignment, in particular, was sensational news. He was about to be named to multiple All-American teams and, in a remarkably ill-timed print run mailed to subscribers on the eve of the scandal, was named national player of the year by the *Sporting News*.

Within 24 hours of the first arrests, the search for solutions had already begun. "Coaches, sports officials and college authorities were divided on the cure," one of the earliest reports noted, "but a majority appeared to favor a return of the game to the campus court." Blacklisting Madison Square Garden was a common proposal, one that was especially popular outside of greater New York. "Isn't it about time college faculties called the boys back home," one St. Louis columnist asked, "and declared New York out of bounds, as far as university basketball, privately promoted for profit, is concerned?"

One year removed from a heartbreaking loss to CCNY in the 1950 NIT finals, players at Bradley voted unanimously not to accept a bid to the 1951 NIT even if one were offered. And Bradley's president said it was doubtful that the Braves would schedule a game at the Garden for the following season. There were also calls for the appointment of a "czar," either of college basketball or perhaps one overseeing all of intercollegiate sports. Phog Allen's name was often mentioned in connection with these discussions. "Out here in the Midwest, this condition, of course, doesn't prevail," the 65-year-old Kansas coach said when the scandal first broke, "but in the East the boys, particularly those who participate in the resort hotel leagues during the summer months, are thrown into an environment which cannot help but breed the evil which more and more is coming to light."

The "evil" feared by Allen came to light because of Junius Kellogg. Manhattan's first Black player had been offered $1,000 to throw the Jaspers' game against DePaul at the Garden in January 1951. Kellogg was told the money would be his if the Jaspers lost by at least five. In fact, Manhattan was favored over the Blue Demons by three. He promptly reported the incident to his coach, Ken Norton, who in turn referred him to the office of the district attorney. From the Jaspers' perspective, the good news was that Kellogg had done the right thing. The bad news was that the person trying to get Kellogg to throw the game was not some shadowy underworld figure but rather former Manhattan teammate Henry Poppe. The next time Kellogg was approached to alter an outcome, he was wearing a wire. Prosecutors secured audio of him being asked to "throw hook shots over the basket" and "miss rebounds occasionally."

For three days, every charge brought forth by Hogan's office had stemmed from games played at the Garden. As the scandal continued to dominate the headlines, however, it became apparent that gamblers had approached players in the rest of the United States too. Former San Francisco guard Frank Kuzara told a reporter that he and Don

Lofgran had rebuffed a $1,200 offer to shave points in the Dons' game against USC in January 1950, a contest USF won by 14 and that was played at Kezar Pavilion in San Francisco.

As the "return to campus" movement gained traction, officials at Bradley stepped forward with a proposal to host their own "national campus basketball tournament" in Peoria, Illinois, in late March. The event was timed to coincide with the NCAA tournament, in order to offer a postseason showcase for teams that weren't playing in that event. While in theory not conflicting with the NIT on the calendar, this new tournament was plainly intended as an alternative postseason destination to Madison Square Garden.

When Bradley athletic director Arthur E. Bergstrom sent out 25 "feeler invitations" in preparation for assembling an eight-team field, he reportedly received encouraging responses from DePaul, Duquesne, San Francisco, and La Salle. Though not on Bergstrom's original list of 25, Siena was fresh off its title at the 1950 National Catholic Invitational and contacted Bradley asking to be considered. The Saints' interest was unrequited, however, and, in the end, the Peoria tournament's field consisted of Duquesne, Villanova, Syracuse, Wyoming, Toledo, Utah, Western Kentucky, and the host team. Syracuse took home the championship with a thrilling 76–75 win over Bradley. It was the first and last "National Campus Basketball Tournament" ever held.

Just four months after that game, the *New York Times* ran the latest on college basketball improprieties in a series of front-page stories, and one headline called out the formerly irreproachable Braves: 8 BRADLEY PLAYERS INVOLVED IN FIXING BASKETBALL GAMES. "Stunning," said the *Chicago Tribune* of the news, which it called "additional evidence of the national mania [for] trying to get something for nothing." The *Tribune* noted that for decades, proposals had been advanced to allow college athletes to receive a portion of the revenue that their games earned for the schools. This new generation, however, had taken things one step further: "They not only ask money for the privilege of representing a university on the basketball court, but they get extra dough for controlling the score."

While it was clear the scandal was no longer confined to the Garden and that it had even infiltrated the nation's heartland, the imbroglio's largest single disclosure was still to come. On October 20, 1951, Hogan dropped his final bombshell. Kentucky's Ralph Beard, Alex Groza, and Dale Barnstable told authorities that, in the *New York Times*'s words, "they had accepted $1,500 to 'throw' a National Invitation Tournament" game against Loyola Chicago in the 1949 quarterfinals. A 12-point favorite before tip-off, the Wildcats had lost to the Ramblers 67–56. Within days of losing to Loyola, Kentucky would record an average margin of victory of 13 points against three opponents all ranked higher than the Ramblers on the way to a second consecutive NCAA tournament title. The rankings of every team involved are known because the AP's basketball poll rolled out that very season.

In real time, no one had been more mystified by the loss to Loyola than Rupp. His team's defeat at the hands of an inferior Jesuit opponent would subsequently rank as arguably one of the sport's most consequential and far-reaching game results. Certainly, one proximate consequence of the Wildcats' brush with point shaving would be the rise and tacitly accepted establishment of a modern regulatory NCAA. When Hogan's criminal probe of college basketball led civilians at both the NCAA and the Southeastern Conference to undertake investigations, UK was accused of giving its players impermissible benefits. This 1952 enforcement action was literally "Case Report No. 1" for the NCAA's new Subcommittee on Infractions. The organization's newly installed executive director, Walter Byers, then famously handed down what would later be called "the death penalty" and barred Kentucky from playing any intercollegiate sports in 1952–53. Officials in Lexington acquiesced, and a precedent was set.

An even more enduring legacy remains from the point-shaving scandal writ large, and specifically from the 1949 NIT. That particular newly expanded 12-team bracket was a veritable who's who of programs about to be ensnared in the New York district attorney's investigation. UK, Bradley, CCNY, Manhattan, and NYU were all there at the Garden that March. Yet even if every team in the field besides Kentucky had been playing it straight and exerting itself to the utmost, the tournament would still be tainted, because UK failed to play to win in one game. San Francisco's title that year is diminished through no fault of the Dons and despite the fact that they never played the Wildcats.

Referring to a death penalty in intercollegiate sports, of course, was and is a blithe misnomer. Sanctions visited upon Kentucky or any athletic department were measured in games, scholarships, and dollars. Punishments inflicted upon individual players were far more consequential and lasting. LIU's White was incarcerated for almost nine months at Rikers Island, which even in the 1950s was notorious for its conditions. It was an unconscionable act by prosecutors, a Dickensian if not medieval response to the fact that college students were being groomed, used, and, in White's case, threatened with violence by gamblers out for easy money.

After graduating from Manhattan, Junius Kellogg accepted an offer to play for the Harlem Globetrotters. In April 1954, he was traveling with teammates when a car accident in Pine Bluff, Arkansas, left him paralyzed for life. Kellogg spent his later years in a Riverdale high-rise, overlooking the campus of his alma mater. He passed away in 1998, one year after receiving a special citation from Governor George Pataki of the state of New York:

> Your story is nothing short of an inspiration. Your early days
> in college basketball, where your integrity was instrumental
> in bringing to a halt a point-shaving scandal that forever
> altered the landscape of college basketball.

5.

The Catholic Moment
at the NIT

In terms of origin stories, the jump shot is the notorious opposite of the sport itself. The invention of basketball is catalogued tidily under one inventor, one spot on the map, and one date on the calendar. The jump shot affords no such clarity. We know only that by the time Paul Arizin was draining jumpers for Villanova in the late 1940s, he was indebted to innovators like Hank Luisetti, Kenny Sailors, and Joe Fulks, among others.

We also know that in his era Arizin was the exception to the rule. Viewed as a herd, coaches were hardwired to resist any novelty that did not come from another coach. Coaches therefore tended to be suspicious of, if not manifestly hostile toward, the jump shot, and the new method for launching a basketball faced a presumption of tactical depravity well into the 1950s. If you have to jump to get an open look, the thinking ran, you must not be open. Credit for Arizin's brilliance as a first-team All-American therefore resides not only with the South Philadelphia native but also with his farsighted college coach, Al Severance.

Arizin never played high school basketball, and, in fact, was cut when he tried out for the team for the first time as a senior at La Salle College High School. "I'm not talking Michael Jordan being demoted to JV," Arizin's son, Michael, would emphasize some 70 years after the fact. "We're talking, 'Get your ball and go home.'" Arizin was paying his own way at Villanova and playing basketball on the side when Severance spotted him at an open tournament where college players mixed with CYO standouts. Impressed, the coach approached him after the game and asked if he had ever considered Villanova. "I'm there already," Arizin replied.

Tom Gola entered La Salle College High School one year after Arizin graduated, and his college recruitment followed a markedly different path than that of his predecessor. Gola may even have been the first modern recruit. He was certainly written up that way. An Associated Press piece reprinted in newspapers from Florida to Montana in March 1951 stated that the high school senior had received 57 scholarship offers. Ironically, the specific number that apparently made the article so irresistible to editors nationwide—not 50 offers or 60, but exactly 57—may have been an understatement. Gola's family members estimated that their celebrity relative instead received over 100 such overtures.

Future Temple coach John Chaney was another renowned Philadelphia player from the same era, and he would later describe Gola as, among other things, an outstanding defender. "If he was playing defense on you and you went around him, he would do this wraparound and tap the ball away and take off," Chaney would recall. "He even did that in the pros." In a sport that had seemed to be trending toward specialists of wildly differing statures, Gola was midsized and multidimensional. The AP summed him up as "an 18-year-old 6-foot-6-inch lad who scales 205 pounds, pours basketballs through hoops in machine-like fashion and runs like a jackrabbit." Gola took a long look at North Carolina State before deciding to stay home and play collegiately at La Salle. Like all players nationally who graduated from high school in 1951, Gola was allowed to play varsity basketball immediately, thanks to a one-year-only reintroduction of freshman eligibility. This "drastic step" was taken in response to the reinstatement of the military draft with the outbreak of the Korean War.

In the season before Gola's arrival, the Explorers had posted a 22–7 record. One of those seven defeats was the source of particular bitterness for coach Ken Loeffler. In a 76–74 loss at NC State in January 1951, La Salle was assessed four technical fouls in the second half alone. The following day, over the course of a long and notably irate phone interview with the *Philadelphia Inquirer*, Loeffler termed the game "one of the biggest steals since the Louisiana Purchase." As chance would have it, that summer he would find himself across the aisle from none other than Wolfpack head coach Everett Case on a commercial flight taking both men to the same coaching clinic. When he glanced over and saw that the NC State coach was fast asleep in his seat, Loeffler crossed the aisle and shook his counterpart awake—suddenly and with some vigor. "The plane's in trouble," he told the startled Case, "and we may not make it. Quick, before we go down, admit those officials in Raleigh were terrible."

Gola was arguably the nation's No. 1 recruit, a fact that did not translate into correspondingly elite status for the Explorers in 1952. National championship chatter that February was instead centered on the likes of Kentucky, Illinois, Duquesne, Kansas, and Saint Louis. La Salle, by contrast, was branded a dark horse. While 20–5 overall, the team had limped through a 7–4 closing stretch that included back-to-back 11-point losses at Duquesne and at Youngstown State, the latter program being at the time the equivalent of what would later be termed a Division II opponent. The Explorers also lost at Convention Hall in Philadelphia to a Georgetown team that would finish the year 15–10. By the time Loeffler's group accepted an NIT bid, the event had already handed out its top seeds and first-round byes to Duquesne, Saint Louis, St. Bonaventure, and St. John's.

This Catholic clean sweep at the top of the bracket was fast becoming par for the course at Madison Square Garden. Fully 64 percent of teams competing in the event from 1951 through 1959 represented Catholic institutions. The 1952 bracket was particularly impressive, with nine teams ranked in the top 20 nationally. To the extent that the statistical heft of mid-20th-century tournaments can be measured, the field that played in the 1952 NIT stands out as both unusually strong and, more particularly, stronger than any National Invitation field to come over the ensuing years. When Saint Louis played Dayton in the 1952 event, for example, the collision of national top-15 programs took place in the quarterfinals. In this embarrassment of riches at the NIT, unranked La Salle would have to defeat four ranked Catholic opponents in order to win a title.

Seton Hall was the first domino to fall, as Gola scored 30 and Fred Iehle added 25, to give the Explorers a four-point victory over star player Walter Dukes and the Pirates. Dukes fouled out with eight minutes remaining, and Iehle poured in 20 of his points on 10-of-15 shooting from the floor in the third and fourth quarters alone. (In March 1951, basketball's national rules committee had announced that games would henceforth be played in 10-minute quarters. The change was implemented with what appears to have been a minimum of controversy or even comment.) La Salle then won by six in the quarterfinals against a St. John's team that committed 42 personal fouls and recorded an 11-of-26 performance at the line. In this final year when teams were still allowed to enter both of the sport's major postseason events, the fear at St. John's was that any NCAA tournament hopes had been dashed by the loss to the Explorers. It would be an anxious 48 hours for Coach Frank McGuire and his team.

By the time La Salle met top seed Duquesne in the semifinals, the thinking at the Garden with regard to Loeffler's group had changed. Holy Cross coach Buster Sheary, whose team had just lost to the Dukes in the quarterfinals, flatly predicted a win for the Explorers. Sheary was prescient. The 13-point La Salle victory, in which Duquesne never once led, turned out to be the Explorers' easiest game yet. When Dukes coach Dudey Moore switched to a zone with his team down 10 after halftime, La Salle held the ball for two minutes and forced Duquesne back into a man-to-man defense.

NCAA bids were announced that day, creating an odd juxtaposition in which the Dukes were awarded a tournament berth, along with St. John's, while the opponent that was in the process of having defeated them both was passed over. Moore shared the good news with his play-ers at halftime in an attempt to inject some life into them. After that effort had failed, Loeffler received a note in the winning locker room: "Your victory made the NCAA committee look bad." And Loeffler kept right on making the committee look bad. The Explorers beat still another NCAA tournament team, Dayton, by the score of 75–64, to capture the 1952 NIT title.

La Salle additionally holds the distinction of being the first Catholic NIT or NCAA champion that was not all-white. Jack Moore was selected to the All-NIT first team, along with teammates Tom Gola and Norm Grekin, after he pulled down 15 rebounds in the title game against Dayton. Now, the Explorers would recuperate, practice, and watch no fewer than three teams they had defeated in the NIT go on to play in the 1952 NCAA tournament. La Salle was waiting for its shot in that year's Olympic qualifying tournament.

The good news for St. John's that March was that, despite the six-point loss to La Salle in the NIT, the team did receive a bid in the 16-team NCAA tournament. The bad news was St. John's was bracketed to play NC State on the Wolfpack's home floor at Reynolds Coliseum. Nevertheless, a 9–0 run for McGuire's men after halftime propelled the visitors to an 11-point victory in front of "a shirt-sleeved crowd" on a warm night in Raleigh. The win brought St. John's face-to-face with No. 1–ranked Kentucky. Curiously enough, the Wildcats had been linked in national headlines for months to, of all opponents, a Catholic school in New York.

In 1950, Kentucky opened a new 12,000-seat venue, Memorial Coliseum. McGuire had just accepted UK's offer of what was said to be "a fabulous guarantee" for a home-and-home series at the arena during the 1951–52 season when, according to one account, Kentucky raised an objection. Solly Walker would join the varsity as St. John's first Black player, a fact conveyed to Adolph Rupp when the Wildcats played McGuire's team at the Garden in December 1950. Told that Walker would be on McGuire's roster the following season, Rupp was reported to have "dramatically raised his eyebrows and wanted to know 'What's going to happen at Lexington?'"

With the support of St. John's athletic director Walter McLaughlin, McGuire reportedly phoned Rupp and stated that he would refuse to bring his team to Lexington if Walker were barred from playing. When the *Brooklyn Daily Eagle* published this version of events in the summer of 1951, Rupp flatly denied having ever wondered what would happen in Lexington. "We always handle such problems in a gentlemanly manner," the coach said, with "problems" being a particularly interesting word choice. In the end, the game was played as scheduled, Walker became the first African American to take the floor at Memorial Coliseum, and St. John's suffered its largest defeat in program history. "It was the worst performance I've seen a St. John's team turn in in [my] 15 years as a player and coach of the school," McGuire said after the 81–40 debacle. The Wildcats would reign atop the AP poll as the nation's No. 1 team for eight of the season's 13 weeks, including the last six in a row leading into the postseason.

McGuire and Rupp appeared in the headlines together again in January 1952, when *Look* magazine published a piece by sports editor Tim Cohane titled "How Basketball Players Are Bought." Cohane depicted a conversation said to have taken place between the two coaches regarding Brooklyn recruit Dave Gotkin. "You're wasting your time, Adolph," McGuire was portrayed as telling Rupp. "Gotkin wants to go to Navy. He can't be had." *Look* reported the Kentucky coach's response as follows: "Rupp drew himself up in baronial hauteur. He reached into his pocket, extracted a couple of greenbacks and brandished them. 'Anybody can be had,' boomed Adolph, 'if they are shown enough of this stuff.'" For the second time in the span of six months, Rupp strenuously denied a published report that also involved St. John's. While he was at it, the UK coach termed the article "stupid," and sued *Look* for $250,000. This time, McGuire agreed with his counterpart from Lexington.

These two teams—and, particularly, these two coaches—had a history together when they took the floor at Reynolds Coliseum to determine which program would advance to the 1952 national semifinals.

Kentucky had won 23 straight contests and hadn't lost an NCAA tournament game since 1945. Both streaks came to an end as St. John's recorded a 64–57 upset that shook the entire bracket. McGuire believed he had made a coaching mistake in December by trying to run with the Wildcats in Lexington. For the rematch, St. John's instead played what its coach called an "old-fashioned New York type of possession game." When Kentucky "came out to meet us," McGuire said, "we drove past 'em." Zeke Zawoluk riddled the UK defense with made hook shots on his way to 32 points.

Having defeated the No. 1 team in the nation in Raleigh on Saturday, St. John's would travel across the continent to Seattle for a Tuesday game against No. 2 Illinois. The 1952 NCAA tournament marked the arrival of the first "true" Final Four. Previously, winners and losers from two semifinals that were played in two different spots would gather in one city for a national title contest and a third-place game. In Seattle, the national semifinals and the championship game would all take place at Hec Edmundson Pavilion on the campus of the University of Washington. That's where St. John's continued its run of upset victories, with a 61–59 win against the Fighting Illini. A half-court heave by Illinois's Jim Bredar missed the mark as time expired.

In any ordinary season, St. John's, even at 25–4, might have been labeled a Cinderella. After all, the Associated Press reported that a Seattle hotel was receiving mail that had been addressed, days in advance, "Care of Kentucky basketball team." In this particular March, however, that limelight was being shared with both La Salle and with a Santa Clara team that was paired with Kansas in the other semifinal. The Broncos, at 15–10, were surprised just to receive a bid, and, after SCU beat UCLA and Wyoming in Corvallis, Oregon, officials back at Santa Clara worried about their players missing so many classes. When they proceeded north from Corvallis to play the Jayhawks, Bob Feerick's men were required to attend courses at the local Jesuit institution, Seattle University.

Santa Clara's center was Ken Sears, who would later share what he called his "biggest memory of the entire Final Four experience":

It happened right as we checked into the hotel where all four teams were staying. I got off the bus and walked over to the elevator to go up to our room. The elevator door opened and this huge man was standing there. He was wearing this immense overcoat and a 10-gallon cowboy hat. He must have weighed 270 pounds. And I'm this skinny 185-pound freshman. I thought, "Look at this guy!" And I knew exactly who it was.

It was Clyde Lovellette. KU's star was in the midst of what is still one of the great individual NCAA tournament runs in the event's history. Lovellette had scored 31 and 44 points in the Jayhawks' wins over TCU and Saint Louis, respectively, to reach Seattle. He then crushed Sears and Santa Clara to the tune of 33 points as Kansas recorded an easy 19-point victory. The win over the Broncos was a preview of the title game, when, for the second time in 24 hours, KU would easily dispense with a Catholic opponent. Lovellette rang up another 33 points against St. John's in leading his team to an 80–63 triumph and the program's first tournament-era national championship. McGuire would one day reflect on the scene he witnessed as time expired in that title game. "After the gun went off," he would say, "everybody mobbed the Kansas players, and there we were—me and 12 basketball players. We were second in the United States. But we might as well have been 50th. It was a lesson."

Because it was an Olympic year, Kansas, St. John's, and La Salle all had more basketball to play. The US Olympic Committee still gave bids in its qualifying tournament to both NCAA finalists as well as to the NIT winner. Having won a national title in Seattle on Wednesday night, Kansas would take the floor in Kansas City on Saturday night against Southwest Missouri State, champions of the National Association of Intercollegiate Basketball tournament. (The NAIB would change its name to the NAIA later that year. Southwest Missouri would become Missouri State in 2005.) The Jayhawks barely had time for a victory celebration on their home campus, one that took place on the streets of

Lawrence after midnight in the early hours of Friday morning. Thousands of KU students built bonfires out of copies of *Look* magazine, which had seen fit to leave Lovellette off its All-American team.

St. John's faced an even more daunting itinerary. It's possible no college team in the history of the sport to that time had traveled as many miles to play four games in one week as did Frank McGuire's group at the end of March 1952. After defeating Kentucky in Raleigh on Saturday night, St. John's was in Seattle for games on Tuesday and Wednesday before flying all the way back to Madison Square Garden to meet La Salle the next Saturday evening. Give the "travel-weary" host team credit. After trailing by 15 with a little more than six minutes remaining, St. John's drew to within 66–62 before losing by nine. Kansas had defeated Southwest Missouri State the previous evening, meaning the Jayhawks and the Explorers would meet. This would be the first game in seven years between the champions of the NCAA and National Invitation tournaments. The winner would, along with the champion from the AAU/YMCA side of the bracket, send players to the Olympics in Helsinki.

The game between KU and La Salle was scheduled for Madison Square Garden. Lovellette scored 40, and Kansas won 70–65. Loeffler's Explorers played without Moore, whose mother had passed away shortly before the game. The following night, the Jayhawks lost by two to the Peoria Caterpillars AAU team in a game that determined little more than that Warren Womble would be Team USA's official head coach. Gola and Grekin from La Salle were named Olympic "alternates," as was Ron MacGilvray from St. John's. Alternates turned out to be unnecessary, however, and the US team that landed in Finland was made up entirely of players from KU and Peoria, along with two members of the Phillips 66 AAU team (including, once again, Bob Kurland). Despite a close game against Brazil, Team USA went 8–0 and won the gold medal.

Less than two weeks after the closing ceremonies in Helsinki, Frank McGuire was named the new head coach at North Carolina. A St. John's official said McGuire "caught us completely by surprise last

Friday when he came and asked us for his release." With McGuire rebuilding North Carolina and Kentucky serving its "death penalty" year in 1952–53, two of the game's most prominent figures from one season were far less visible the next. Attention that next year would be focused instead on teams like Indiana and Seton Hall, including one notorious night experienced by the Pirates on the road.

In its basketball program's history, Seton Hall has produced three consensus first-team All-Americans: Myles Powell (2020), Walter Dukes (1953), and Bob Davies (1942). Davies additionally happens to have recorded possibly the most impressive individual feat in the history of organized basketball.

Starting in the fall of 1946, Davies appeared in 32 games and averaged 14 points per contest for the Rochester Royals on his way to winning the National Basketball League's most valuable player award. In that very same 1946–47 season, he served as head coach at Seton Hall and led the Pirates to a 24–3 record. "I took a lot of overnight sleepers," Davies later explained. He also coached the SHU baseball team that year.

When Davies returned to more or less full-time duty as a player with the Royals the next season, he immediately spotted Dukes at Rochester's East High School. As a 6-foot-5 sophomore, Dukes had led the City Scholastic League in scoring, a feat he repeated in 1947–48 as a 6-foot-7 junior. Davies encouraged and, eventually, persuaded the best high school player in Rochester to transfer to Seton Hall Prep, then in South Orange, New Jersey, for his senior year. By the time Dukes joined Seton Hall University's varsity team for the 1950–51 season, he was 6 foot 11 and well on his way to becoming a star the likes of which major college basketball had never seen before.

As it happens, college basketball would see a few select legends with similar combinations of size and athletic ability *after* Dukes. This meant that the Seton Hall standout was fated to be the lesser-known figure in comparative sentences written ever after. Before there was Wilt Chamberlain, such sentences run, before there was Bill Russell, there was another remarkable player you may not have even heard of. It is said Walter Dukes was the game's first truly dominant African American center. Certainly, the impact Dukes had on his program was Chamberlain- or Russell-like. As a senior, he set an NCAA single-season record for rebounds that still stands. Of course, Dukes was playing at the perfect historical moment to set a mark that may never be broken. In 1951–52, college basketball as a whole had just averaged what is still the all-time high for shot attempts per game. The following season, when Dukes was a senior, that number was still quite high, and, anyway, Seton Hall opponents were held to 31 percent shooting from the floor. Dukes recorded 734 rebounds over the course of 33 games. No other player in college basketball history has had more than 600 in a season.

For three years in the early 1950s, Dukes and Richie Regan were Seton Hall's leading scorers. The Pirates may even have been better when Dukes and Regan were juniors than when its two stars were seniors. In 1951–52, Honey Russell's men earned a 25–3 record and the unqualified praise of La Salle coach Loeffler, who termed his team's 80–76 win over the Pirates in the first round of the NIT the toughest victory his Explorers recorded on their way to the title. That year, Seton Hall outscored its opponents by an average of almost 17 points per game. The margin of victory narrowed to 13 in 1952–53, but the wins grew more numerous. Indeed, no fewer than 27 of them were sequenced consecutively from the start of the season all the way to March. The Pirates were what a later era would term "clutch," winning eight games decided by nine points or less over their first 27 outings.

By the time the AP called Honey Russell in late February 1953 for his reaction to Seton Hall's being voted the nation's No. 1 team for a sixth consecutive week, he was on a 52–3 run across two seasons with Dukes and Regan. Perhaps that explains why the coach avoided the standard "It doesn't mean anything until we prove it" response. "We don't think we'd give quarter to anybody," he said, "and that includes Indiana." In his Straight Stuff feature, *Indianapolis Star* sportswriter

Bob Stranahan fired back with a prediction: "I'm quite sure the Hurryin' Hoosiers will uphold Western Conference basketball honor very well in the NCAA tourney while Seton Hall is playing in that Garden abortion called the NIT."

The distinction between the National Invitation and NCAA tournaments was indeed stark that season. Starting with its 1953 tournament, the NCAA implemented two changes that would, in time, doom the NIT to second-class status. First, the NCAA field was expanded from 16 to 22 teams. More teams flowing into the NCAA tournament did not portend good times to come for the NIT, but the second formatting change made to the postseason was even more damaging to the event at Madison Square Garden. Teams were now required to pick either the NIT or the NCAA tournament. Programs could no longer play in both events in the same season.

Had the stars aligned differently, in the form of a "down" season for independents east of the Mississippi, it's conceivable the NIT might have dipped in quality that first year. Instead, February and March 1953 proceeded largely according to a script established in previous postseasons. NIT organizers decided the one team they had to have at the outset was defending champion La Salle. The Explorers were 20–2 and ranked No. 4 in the nation when they received the NIT's offer in mid-February. Loeffler left the decision up to the players, and they voted unanimously to play in the NIT. "The boys would rather play close to home," Loeffler said, "where their fellow students can see them play."

Two days later, the NIT added both No. 1 Seton Hall and No. 9 Western Kentucky. Nevertheless, if there were ominous notes sounded regarding the NIT's future even as early as 1953, they were perhaps to be found on opposite coasts. Out west, no less a Catholic independent than No. 14–ranked Seattle opted to play instead in the NCAA tournament. Geography trumped Jesuit affiliation for coach Al Brightman and his sensational scorer John O'Brien. Meanwhile, in the Garden's own backyard, it was reported that Seton Hall's players were not unanimous in their postseason voting the way La Salle's had been.

opponent than the Dayton team that had already knocked off the Pirates. Peck Hickman's team didn't require any assistance from the officials to win at home against Seton Hall. Just the same, it's possible the Cardinals received such assistance.

College basketball was then in its second season of what would be a three-year experiment with 10-minute quarters. In the second quarter alone, Seton Hall was called for traveling no fewer than six times as the team committed 11 turnovers. The game nevertheless remained tight, and with exactly three minutes remaining in the contest and Seton Hall trailing 66–64, Regan went to the line for what he assumed would be two shots. The rule at the time stated that any foul committed in the last three minutes of the game resulted in two free throws. Instead, official Jim Biersdorfer informed Regan that he would be given one shot. When questioned about this at the scorer's table, the official said that the rule "doesn't go into effect until 2:59."

"Then it's misnamed," a reporter on press row said to the referee. "It should be called the 2:59 rule."

"If it was the 2:59 rule," Biersdorfer replied, "it wouldn't apply until 2:58."

Seton Hall was given one shot, and Louisville went on to record a 73–67 win.

"The Louisville players wanted to win pretty badly," Russell said afterward, "and were tackling, tripping, and throwing elbows at us." Two photos of game action in the next day's Louisville *Courier-Journal* show Dukes being besieged with some gusto by the opposing team. Accounts offered by teammates decades after the fact would assert that Dukes was struck in the face, and then when he crumpled to the floor with the ball, he was called for traveling. If such events did occur, and if the Pirates were moved to respond in kind, the response may have taken the form of an elbow to Louisville's Corky Cox as time expired. This was the version of events offered by Cox's teammate, Chet Beam, who said Seton Hall's Harry Brooks delivered the elbow in question.

As soon as the game ended, Beam approached Brooks to, Beam would later insist, shake hands. Brooks interpreted a different motive, and a fight erupted. What happened next at the Jefferson County Armory was not so much a player altercation as a mass riot, one forever captured by an infamous *Life* magazine photo of the Pirates' Mickey Hannon lying unconscious on the court.

Regan would be a fixture at Seton Hall for the rest of his life, serving as head basketball coach throughout the 1960s, athletic director from 1971 to 1985, and executive director of the school's athletic fund until 1998. For years, he would be asked what took place that night in Louisville. For years, he would say the same thing: "It was 7,000 against 12." Seton Hall hurriedly made its way north, recorded a 27-point win over John Carroll at Cleveland Arena, and then headed home to New Jersey at 28–2 to prepare for the NIT.

The 1953 National Invitation bracket was set up for a marquee showdown in the final game: La Salle versus Seton Hall. Gola versus Dukes. At least it would have been if it had ever occurred. Instead, the Explorers fell 75–74 to St. John's in the quarterfinals. La Salle fans were so incensed by the calls made by referee Red Mihalik that they waited for him outside Madison Square Garden. The mob "made a rush for [Mihalik] when he stepped outside," but the official "ducked back into the Garden until police arrived and whisked him into a cab."

Seton Hall came close to meeting La Salle's fate and losing in the quarterfinals. The Pirates trailed Niagara by four at halftime, and Dukes had fouled out with more than nine minutes left in the game before Regan stepped in to guide his team to a five-point win. It was the closest any opponent would come to Seton Hall in that year's NIT. Many at the Garden were hoping for a rematch between Louisville and the Pirates, but that was taken off the table when Manhattan recorded a 79–66 win over the Cardinals. Instead, Seton Hall cruised to its first National Invitation title with victories by 18 and 12 over Manhattan and St. John's, respectively. For a second consecutive year, a Catholic NIT champion had faced nothing but Catholic opponents on its path to the title. A robust debate has raged ever since over whether the Pirates or NCAA tournament champion Indiana would have prevailed in a "true" 1953 national championship game.

Walter Dukes had, incredibly, averaged a 26–22 double-double for the season. The Knicks made him their territorial draft pick, and his hometown of Rochester, New York, held a Walter Dukes Day. On May 23, he was presented with a car at a ceremony held in Franklin Square. Two weeks later, Dukes attended a press conference at Toots Shor's in Midtown Manhattan. Harlem Globetrotters owner Abe Saperstein had a wheelbarrow filled with 3,000 silver dollars rolled into the restaurant. Saperstein announced that he had signed Dukes to a $25,000 contract. The silver dollars had been a token gesture, offered when Dukes happened to mention he had never seen that particular coin before. After he was photographed smiling joyously behind neatly stacked columns of silver dollars, Dukes left with Saperstein and together they boarded a flight for London. The newest Globetrotter would join the team there.

"Walter's case is mystifying," an NBA front office official said in 1992. "He's eligible for pre-pension benefits, and we have no idea where he can be." In the four decades between signing with the Globetrotters and the headline FEW CLUES IN MYSTERY OF THE MISSING DUKES, the greatest player in Seton Hall history charted a path of steadily diminishing contact with the outside world.

At first, all seemed well. Dukes played two years with the Globetrotters, followed by eight seasons in the NBA. He was an All-Star in 1960 and 1961 with the Detroit Pistons, and in the former year he graduated from New York Law School. But there were challenges awaiting Dukes in both his chosen careers. He battled knee injuries and, after his retirement from the NBA in 1963, he would be remembered primarily as one of the most foul-prone players in the league's history. Indeed, it would be Dukes's misfortune to serve as an example of a dominant big man coming out of college who, all in all, did not pan out as a player in the NBA. In the 1990s, for example, Red Auerbach would reflect on his own career and insist that drafting Bill Russell had actually carried a high degree of risk. After all, look at what could have happened. "You take a guy like Walter Dukes," Auerbach would say. "He was bigger, stronger, and he could shoot much better than Russell."

One somber irony presented by Dukes is that both of his professional trajectories were so similar. He would eventually be suspended from the Michigan bar for failure to pay dues. In 1975, after a six-day trial in Manhattan Criminal Court, Dukes was found guilty of practicing law without a license. By 1978, when he gave an interview to the New York *Daily News*, he was said to be an assistant coach at Hunter College on Manhattan's Upper East Side. He was still at least answering the phone as late as 1989, when the entire sportswriting world called Dick Vitale (Seton Hall class of 1963), Regan, and Dukes, in that order, for reactions on the Pirates' run to the Final Four. Dukes said no to every interview request, but he could still be reached. *Newsday* explained that Dukes "has fallen on difficult times and has become reclusive." Four years later, he answered the phone for one of the last times and spoke long enough to promise to attend the 40th anniversary celebration of the 1953 team. After that, nothing.

Nothing until February 8, 2001, when a Newark *Star-Ledger* sportswriter flew to Detroit for a game and, on a whim, knocked on the door on Chicago Boulevard that, according to one database, matched an old address for Dukes. Sure enough, that's where Dukes was huddled around a space heater in his kitchen with his sister. The heat had been cut off by the utility company. Sadly, that was one of the last times Walter Dukes was seen alive. His body was found in his bed by his sister on March 13 of the same year. Authorities said Dukes had died of natural causes and estimated that he had passed away almost a month before.

In his final days, Dukes spoke of having spent five years bedridden in hospitals due to a 1971 car accident. However, that account doesn't seem to align with newspaper coverage of his public appearances from the early 1970s. Perhaps there was a serious incident around that time. In the end, we don't know exactly which set of challenges Dukes faced. We do know that he was a remarkable college basketball talent, one who preceded and, in some ways, equaled many far more celebrated names to come. His name merits mention alongside theirs.

6.

Gola and Russell

few months before the NBA adopted its shot clock, Yale coach Howard Hobson proposed that college basketball adopt a shot clock of its own. In February 1954, Hobson floated a proposal for a 30-second clock, saying it would improve the game. "I'd give a team the regular 10 seconds to get the ball past midcourt," Hobson said, "and 20 more to try for the goal. If the team failed to take a shot in time, I wouldn't take away possession. That would be too severe. I'd advocate a jump ball." The pros and cons of having a shot clock in college basketball would be debated more or less without pause for the next 30 years.

The pros and cons of the NCAA's regulatory actions would be a matter of dispute for even longer. In the same month that Hobson launched his trial balloon for a shot clock, news leaked that Seton Hall's basketball program was under investigation by the NCAA. The Pirates had allegedly used the occasion of their otherwise geographically aberrant road game against Loyola Chicago in February 1953 as an opportunity to hold tryouts for area talent at Chicago Stadium. That was a violation, the same kind of transgression that simultaneously landed the Kansas State and NC State basketball programs in hot water with the NCAA.

The Wildcats and the Wolfpack were placed on probation, with Everett Case's team in Raleigh additionally being ruled ineligible for the 1955 NCAA tournament. Seton Hall escaped with merely being officially and "severely" reprimanded.

A different NCAA rule entirely would have a significant impact on the 1954 postseason. On January 25, a sportswriter spoke to Adolph Rupp and asked the Kentucky coach whether he was aware that his three leading scorers were almost certainly ineligible to play in the NCAA tournament. It was reported the following day that "Rupp appeared shocked when told of these developments." With Cliff Hagan, Frank Ramsey, and Lou Tsioropoulos in the lineup, the Wildcats were undefeated, ranked No. 1 in the polls, and, statistically speaking, far and away the strongest team in the nation. The problem in the NCAA's eyes was that the trio had continued to attend classes and earn credits during UK's "death penalty" year in 1952–53. Now, in January of 1954, Tsioropoulos was already working on a master's in physical education, and Hagan and Ramsey were days away from graduating with their bachelor's degrees. NCAA rules at the time specified that only undergraduates could compete in the association's postseason tournament.

Kentucky was still free to play in the NCAA tournament without Hagan, Ramsey, and Tsioropoulos. When the news first broke, however, speculation centered instead on whether the Wildcats would elect to play at full strength in the NIT. The Southeastern Conference, like the Atlantic Coast Conference (and, for that matter, like the future NCAA), allowed players to continue to compete after they had received their degrees. The NIT required merely that teams be eligible according to their conference's rules. Might postseason history have taken a different turn if the highly Catholic NIT had been both sustained and reoriented by the appearance of a state school with one of the strongest teams of the decade? We'll never know. One of Kentucky's acts of contrition in the wake of the point-shaving scandal had been the adoption of a new Policy on Intercollegiate Athletics. On July 26, 1952, the school vowed that its "basketball team shall not participate in any postseason

tournament other than the tournaments of the NCAA or of the SEC."
The Wildcats would not appear in the NIT again until 1976.

The 1954 National Invitation Tournament would have to find its
elite teams elsewhere. Today, we look back on that year and note that
for the first time the champions of both major national tournaments
represented Catholic institutions. La Salle won the NCAA tournament, and Holy Cross was crowned as champion at the NIT. Catholic
basketball's shining hour, however, was another subtle indication of
the NIT's gradual decline. In February, it was undefeated and No.
2–ranked Duquesne that NIT organizers felt they absolutely had to
capture. Even the usually circumspect NCAA gave public assurances
in advance of an official invitation that the Dukes were virtually assured of receiving a bid. While conference champions were of course
locked into the NCAA tournament, Dudey Moore's team was viewed
nationally as the key independent program in the tug-of-war between
the two postseason events. How the NIT won this largest of battles
yet continued to lose the war against its postseason rival makes for an
instructive parable.

Imperiled by the NCAA tournament's expansion and by the requirement that teams choose one postseason showcase only, NIT organizers
sought to lock teams into their bracket earlier than ever before.
Duquesne received its NIT bid on February 1, a full five weeks before
postseason play would commence. No at-large team was going to
earn an NCAA bid that early, but NCAA tournament committee chair
Doug Mills reportedly "assured the university that an invitation was
certain." It was going to be a difficult decision for the Dukes. Players
from the New York area naturally saw an advantage to spending their
postseason at Madison Square Garden. Still, it was reported that a fair
number of Duquesne players from other parts of the country "would
like to get a crack at the big-name teams of the NCAA."

While the Dukes mulled their options, observers were already fore-
casting that a La Salle program that to date had appeared in five NITs
and zero NCAA tournaments would, in fact, be gracing the NCAA's
event in 1954. On the surface, this prediction appeared to mark a

dramatic departure for a program whose players had voted unanimously just one year before to play in the NIT. What had changed in the interim were not preferences but procedures. There would be no vote held among the Explorers this time. Instead, coach Ken Loeffler and his team had to abide by rules set forth by the Middle Atlantic States Collegiate Athletic Conference.

Nominally composed of no fewer than 38 members with wildly differing basketball pedigrees, the MASCAC was more an institutional federation than a basketball conference. But, as of the 1953–54 season, the MASCAC did have one rule that was all about basketball. Unless a member had indicated before the season that it was forgoing postseason participation entirely, any team chosen by the MASCAC's selection committee was required to play in the NCAA tournament. La Salle had, by far, the best team among member schools. On February 20, it was official: Tom Gola and his teammates were, for the first time in program history, going after what the press termed "the biggest prize of 'em all." The Explorers would play in the NCAA tournament "with 24 of the nation's finest quintets." A few days later, 24–2 Duquesne accepted a bid as the top seed at the NIT.

Within this brief historical window where the National Invitation and NCAA tournaments actively competed against each other in an either-or setting as approximate, or at least potential, equals, Duquesne's reasons for choosing to play at the Garden spoke volumes. Already by 1954, it was virtually conceded by an elite Catholic program electing to play in the NIT that the NCAA tournament was in fact the more prestigious event. The obstacle to the Dukes' participation in the emerging national championship tournament was simply that the NCAA did not confer upon independents their due measure of prestige. When postseason decisions were left to coaches or schools in real time, the NIT could still compete for independents like Duquesne that had a long history at the Garden. This slim but no less vital opening for the NIT stemmed from the second-class status afforded nonaffiliated programs in NCAA bracketing.

In cases where conferences or teams adopted postseason decision

One report even stated that Dukes had told a writer that he personally would prefer to play in the NCAA tournament. He was overruled, however, and the Pirates chose the NIT.

To this point in its undefeated season, Seton Hall had journeyed far from home just once. The Pirates had scratched out a 52–49 win against an 8–13 Loyola Chicago team at Chicago Stadium. George Ireland was in his second season as coach of the Ramblers, and better times were still to come for the program. That single win for Seton Hall notwithstanding, the team had yet to play a game west of Scranton, Pennsylvania. This eastern emphasis was about to change: Russell's men were booked for a three-game road trip, with dates scheduled at Dayton and at Louisville, leading into a contest against the Jesuits of John Carroll in Cleveland. After this three-game swing, the Pirates would take a few days off and then proceed directly to Madison Square Garden for the NIT.

The undefeated status didn't last long on the road. Despite a 14–13 record at tip-off, Dayton defeated the Pirates 71–65, in front of what was reported to be the largest crowd ever to see a game at the then two-year-old Fieldhouse. With Seton Hall scheduled to play at Louisville the following day, the Pirates arrived at their next destination the night before the game and slept on the train at the station. In later accounts, players would recall that Louisville hotels would not allow Dukes and teammate Frank Minaya on the premises. The team's cramped sleeping arrangements would turn out to be perhaps the best part of their stay, one that was actually a return visit. Seton Hall had won a road game at Louisville by two points the previous year. While the team was presumably forced to sleep on the train on that earlier occasion as well, the game itself, for better or worse, did not appear to raise any red flags with Russell. He'd again agreed to a home-and-home series with the Cardinals for 1952–53.

After Seton Hall's experience in Louisville in 1953, no such agreement would be signed for the following season. The Pirates and the Cardinals would not play each other again for 49 years.

Ranked No. 18 nationally, Louisville was a significantly stronger rules in advance, however, those procedures invariably favored the NCAA tournament. We see this not only in the case of La Salle, but also, paradoxically, in the example provided by eventual 1954 NIT champion Holy Cross. Buster Sheary had his best post-Cousy-era team that year. Future NBA players and fellow Union City, New Jersey, products Togo Palazzi and Tom Heinsohn were on the floor together as a senior and sophomore, respectively. When the Crusaders rolled up 11 consecutive wins, the Associated Press assumed Holy Cross was mounting a "drive for the New England NCAA championship tournament berth." The District 1 selection committee chair was John Bunn, athletic director at Springfield College. He said his campus would host a four- or possibly even eight-team tournament, and the champion would earn the district's NCAA bid.

What occurred instead was an insurrection, or perhaps an example of passive resistance. Holy Cross and Connecticut jointly decided, with some justification, that they were the two best teams in New England. The Crusaders and the Huskies boasted a combined record of 42–3 when the two teams met at Worcester Auditorium on February 27. Sheary and UConn coach Hugh Greer made a gentleman's agreement before tip-off that the winner would take the NCAA bid. The Holy Cross coach doubtless felt he had the better part of that bargain, since his team hadn't lost a game at "the Aud" in five years. But Connecticut overcame a 38-point performance by Palazzi and won 78–77 on a last-second shot by Worthy Patterson. After the game, both coaches proclaimed their teams "unavailable" for any District 1 tournament, giving the Huskies the NCAA bid and leaving Bunn to protest weakly that "we're not going to bump our heads against a wall." Even in New England in 1954, hardly an NCAA stronghold, it was assumed that the winner of a game between the region's two best teams would go to the NCAA tournament. The NIT scooped up the 22–2 Crusaders and awarded them the No. 3 seed behind Duquesne and Western Kentucky.

Holy Cross recorded 35 points at the line in an easy quarterfinal win over St. Francis (the Terriers at last crossed the East River to make their first NIT appearance) before Palazzi scored 32 in a slight upset over Western Kentucky, the No. 4 team in the nation. After time expired against the Hilltoppers, fans of the Crusaders managed to storm a neutral court at Madison Square Garden. That game would turn out to be the toughest test for Holy Cross. In a 71–62 victory in the final against star forward Dick Ricketts and Duquesne, the Crusaders never trailed and, after halftime, the Dukes never drew closer than eight. "This is not quite the team that Holy Cross had in 1947," former CCNY coach Nat Holman remarked to a reporter that night. "It doesn't have the great individual stars. But it worked together beautifully as a unit." The following evening, Sheary and his team made an appearance on *The Ed Sullivan Show*.

Gola didn't even need to be part of a championship team to earn an invite from the show. He was asked to appear even before La Salle's opening tournament game against the Fordham Rams. Loeffler vetoed the idea, since the show would have been broadcast from Midtown Manhattan the night before the Explorers were to meet the Rams at Buffalo Memorial Auditorium.

La Salle was younger than it had been when it was upset by St. John's in the 1953 NIT. Norm Grekin and Jack Moore were gone, but Gola and his mostly shorter and less experienced teammates had put together a 21–4 record and entered the 1954 NCAA tournament ranked No. 8 in the nation. In Buffalo, they would face an 18–5 Fordham team appearing in its second consecutive NCAA tournament. Loeffler was not the type of coach to feign concern about an opponent in front of the press, so when he said, "I wish we were playing against anyone but Fordham," he likely meant it. Anyway, his apprehension turned out to be well-founded. "It looked as if La Salle was doomed," the *Philadelphia Inquirer* stated succinctly.

With the score tied at 66, Fordham held the ball for the final two minutes to get the last shot. The Rams' Dan Lyons then rebounded an Ed Parchinski miss and gave his team a two-point lead with eight seconds remaining. Loeffler called two time-outs in four seconds of game clock to advance the ball to half-court. He then drew up a play for

Gola to come off a screen for an open shot. But Gola was surrounded when he received Fran O'Malley's inbound pass above the free-throw line. O'Malley cut straight to the basket, Gola got him the ball, and the sophomore tied the game as time expired. At the beginning of over-time, a deep Charlie Singley set shot from the left side and two Gola free throws gave La Salle a lead it would never surrender on its way to a 76–74 victory.

The perilous win in Buffalo gave the Explorers the opportunity to play their way into the Final Four in the familiar environs of the Palestra in Philadelphia. That's where La Salle faced NC State, the only ranked opponent the Explorers would see in their five-game NCAA tournament run. Loeffler's team scored 17 points in the last two minutes to win 88–81. By the time La Salle recorded a 16-point victory over an "outclassed" Navy team in the regional final, local fans were already looking ahead and noting that the rest of the NCAA bracket in 1954 had collapsed. No. 1–ranked Kentucky had finished 25–0 and didn't even enter the tournament. No. 2 Indiana, the defending champion, had lost by one in the regional semifinals to No. 6 Notre Dame. Unranked Penn State then eliminated the Fighting Irish. The Explorers would be joined at the Final Four by three unranked teams: Bradley, USC, and the Nittany Lions.

After winning games by two, seven, and 16 points, La Salle extended this trend of steadily decreasing drama and increasing euphoria at Municipal Auditorium in Kansas City. The Explorers defeated Penn State by 15 and Bradley by 16 to capture the national championship. In the span of just three seasons, Loeffler and his group had won both the National Invitation and NCAA tournaments. It was of course La Salle's success in the latter event that would forever enable the program to have claimed to have won "the" national championship. Ironically, however, and through pure chance, the 1952 NIT title was the far more impressive achievement. To win the National Invitation that year, Loeffler's team had defeated four opponents ranked in the top 15 nationally, up to and including Walter Dukes–led Seton Hall and a St. John's team days away from advancing to the NCAA's final game. It was a nice Gola-era problem to have if you were La Salle, trying to determine which of your national tournament titles was more amazing.

In addition to hosting the renaissance of a sport in which Catholic programs were thriving, the mid-1950s also ushered in a decision that has determined the basic format of college games played ever since.

Yale coach Howard Hobson was still lobbying for his 30-second shot clock, and he presented his proposal to fellow National Association of Basketball Coaches members at the 1954 Final Four. His motion for a clock was defeated in "emphatic" fashion and, in fact, drew just one supporting vote. The assembled coaches did however adopt one recommendation intended to reduce what was termed "stalling." Now that 10-minute quarters had been used in college basketball for three years, the coaches recommended that the basketball rules committee return the sport to 20-minute halves. According to the NABC, the problem with quarters was that teams were playing for the last shot for one to two minutes or even longer at the end of each 10-minute period. While a shot clock would have prohibited holding the ball, coaches instead chose to reduce the number of cues to hold the ball.

When college basketball finally adopted a shot clock for all games including the NCAA tournament as of the 1985–86 season, this original rationale for 20-minute halves was rendered a dead letter. Nevertheless, halves endure. To this day, college basketball in the United States stands out as one of the few forms of the men's game anywhere in the world that uses halves instead of quarters. Ultimately, this eccentricity stems from one gathering of coaches in the Grand Ballroom of Kansas City's Hotel Muehlebach on March 19, 1954.

At the beginning of that same 1953–54 season, the *San Francisco Examiner* had run a large photo from an opening-night game on the front page of its sports section. The picture was captioned: "A Bucket? No." In the photo, the shooter has elevated for a layup and is about to release the ball. The defender is still flat-footed, on the ground below. Yet the shot was blocked.

The defender was Bill Russell of the University of San Francisco. The unlucky opponent was California's Bob Matheny. Of the two, Matheny was by far the more celebrated player in December 1953. He had been named Northern California high school player of the year in 1952, while Russell toiled in obscurity for his high school team in Oakland. Russell's block against Matheny was one of 13 the sophomore would record in his varsity debut, as the Dons defeated the Golden Bears 51–33 at Kezar Pavilion in San Francisco. Cal was a quality opponent, and, in particular, 6-foot-7 junior Bob McKeen entered the season touted as an All-America candidate. His candidacy got off to a rocky start. One writer reported that Russell left "McKeen so frustrated that the lanky Cal man had his best look at the basket from the bench." McKeen was outscored 23–14 by Russell, and the game seemed to signal a changing of the guard in West Coast basketball.

It didn't happen that way, though, at least not that season. USF turned out to be, as coaches like to say, a year away. In the *Examiner's* picture of Russell's incredible soon-to-be block, teammate K. C. Jones appears to be wearing a pained expression and his jaw is clenched. The Dons were scheduled to play their next game on the road in Fresno, which is where Jones was hospitalized, at Saint Agnes, with a ruptured appendix. He missed the entire season except for that one game against the Bears, a fact that would loom large for his eligibility in the 1956 NCAA tournament. As for the 1953–54 team, it would be said in later years that chemistry had been an issue. Russell was a sophomore. The white seniors felt they had paid their dues in Phil Woolpert's program and that this was to be their year. San Francisco finished 14–7, with Russell as its leading scorer.

At first it appeared the following season might bring more of the same for USF, even with a healthy Jones rejoining the lineup. San Francisco opened 1954–55 with a 2–1 record, courtesy of a 47–40 loss at UCLA. Still, Russell reportedly "blocked at least a half-dozen Bruin shots" in that game, and, even in defeat, the Dons left an indelible impression on head coach John Wooden and his players. UCLA's Willie Naulls would recall that, as the Bruins were coming out for warm-ups before tip-off, he could hear his team's own fans cheering the USF players and their impressive display of dunking during pregame drills. Once the Bruins were out on the floor, Naulls and his teammates found that they, too, couldn't help but watch the Dons. Wooden became so upset he ordered his team back into the locker room and scolded them for letting an opponent intimidate them. The Bruins were at least correct to be impressed. One week later, with Hal Perry replacing Bill Bush in USF's starting lineup, San Francisco crushed UCLA in a rematch at the Cow Palace in San Francisco. While on paper the Bruins lost by 12, the Dons were leading 54–29 with five minutes remaining when Woolpert cleared his bench. UCLA didn't score from the field until midway through the first half. The following week, USF was ranked in the top 20 for the first time since 1950.

The shift from Bush to Perry in the starting lineup carried symbolic weight. Perry was an African American player from outside the Bay Area. Bush was a white graduate of St. Ignatius High School, which shared both a neighborhood and a history with Jesuit USF. Until 1930, the University of San Francisco itself had been St. Ignatius College. Woolpert had been a teammate of Pete Newell's in Los Angeles at the school later known as Loyola Marymount. After Newell left the Dons' head coaching job to go to Michigan State in 1950, Woolpert moved over from leading the USF freshman team to coaching the varsity. Woolpert had also coached at St. Ignatius High, SI to the locals. Putting Perry in the lineup alongside Russell and Jones would earn the coach praise in later years, for flouting an unwritten rule and starting three Black players. In real time, the true "unwritten rule" was arguably one requiring five white players. Where that assumption was overturned, the abuse heaped upon Black college players exhibited little correlation to whether one, two, or three persons of color appeared in a starting lineup. Such quantitative distinctions were a luxury afforded after the fact. Woolpert is said to have received hate mail throughout the years that Jones, Russell, Perry, and reserve Warren Baxter were on campus. In addition to anonymous letters, the coach was subjected to criticism from within the church by local educators. They felt USF basketball scholarships should be awarded to white graduates of Catholic high schools.

While Woolpert received pushback for his pioneering ways, he had company in his trailblazing. The so-called unwritten rule was being violated by more than one major college coach in 1954–55, a development celebrated by the African American press nationally. The venerable *Pittsburgh Courier* paid tribute that season not only to San Francisco's remarkable nucleus but also to starting trios at Duquesne (Si Green and brothers Dick and Dave Ricketts) and at UCLA (Naulls, John Moore, and Morris Taft). While singing the praises of La Salle starter Alonzo Lewis as well, the *Courier* remarked that "Negroes and success in big time collegiate basketball are becoming more synonymous each year." Perry, in particular, gave Woolpert a second tenacious backcourt defender to pair with Jones, one who, at 5 foot 10, specialized in harassing larger opponents and then beating them down the floor after still another blocked shot by Russell.

With Perry having started two games, San Francisco was 4–1 and ranked No. 17 in the nation. USF's breakthrough was about to occur in, of all places, Oklahoma. Anticipating a special team in 1954–55, Woolpert had booked San Francisco for the All-College tournament in Oklahoma City's Municipal Auditorium. The event proudly billed itself as older than both the National Invitation and NCAA tournaments. However, nearby hotels would not serve Russell, Jones, and Perry, and the entire team instead stayed in a dormitory at Oklahoma City University. And when the Dons took the floor at the Auditorium for their scheduled workout, they were pelted with coins by spectators. Russell responded outwardly with studied nonchalance, scooping up the pennies as though collecting easy money and asking Woolpert to hold them for him. "I thought that was awesome," Jones would say decades later.

That year's All-College bracket had been built for a title game between two national top-15 teams, Wichita State and George Washington. Unfortunately for the Shockers, they were paired with San Francisco in the tip-off for the entire tournament. After seven minutes of basketball, WSU trailed 25–3. Jerry Mullen scored 23 points for USF before halftime. In what was rapidly becoming a pattern, the final score, 94–75, obscured how unequal the contest had actually been. The next opponent, Oklahoma City University, eked out 29 points in 31 minutes, until Woolpert pulled his regulars. In the championship game, Russell posted a 23–30 double-double in a 16-point win over George Washington. In 120 minutes of basketball, the junior had gone from having made some all–Pacific Coast teams in 1953–54 to being ranked among the greatest ever to play the college game. A shocked *Oklahoman* newspaper reported that "coaches mince no words about elevating [Russell] above such men as [Oklahoma] A&M's Bob Kurland and Clyde Lovellette of Kansas." It went without saying, now, that USF was "a definite national championship contender."

Woolpert had built his contender with equal measures of hustle and good fortune. If the coach was ahead of some of his peers in starting three Black players, he was also ideally situated in place and time with all three recruits. Jones had arrived in 1951 after a successful career at Commerce High School in San Francisco, making him the most celebrated recruit on the Dons roster. Celebrated yet bypassed: Jones's only scholarship offer had been from Woolpert. The following year, Perry secured a tryout with USF after he was turned down by Cal and Oregon State. When he was guarded by Jones during the entire work-out, Perry was, predictably, shut down completely. Undeterred, the Baptist from the relative hinterlands of Ukiah, California, proceeded to talk Woolpert into a scholarship at the Jesuit school by asking the coach to pray about the matter. Russell had been so obscure at Oakland's McClymonds High School that Jones had never heard of him until they became college teammates. "Russ wasn't even the best player on our school team," his coach, George Powles, would marvel in 1955. Nevertheless, USF's Dick Lawless was impressed when he was guarded by Russell in a pickup game, whereupon Woolpert dispatched Hal DeJulio as a scout. A member of San Francisco's 1949 NIT title team, DeJulio saw something in Russell, who was 6 foot 7 when he arrived on campus.

After Russell set a record by averaging 20 a game for the freshman team, he was approached by other schools with offers to transfer. Woolpert's recruit elevated his game exponentially at the same time that he added three inches in height. The combined impact of those developments changed the sport itself. Perhaps no one in the history of the game has made a more dramatic transformation from high school to college player than did Russell. Give all due credit to DeJulio and Woolpert for what was, strictly speaking, college basketball's greatest single player evaluation ever. Then again, a program stronger than USF was in 1952 would have been far less likely to expend a precious scholarship on a project like Russell. In this instance, San Francisco benefited from its perceived status as being a level down from Cal, Stanford, UCLA, and even, by the early 1950s, from its Jesuit rival Santa Clara. Once Russell had become *the* Bill Russell, circa 1955, Woolpert was asked what lessons in skills development he could share with his peers. "Under my coaching," he replied, Russell "improved so much that he is now a 6-foot-10-inch player. You understand now what coaching genius is."

The changing of the guard in West Coast basketball had come to pass after all, and it became official at the Cow Palace in January 1955. San Francisco and Santa Clara would each play Stanford and Cal on consecutive nights in a four-game test of the upstart California Basketball Association's strength relative to the established and preeminent Pacific Coast Conference. The CBA had been launched prior to the 1952–53 season, with USF, SCU, Saint Mary's, San Jose State, and College of the Pacific as founding members. (COP would later become UOP: University of the Pacific.) In its first two seasons, the CBA had twice sent Santa Clara and its star Ken Sears to the NCAA tournament. Now, San Francisco was pillaging the conference in the league's third season of existence. "There's only one way to beat Russell," Saint Mary's coach Thomas Foley observed. "That's to kidnap him. On second thought, where are you going to hide that big character if you do?"

PCC teams didn't fare any better against Russell than Foley had. USF blew Stanford off the floor 76–60 before turning around the next night and running up a 20–0 lead on Cal en route to an 84–62 victory.

First-year Stanford coach Howie Dallmar was stunned yet admiring. "We had three defenses ready for the Dons," he observed. "The first, second, and third, or 'panic stage,' which we hoped we wouldn't have to use. Well, we were in the 'panic stage' before the game was seven minutes old." San Francisco replaced Kentucky as the No. 1 team in the national polls in early February and remained there for the remainder of its 23–1 regular season.

There was never any real doubt that Jesuit USF, which had been a proud independent just three years before, was going to play in the NCAA tournament. NIT officials at Madison Square Garden apparently assumed they had no shot with the greatest Catholic college basketball team to date. They were right. The CBA regular-season champion was required to enter what at the time was called the NCAA "playoffs."

Instead of expending effort on what was sure to be a futile pursuit of San Francisco, the NIT again went after Duquesne. The Dukes were again ranked among the top five teams in the nation, but this time there was less drama and discussion about what to do in the post-season than there had been in 1954. Dudey Moore's program just said yes, and did so earlier than any NIT team had in the event's history. "We like it in New York," Moore explained. "There's no problem of traveling, because the play is in the one city, and well, it seems we just always go to the NIT." Dayton quickly joined Duquesne in the field at the Garden, with the added kicker that the Flyers had an official NCAA bid in their pocket and chose instead to play at the NIT. The Dukes and UD were alike in that they were outstanding Catholic independents putting together excellent runs in the mid-1950s. Both fan bases had already demonstrated the vital ability of showing up in force on Eighth Avenue to support their teams.

Geographic proximity, independence, and Catholicity were traits that worked consistently in the NIT's favor, but Villanova proved they weren't everything. The Wildcats checked all three boxes yet turned the National Invitation down flat to say yes to the NCAA in 1955. But the biggest single surprise on the NCAA vs. NIT front was supplied by Marquette. The Warriors, as they were then known, spent the balance of 1954–55 extending the nation's longest win streak, one whose start predated even San Francisco's. Jack Nagle's men would eventually reel off 22 straight victories, but by the time Marquette got to 17 in a row, the NCAA had seen enough. MU accepted its first-ever NCAA tournament bid on February 12, putting the NIT on notice that its rival was perfectly happy to poach independent Jesuit programs when it saw fit. However, not every team fitting that profile was as fortunate as Marquette. Coming off two consecutive NCAA tournament appearances, Fordham confidently rejected a 1955 NIT bid. The Rams then missed the NCAA tournament entirely.

If Fordham had chosen to play at the Garden, perhaps the school could have delivered the tristate area its second title at the event in three years. Instead, Duquesne won the NIT, on its eighth try. Moore had two All-Americans, in Si Green and Dick Ricketts, and the Dukes recorded relatively easy wins against Louisville and Cincinnati before meeting fellow NIT stalwart Dayton in the title game. Green and Rickets scored all 35 of Duquesne's first-half points on the way to a 70–58 victory. Fans in Pittsburgh were so overjoyed that when the team arrived home the locals did a fair reenactment of Charles Lindbergh's landing at Le Bourget in Paris. A crowd estimated at 5,000 "broke onto the airport landing field" at Greater Pittsburgh Airport as the Dukes' plane touched down.

While Moore had enjoyed the luxury of knowing the 12-team NIT field a week in advance, his counterpart at San Francisco had to wait until the last minute to learn which opponent his team would play in its first NCAA tournament game. The Dons were bracketed to face the champion of the Border Conference, and that title race came down to the last night of the season, when league leader Texas Tech played at Texas Western (later known as the University of Texas at El Paso, or UTEP). After losing 79–71 at El Paso County Coliseum, Texas Tech also came up on the short end of a postgame coin flip to determine the league's representative in the NCAA tournament. USF would instead face the West Texas State Buffaloes at the Cow Palace.

Woolpert knew nothing about West Texas State, a team that turned out to have a deplorable plan, such as it was, with regard to Russell. Twice in the game's opening minutes, the Buffaloes submarined Russell when he was in midair. Woolpert rushed onto the court in protest after the second incident as a chorus of boos rained down on West Texas State. Russell had an even better response: He scored 20 in the first half. San Francisco won by 23, and the Dons proceeded to Corvallis, Oregon, for a regional semifinal against Utah. Utes coach Jack Gardner was given an unsolicited scouting report on USF from one John D. Wagner, a former Provo resident now living in San Francisco. "If any type of offense can be concocted to cause the Dons to lose one or two men on the fouls," Wagner wrote, "they would lose much of their effectiveness and become an average team." The Utes never got the chance to try Wagner's plan. USF sprinted out to a 41–20 halftime lead and won by 19 with no Don picking up more than three fouls. San Francisco would meet Oregon State in the regional final.

All season long, Russell had dominated opposing players who were both overmatched and undersized. The second part of this dynamic, at least, was supposed to be reversed by the Beavers. At a listed height of 7 foot 3, OSU's Swede Halbrook had five inches on Russell. UCLA had been outfought for the Pacific Coast Conference's bid by Oregon State, and the Bruins coach offered his opinion that Russell was at long last about to meet his match. Wooden was apparently unaware of a photo that might have altered his assessment. At a press availability in Corvallis before the regional semifinals, a photographer attempted to stage a publicity shot where Halbrook would hold the ball as high as he could and Russell would reach for it in vain. "Just reach as high as you can, Bill," the photographer told the Dons star.

Instead, the photo's caption had to be reworded. "SAN FRAN-CISCO'S All-American Bill Russell (left) stands only 6-10 but his arm reach matches that of Oregon State's 7-3 Center." Russell's standing reach was so telescopically prodigious that he easily grasped his half of the ball that Halbrook was holding aloft. "I've never been measured," Russell would respond when asked about his wingspan. Russell used that wingspan to score 29 against a "towering" OSU front line that featured Halbrook, 7-foot-0 Phil Shadoin, and 6-foot-7 Tex Whiteman. USF needed every one of its star's points on the Beavers' home court. Jerry Mullen was San Francisco's second-leading scorer, and he had to be carried off the floor after he injured his ankle 30 seconds into the game.

The Dons led 57–55 with 13 seconds remaining when, with Oregon State about to inbound the ball coming out of a time-out, K. C. Jones was hit with a technical foul for accidentally bowling over OSU's Bill Toole. The Beavers made the free throw and retained possession. Ron Robins then missed a set shot from the corner and, when Jones took the rebound away from Halbrook, a jump ball was called at Oregon State's end of the floor. Whether the 6-foot-1 Jones denied the 7-foot-3 Halbrook a clean tap by jumping early or thanks to one "mighty leap" depends on the storyteller. Somehow, the ball ended up in Hal Perry's hands as time expired. With its 57–56 win over OSU, San Francisco was going to the Final Four. "That Russell may be 6-foot-10," Beavers coach Slats Gill said, "but he plays like he's 7-foot-5."

Mullen's ankle was the top sports story in the Bay Area press that weekend. By Monday evening, he was mobile enough to appear at the Northern California Basketball Writers and Sportscasters Association's annual dinner with several other players. It had already been announced that the media members, assembled at the Press and Union League Club that night, would award their most valuable player award to Ken Sears of Santa Clara. The fact that Russell would win this same award in a walk one year later could offer no justice in real time. He was furious, and he vowed that he would not attend the ceremony. Woolpert responded that such a boycott would be viewed as petulance, a remark that, while correct with respect to how whites around Russell in the 1950s would react, was no less revealing in its own right. In the end, Russell did attend the dinner and even managed a wan smile when photographed with Sears, Mullen, Cal's Bob McKeen, and Stanford's Ron Tomsic.

The Dons flew to Kansas City for the Final Four on a plane shared with area coaches like Santa Clara's Bob Feerick, Stanford's Dallmar, and Newell, now at Cal, a longtime friend of Woolpert's. USF would face Colorado in one semifinal, while La Salle would play Iowa in the other game. The Explorers had breezed to the Final Four, recording wins by an average margin of 32 points over West Virginia, Princeton, and Canisius. Loeffler felt this 25–4 team was stronger than his 1954 national champions, and the statistics backed him up. Sophomores had become juniors, and new addition Alonzo Lewis vied with Charlie Singley for the title of second-leading scorer behind Tom Gola. "He'll be La Salle's big gun next year," the *Philadelphia Inquirer* said of Lewis.

Gola was still the big gun in 1955. Russell and Gola were both well ahead of their times; it just happened to be the latter's misfortune to be so far ahead of his that there was no three-point line on the floor. Gola was an outstanding shooter who converted 75 percent of his free-throw attempts over a four-year career, when Division I as a whole was improving from 63 to 67 percent at the line. Customarily referred to as a center because he was the tallest player on La Salle's roster, Gola in fact overmatched opponents by roaming the floor. It was no coincidence that Loeffler presented a clinic on the topic of screening at that year's NABC meeting in Kansas City. The Explorers often employed a weave on offense, and Gola recorded a fair share of his points away from the basket, either on jumpers or on "one-handed push" shots. He was considerably more accurate from the field than his teammates, despite his role as the highest of high-volume scorers. Gola was also excellent on the boards.

In short, by advancing both Gola and Russell to Kansas City, the 1955 NCAA tournament delivered pure basketball justice. They were quite possibly the two best players the college game had seen to that point, and they finally laid eyes on each other for the first time in the lobby of Kansas City's Hotel Continental the Thursday before the semifinal game. Ideally, it would have been a meeting of the greats, an opportunity to voice reciprocal admiration. Instead, it was a bit prickly. La Salle was coming back to the hotel after practice when a USF teammate nudged Russell and said, "There's Gola." In the description offered the next day by a Philadelphia sportswriter, "Russell, wearing a smirk, drew himself up stiffly to emphasize his height, placed his hands on his hips and said loud enough for Gola to hear: 'At last I meet the great Gola.'" Accounts vary, but Loeffler reportedly snapped back at Russell with something along the lines of "You'll be seeing a lot of him."

Gola later admitted that the ability of Philadelphians in the 1950s to track the doings of the California Basketball Association was limited. "People aren't going to believe me," he would say in hindsight, "but Bill Russell was not a big name on the East Coast...Russell didn't know me, and I didn't know him." Apparently, Russell wasn't a big name in Boulder, Colorado, either. Whether as a motivational ploy for his team or as a statement of genuine belief, Colorado coach Bebe Lee predicted that his men would defeat the Dons. One person ideally positioned to weigh in on that comment was Newell. Cal had lost to USF, while recording two victories in three tries against the Buffaloes. Told of Lee's quote, Newell said, "When I was a little boy, I used to whistle in the cemetery."

Woolpert started St. Ignatius product Bob Wiebusch in Mullen's place against CU, a game-time decision that likely reflected the coach's estimation of the opponent as much as it did the condition of Mullen's ankle. USF opened a 44–26 lead on Colorado before posting a customarily misleading final score, 62–50. Russell hammered home one of his celebrated reverse dunks, and Jones brought down the house with two emphatic slams of his own.

On the other half of the bracket, La Salle had survived foul trouble and its own rather ineffective use of a 1-3-1 zone to post a shaky three-point victory over Iowa. Since the beginning of the tournament, a title game between the Explorers and USF had been widely anticipated and highly desired. It was not, however, televised, even though the previous year's final contest between La Salle and Bradley had been. This invisibility of the 1955 title game is a significant loss to basketball history. Though the game itself wasn't close, two of its individual performances fairly became the stuff of legend.

Russell posted a 23–25 double-double, with 18 of his points coming in a first-half flurry that effectively broke La Salle's will. Phog Allen, hardly an impetuous cheerleader for all that was novel in Naismith's game, called Russell's performance in the opening 20 minutes the most exciting basketball he had seen from a player in 45 years. Conversely, Gola scored 16 on the evening and ended an unparalleled career by passing the torch. The senior "rang down the curtain on four seasons of magnificent basketball," the hometown *Inquirer* eulogized. "But his work was futile and completely overshadowed by Russell." USF won the national title 77–63. While Russell was rightly named the tournament's most outstanding player, he may not have been the evening's top performer. That honor may instead belong to Jones, who outscored his teammate by one while also guarding Gola the entire night.

Within the span of a few hours, San Francisco defeated La Salle in Kansas City, while Duquesne beat Dayton at Madison Square Garden. Across two storied national tournaments, a final four, of sorts, emerged: Jesuit, Lasallian, Spiritan, Marianist. The night of March 19, 1955, was a Catholic college basketball landmark.

It was viewed as a shared landmark, as seen in the following week's African American press:

> What has been threatening to happen for a long while became a reality last week as Negro collegiate basketball stars surged to the head of the class in the cage world.
>
> The facts were so apparent that to deny them would prove hopeless. Two of the biggest titles in the country...were captured last Saturday by teams that have been sparked by beige stars all year.

Mullen and USF teammate Stan Buchanan were seniors. At a victory luncheon attended by over a thousand fans who the filled the Gold Room of San Francisco's Fairmont Hotel to overflowing, Mullen spoke of his team in the third person for the first time.

"They're going to win the championship again."

7.

Perfection

ill Russell's San Francisco teammates for 1955–56 still included K. C. Jones and Hal Perry, who were now joined by new starters Carl Boldt and Mike Farmer, as well as by reserve Gene Brown. Jones had been allowed to play varsity ball as a freshman in 1951–52 due to the same Korean War–era exemption that had applied to Tom Gola. In his "first" junior campaign in 1953–54, Jones had played just one game before his appendix ruptured. Now, prior to the 1955–56 season, he was granted a fifth year of eligibility by the California Basketball Association. The only remaining question was whether Jones would be eligible for the 1956 NCAA tournament. The NCAA would meet in convention in Los Angeles in January, and USF officials would make their case at that time.

Phil Woolpert had to work hard to project his usual worried air with regard to a defending champion returning three of its top four scorers, one that was an overwhelming choice as the nation's No. 1 team in the season's initial AP poll. Woolpert sounded far less concerned when discussing a rule change that pretty much everyone in the country, including and especially Russell, viewed as being specifically targeted at Russell. The lane had been widened to 12 feet, and Woolpert, for once, sounded utterly and correctly nonchalant. "They aren't going to stop [Russell] with puny things like a 12-foot lane," he said. "The only way they'll beat him is to pass legislation that will keep him from lifting his arms."

Woolpert crafted a schedule that was a dramatic departure from the previous year's. In 1954–55, the Dons had played three regular-season games in Oklahoma City and 21 in the state of California (with 17 in the Bay Area). Now, as the defending champion, USF would venture confidently east of the Mississippi for the first time in any of the players' careers. The road trip would include stops at Chicago Stadium, Wichita State, Loyola New Orleans, and, finally, Madison Square Garden. It was an ambitious itinerary that got off to a listless start: San Francisco trailed for much of the game against Marquette in the Windy City. Russell scored just one basket in the first half against the 6-foot-9 Terry Rand before the Dons came to life and prevailed 65–58.

San Francisco looked much more like itself in brushing aside host DePaul by 23 in the holiday tournament's title game. Woolpert was already resting his starters in the first 20 minutes, but Jones somehow still managed to score 17 first-half points. Blue Demons head coach Ray Meyer called Russell "a better defensive man" than DePaul legend George Mikan. By Meyer's count, Russell "blocked 10 shots in the first half and five in the second—all short shots—which against anyone else would have been 'sure' baskets." Blocks were still years away from being tracked as an official statistic, and dazed victim-impact statements like Meyer's are some of the best suggestive hints we have as to Russell's true greatness on defense. Anecdotal evidence suggests Russell may have played as little as 20 minutes in lopsided wins, which, in the case of USF in 1955–56, meant an unusually high number of games. His actual performance statistics, if we could ever glimpse them, would likely be off the charts.

The Dons proceeded from Chicago to Wichita, where Ralph Miller's Shockers had just won by eight at home against UCLA. A 10-point San Francisco victory was distinguished primarily by the fact that fans of the home team were booing and making noise while USF shot its free throws. Miller apologized to Woolpert after the game, though La Salle, for one, had already encountered this new tactic on the road during the Gola years. Accepted etiquette for home crowds was very much in flux. Soon, creating a distraction during the visiting team's free throws would be accepted as the norm.

Playing a true road game against a less prominent opponent like Loyola New Orleans, as the Dons did next, represented a regional homecoming, of sorts, for Russell, a North Louisiana native who'd lived in Monroe until he was eight years old. On a less sentimental level, it was also a sizable gift to the home team. The Wolf Pack were making a concerted effort to raise the profile of their Jesuit institution through basketball, and why not? Russell himself, despite living in Oakland for a decade, had never heard of the University of San Francisco until he received a phone call from its coaching staff. For its part, however, Loyola was learning that USF's rise was easier to admire than duplicate. Faced with, among other things, a very different local attitude toward recruiting Black players, the Wolf Pack's Jim McCafferty was finding it difficult to build his program. Ultimately, the school went for broke, building a new field house and scheduling home games against kindly and accommodating but also powerful Catholic friends like La Salle, San Francisco, and Dayton.

As far as the Dons were concerned, an additional incentive was to help Loyola along in its efforts to at least be seen as hosting African American opposing players even if the Wolf Pack did not yet recruit such talent. USF's lead athletic official, the Rev. Ralph Tichenor, was traveling with the team on the trip, and in Wichita he struck up a conversation with a local journalist. "You know," Tichenor reportedly said, "one of the big reasons we booked a date in New Orleans with Loyola was the school officials there said we could help along their integration program." The new field house in New Orleans was itself an $800,000 wager that longstanding strictures on segregation could be finessed or even subverted. Seating at the new venue was, in the parlance of the time, "mixed," and the local Black press took note. "Negro sports fans of this community and surrounding areas will for the first time be treated as normal, ordinary human beings," the *Louisiana Weekly* stated when the field house opened. La Salle and Alonzo Lewis had already been hosted by Loyola in December of 1954. While struggling on the court, the Wolf Pack program earned praise nationally for "its pioneering of mixed athletic events in the South."

Loyola could control the seating at its field house, but it couldn't tell local businesses how to operate. Upon arrival in New Orleans, the San Francisco traveling party divided up into whites and African Americans. The former stayed at a hotel, the latter on the campus of Xavier, the HBCU that had put together its own dominant run of basketball in the 1930s. The Dons arrived in town to find that tensions had been raised by the Wolf Pack's previous home game. When Bradley's Shellie McMillon had fouled out, he was booed and jeered by the crowd. On that much, everyone agreed. Past that, accounts diverged. The visitors said the crowd chanted "Bye, bye, blackbird" at McMillon, and that the Loyola band started playing "Dixie." Others said McMillon stuck out his tongue or even gave fans the finger, a version that BU coach Bob Vanatta denied.

Whatever had transpired three nights before, San Francisco showed up at Loyola's new field house and won the game by 18 in front of a "non-segregated crowd." In the revealing formulation of the day, one laden with subtext, the game was said to have been played "without incident" (though not without officious mimicry of Black dialect by one referee). The AP noted only that the Loyola band that night "confined its selections to the Loyola fight song and the national anthem." The Dons had visited New Orleans and received "thundering ovations," but this game would prove to be a quiet moment amidst a gathering storm.

Basketball and football teams in the South had played and were playing against African American opponents on occasion, but particularly after *Brown v. Board of Education* was handed down in May 1954, politicians saw a new opportunity to take stands and make news. In the same month that USF played in New Orleans, Georgia's governor vowed to block Georgia Tech's football team from playing Pitt and Bobby Grier in the 1956 Sugar Bowl in New Orleans. "The South stands at Armageddon," Governor Marvin Griffin proclaimed. "We cannot make the slightest concession to the enemy in this dark and lamentable hour of struggle." As it happens, the governor failed to prevent Georgia Tech from playing Pitt. Yet the battles continued and, if anything, intensified. The issue of teams playing against African American opponents would become more hotly contested in the South, not less, after December 1955.

From New Orleans, USF headed north and east. At 7–0 and having won 33 straight games, the Dons were about to play at Madison Square Garden for the first time in five years. The eight-team Holiday Festival included No. 2 seed UCLA, as well as three of the five players who would eventually earn consensus first-team All-American honors for 1956: Russell, Duquesne's Si Green, and Tom Heinsohn of Holy Cross. No longer sharing the limelight with Togo Palazzi as he had on the Crusaders' 1954 NIT title team, Heinsohn was one of the most prolific scorers in the country. Before the year was through, he would record a 51-point and 43-rebound effort against Boston College. But such numbers were not in the offing against Russell and the Dons. Struggling with illness, Heinsohn was held to 12 points as San Francisco prevailed by 16. In the crowd at the Garden that night watching Russell, Heinsohn, and also K. C. Jones intently was Red Auerbach of the Boston Celtics.

The brackets held true, and USF and UCLA would meet in the title game. John Wooden had to be persuaded by Ned Irish and Garden officials to allow Willie Naulls and Morris Taft to play after the two players had violated curfew on their visit to the big city. In the end, the two stars did take the floor, and Wooden planned to stall if the Bruins could get a lead. Instead, the Dons captured the tournament title in convincing fashion, 70–53. In an otherwise lopsided game, Russell and Naulls provided a glimpse of basketball's future, both in terms of entertainment value and in officiating. When Naulls sailed high above the rim only to have his attempt at a two-handed dunk stuffed by Russell, Wooden lobbied the officials for a goaltending call. The ball was obviously heading down, after all, but no one had ever seen a play like this before. Eventually, the call stood as a blocked shot.

Upon their return to San Francisco, the Dons publicly aired their grievances regarding what they called harsh and unfair treatment by the New York writers. "I kind of think I was the most hated man in New York," Russell said, "what with all the catcalls, the boos, and the description of me in the papers." If there was an injustice in how observers evaluated Russell's game, it was found in a persistent reluctance to value him correctly as a scorer. One journalist managed to denigrate the star for shooting 77 percent and scoring 20 points from the floor. In this writer's estimation, Russell "hit 10 of 13 from the field—a good percentage, yes, but not spectacular when it is realized practically all his shots were taken from close range, sometimes directly above the bucket." The player who "couldn't shoot" in fact became his program's all-time leading scorer in his 41st game, breaking a record that Don Lofgran had set over the course of 56 outings. It is often said that Russell changed the game, and he did. He changed it faster than people could change how they thought and wrote about it.

After stops in Chicago, Wichita, New Orleans, and New York, USF would play the rest of its 1955–56 regular-season schedule entirely within the state of California. The Dons would do so knowing that Jones would not be eligible for the NCAA tournament. Officials at San Francisco had always understood that securing a waiver from the NCAA was going to be a long shot. Technically, there was no need for the NCAA to "rule" on the case at all. Jones, as it stood, was ineligible for the tournament. The matter was officially closed on January 11, when the NCAA denied USF's appeal.

For the balance of its 1956 campaign, USF would play a double round-robin in the newly expanded California Basketball Association. The conference now included Loyola Marymount, Pepperdine, and Fresno State. Moreover, in recognition that the national champion was a CBA member, the NCAA granted the league a "true" automatic bid. Instead of facing a qualifying game against the likes of West Texas State at the Cow Palace, the conference champion would now proceed directly to the regional semifinals in Corvallis, Oregon. Other than San Francisco, no CBA team that year would finish with a regular-season record better than 16–10. West Coast basketball fans concluded there was only one game on the schedule in which USF might stumble. The Dons were slated to play Cal in Berkeley at the end of January. It would be a road game, and the gym would be packed to the rafters with 7,200 fans. Maybe "wily" Golden Bears coach Pete Newell would pull a rabbit out of his hat. "You have to be coldly analytical about it," Newell said the day before the game. "The number of our mistakes has to be reduced to the absolute minimum."

A San Francisco win over the Bears would mark the program's 40th straight win, breaking a major college record shared by LIU and Seton Hall teams from before the Second World War. While USF took a two-week break from basketball so that players could complete final exams, pressure mounted throughout the region to televise the game. To do so, Cal officials had to work gingerly but quickly around the Pacific Coast Conference's existing television rights package with CBS. Local educational station KQED had already stepped forward and offered its airtime, but as of 72 hours before tip-off, administrators in Berkeley were still hesitating to be seen as giving away a telecast for free. Finally, USF alumnus Charles Harney, class of 1923, paid $3,000 out of his own pocket to put the game on KQED. The two universities each received $750. "Hundreds of thousands" of viewers would now be able to watch the game. This fact would long be remembered in the Bay Area as a case of "be careful what you wish for."

California froze the ball. "It gave us our only chance to win," Newell said. The home team held the ball without making a single pass for approximately eight minutes in the second half, with the Dons up 26–21. All this time, the ball was in the possession of Cal's Joe Hagler. He was Russell's defensive assignment, but Hagler was near midcourt and Russell saw no reason to defend his opponent in that location on the floor. Instead, Hagler stood alone as the other nine players congregated and even chatted with each other near the basket. "I felt like sitting down," Russell said after the game. Meanwhile, Hagler stood for so long that he later admitted he forgot whether his left or his right foot was his pivot foot. That wasn't his only challenge. "It got a little cold," Hagler told a reporter afterward. "There was a draft coming through the door."

USF went on to record a 33–24 victory. The game was termed "a spectacular flop," as spectators, both those who'd attended in person and KQED's viewers, vented their outrage for days. "I broke my neck to pay 20 bucks to see a bunch of athletes stand still," one fan complained. He was referring to the going rate charged by scalpers for tickets that carried a face value of $1.50. "As a matter of self-preservation," the *San Francisco Examiner* advised, "college basketball should take stalling out of the game by adopting the pro league rule."

Woolpert's men ran the table in the CBA at 14–0, winning their conference games by an average of 24 points. While the Dons were running away with the league title, UCLA was posting a 16–0 mark in Pacific Coast Conference play. Throughout February and into March, anticipation built in advance of the two teams meeting in the NCAA regional semifinals in Corvallis.

By 1956, the postseason rivalry between the NCAA and National Invitation tournaments had largely resolved itself into mere tribal dissonance rather than open warfare. While the postseason choice of this or that independent program could still spark intrigue, the respective populations of each tournament were now fairly distinct. As a result, the tournament decisions made by independents were treated as less momentous than they had seemed in 1953 or 1954. Most notably, such choices were less often discussed in the context of an NIT that could conceivably either die out altogether on the one hand or somehow become superior to the NCAA tournament on the other. It was instead assumed the two tournaments would coexist indefinitely, and that a small but visible community of programs would continue to be culturally inclined toward the NIT. Nor was said community exclusively Catholic. With the exception of four Catholic mainstays (Dayton, Duquesne, Niagara, and Saint Louis), no program would make more NIT appearances in the 1950s than Louisville.

Duquesne was just 9–7 when it became the first team to enter the 1956 NIT field, but Si Green was an All-American and the Garden was happy to host him one last time. The Dukes were soon joined in the bracket by fellow Catholic independents Seton Hall, Marquette, and, most notably, Dayton. Led by Jim Paxson and seven-footer Bill Uhl, the Flyers were ranked No. 2 in the nation behind San Francisco for much of the season. Tom Blackburn's team was even rated as superior to San Francisco by no less a basketball observer than Ned Irish. Perhaps the longtime impresario of both college and pro basketball at Madison Square Garden was biased toward a program making its fifth NIT appearance in six years. In any event, Dayton made Irish look wise by reaching the team's fourth National Invitation final in that span. Irish's claim that UD was the best team in the country would have fared better, however, had the Flyers not posted a 0–3 mark against Louisville. That record included a 13-point loss to the Cardinals in the NIT title game.

In stating his case for why Dayton really was the nation's best team, Irish had termed San Francisco's schedule weak. There, and there alone, he had a point. Holy Cross was ranked No. 7 in the nation when USF faced the Crusaders at the Garden in December. Otherwise, no opponent all season was ranked in the AP top 20 at the time it played Woolpert's group. While UCLA began the year at No. 16, it had dropped out of the rankings by the time it ran across the Dons in New York. Wooden's team then resurfaced in the top 20 in late January and ascended to the top 10 as the Bruins posted a perfect record in PCC play.

Woolpert faced an unusual coaching challenge late in the season. His team fairly coasted to a perfect conference record, but he still had to prepare his rotation for playing in the NCAA tournament without Jones. The coach therefore increased Gene Brown's minutes while also playing his regulars for longer than he otherwise would have in lopsided contests. To Woolpert, these games were "scrimmages" in preparation for the tournament. As for Jones, his last moment in a San Francisco uniform was memorable and came about entirely by accident. USF was blowing out Saint Mary's in front of still another record crowd at the Cow Palace when Woolpert pulled his senior with 9:10 remaining. The coach had intended to give Jones a quick breather, but when spectators saw a tournament-ineligible senior leaving the game with his team ahead 60–34, they deduced that a career had just ended. "There wasn't a person in the vast audience," one reporter wrote, "whether they were of USF or Saint Mary's stripe, who didn't spontaneously climb to his feet and roar appreciation as Jones slowly trudged off the court, head bowed and eyes wet." The ovation lasted three minutes. "I was so stunned I even forgot to shake K. C.'s hand," Woolpert admitted. Jones watched that final 9:10 from the bench, his coach having correctly decided that it "would have been anticlimactic to put [Jones] back in there after that ovation."

While the Dons prepared for UCLA, the 1956 NCAA tournament tipped off on the East Coast with one of the best two-game sets in Madison

Square Garden history. In the first game, Temple defeated Holy Cross 74–72 when officials ruled that Tom Heinsohn's would-be game-tying shot went through the basket *after* time expired. Fans of the Crusaders disagreed and charged the floor. At the precise moment when the officials thought they had safely escaped the mob, one referee was reportedly punched by a Holy Cross supporter just short of the dressing room.

In the nightcap, little-used reserve Fran Corcoran hit the game-winner at the end of the fourth overtime as Canisius defeated the No. 2 team in the country, NC State, 79–78. Corcoran was on the floor only because three starters had fouled out. The Golden Griffins would fall to the Temple Owls by two at the Palestra in the regional finals, marking the Jesuit program's second consecutive Elite Eight. One year later, Joe Curran's team would play eventual national champion North Carolina tough before losing by 12 in the regional semifinals. The 1950s were truly the golden age of Canisius basketball.

NC State's sudden fall from grace instilled a belief among some observers that anything could happen, even with a defending national champion on a 51-game win streak. USC coach Forrest Twogood predicted that UCLA, with a 17-game win streak of its own, would defeat USF. "Just remember that K. C. Jones is gone," Twogood explained, "and they're really going to miss him." Conversely, a meeting of Northern California coaches returned a unanimous prediction that the Dons would prevail. Santa Clara coach Bob Feerick said he was putting his faith in the fact that Woolpert and San Francisco had never lost in the NCAA tournament while Wooden and the Bruins had never won a game.

The game between the Dons and the Bruins was the only regional semifinal that pitted two top-10 opponents against each other. Surprisingly, Woolpert was able to give a fiery pregame speech about being disrespected to what was demonstrably the most successful college team in history to that point. The coach's talk actually had some basis in fact. USF's schedule was indeed being denigrated as soft, and the team really would be playing without Jones. Moreover, a group of Southern California writers really had declared themselves unimpressed by what they saw in San Francisco's road wins over Pepperdine and Loyola Marymount. Somehow, there were doubts still attached to this team.

The Dons needed just a few minutes of basketball against the Bruins to answer every one of them. UCLA was held scoreless for 11 minutes in the first half as USF's lead reached 39–19 shortly before the intermission. The Bruins did draw to within 57–48 with five minutes left, but San Francisco scored the next six points on its way to a 72–61 victory. Brown was a revelation, leading all scorers with 23 points. "The Dons need Jones like Texas needs another cow," muttered the *Los Angeles Times*. Russell recorded an estimated eight blocks to go along with his 21–23 double-double. Two of those points came when Mike Farmer inbounded the ball over USF's own backboard for a Russell midair catch and dunk. Here was yet another wrinkle not previously anticipated by earthbound mortals who wrote rule books, one that would soon be prohibited. In a somewhat anticlimactic regional final against Utah, San Francisco paid a price for not having Jones on defense and fell into a shoot-out with the Utes, one the Dons won 92–77. Russell was in foul trouble for one of the few times in his career yet still scored 27. Utah coach Jack Gardner closed out the weekend in Corvallis with a final word: "Russell is to basketball what Babe Ruth was to baseball."

USF would face Southern Methodist in the Final Four, with Iowa bracketed against Temple in the other national semifinal. The tournament's final games were played in McGaw Hall, which had opened in 1952 on the campus of Northwestern University. (The venue would be renamed Welsh-Ryan Arena in 1983.) Scouting was still something of a technological and logistical challenge. To gather information on the Mustangs, Woolpert was reportedly reduced to sifting through newspaper clippings. His research proved to be sufficient, though, as his team advanced 86–68. The title game against the Hawkeyes, on the other hand, gave San Francisco one of its biggest scares since Oregon State the year before. Iowa hit its first six shots and led 15–4 until Woolpert switched defensive assignments and put Brown on Carl Cain. USF rallied but was still up by just five at halftime when Cal coach Newell was asked on the game's radio broadcast if he would be worried if he were in Woolpert's shoes. "I don't know if I'd be worried," Newell replied, "but I'd sure be uncomfortable. He wears a size smaller than I do." There was no call for worry or discomfort. The Dons recorded an 83–71 victory behind a 26–27 double-double by Russell. At 29–0, San Francisco had become the first team ever to win the NCAA title with a perfect record.

USF fans were outraged, however, when Temple's Hal Lear was named the tournament's most outstanding player. Lear went off for 48 points in the third-place game against SMU, still one of the 10 highest-scoring performances in tournament history, and ballots were distributed to the press at halftime of the championship game, when it appeared that Iowa might have a fighting chance against San Francisco. Timing worked against Russell in the historical sense as well. If the 1956 Final Four had instead been played at any point after 1981, he would have been named MOP—and quite possibly as a unanimous selection. There would have been no third-place game.

In any event, Russell and Lear were teammates soon enough. They competed together on a college all-star team against AAU opponents at the 1956 Olympic qualifying tournament in Kansas City. Rather than having entire college teams enter the Olympic trials as St. John's and La Salle had done in 1952, the USOC was selecting individual players for the Melbourne Games. The three collegians who made Team USA were Russell, Jones, and Iowa's Cain. Russell was the Olympic team's leading scorer as the USA won every game by at least 30 on its way to a gold medal. When he dunked in one of the team's early games, the referee had literally never seen such a shot before in his life. The stunned official therefore declared that what had just happened must somehow be prohibited and disallowed the basket.

In addition to fostering a greater international understanding of dunking, Russell's participation in an Olympiad that took place in the Southern Hemisphere would delay the start of his career with the Boston Celtics. Red Auerbach hadn't forgotten what he had seen that December when USF played Holy Cross at the Garden. In one fell swoop, he gathered up Russell, Jones, and, as a territorial pick, Heinsohn. To acquire the No. 2 pick needed to get Russell, the Celtics traded Ed Macauley and Cliff Hagan to the St. Louis Hawks. The team that passed on Russell at No. 1 was Rochester. The Royals instead drafted Si Green out of Duquesne.

USF recorded victories in its first five games of 1956–57, extending the streak to an incredible 60 wins in a row. Coming off a 19-point triumph at Loyola Chicago, the Dons traveled south to face Illinois in Champaign. By this time, San Francisco had not lost an official game in over two years. ("Official" meaning that the exhibition loss to Russell, Jones, and the rest of the US Olympic team at Chicago Stadium after the Loyola game didn't count.) That streak came to a shuddering halt the night of December 17, 1956, against the Fighting Illini in Huff Gym, when Illinois breezed to a 62–33 win. The Dons would regroup, post a respectable 18–6 record in the regular season, and even reach the 1957 Final Four before bowing out against Wilt Chamberlain and Kansas. USF's record of 60 consecutive wins would stand until Wooden and UCLA won 88 in a row between 1971 and 1974.

Soon there were "Russell rules" on the books in college basketball. Offensive goaltending was prohibited, the two positions closest to the basket on free throws were both reserved for the defense (previously those spots on the lane had been marked H and V for home and visitor), and players were required to stay outside the lane until a free throw hit the rim or backboard. Bill Russell quite literally changed college basketball, and San Francisco changed the game visually, strategically, normatively, and, no less, culturally. College basketball at its best was now played above the rim.

The Russell revolution, however, did not herald a new dawn of Catholic hegemony in the game. The next three national champions would be all-white teams from flagship state universities. Nevertheless, San Francisco did point the way to the future. Today, as inhabitants of that future, we feel a shock of recognition when we look at USF teams from 1954 to 1956. This is the earliest program in the sport's history that registers on our basketball consciousness as one that we immediately and instinctively recognize. The Dons are still the only Catholic program ever to have won two consecutive NCAA titles. Holy Cross made a valiant effort at repeating in 1948. Georgetown, of course, came within three points of doing so in 1985. Villanova earned the opportunity to defend its 2016 title as a No. 1 seed in the 2017 NCAA tournament. Yet only San Francisco closed that deal. The Dons locked in Catholic basketball's place on the historical map.

8.

Polarization

C ollege basketball in the late 1950s and early 1960s was played
out against a backdrop of regional tension and outright conflict. One event that both encapsulated and catalyzed this
dynamic was the state of Louisiana's 1956 ban on all interracial sports
competition. While the statute applied to all sporting events and would
cause challenges for Shreveport's minor league baseball club in particular, the measure was discussed nationally and debated by
lawmakers in Baton Rouge primarily in terms of what it might mean
for intercollegiate revenue sports. The bill's author in the state legislature, Lawrence Gibbs, dismissed fears that Louisiana as a whole would
be bypassed by college teams from much of the rest of the country. He
predicted that, instead, the money and prestige attached to events like
the Sugar Bowl football game and to the annual Sugar Bowl basketball
tournament would still offer out-of-state athletic programs "a strong
inducement for leaving their colored players at home."

The law would be invalidated three years later under a suit brought
against it by an African American boxer, but in 1956 the measure's
impact was felt immediately. Contrary to Gibbs's assurances, the
University of Wisconsin withdrew from a home-and-home series with

Louisiana State in football. The new law was also a source of concern for civic and business leaders in New Orleans. In addition to hosting the annual Sugar Bowl, the city was the site for a weeklong festival of sporting events and celebrations leading up to the football game. The annual Sugar Bowl basketball tournament was a particularly popular event, and the December 1956 field was originally scheduled to feature Kentucky, Dayton, Notre Dame, and Saint Louis.

Behind the scenes, officials with the Sugar Bowl basketball tournament had encouraged Billikens head coach Ed Hickey, for one, to send a telegram opposing the bill to Louisiana's governor, Earl Long. When the bill was signed into law anyway, tournament organizers were reduced to asking all four universities if they were still planning to attend. Dayton, Notre Dame, and Saint Louis all indicated that, no, they would not be participating. The University of Dayton responded in writing that it still held out hope that the state of Louisiana would reconsider its position. "Our association with your executive committee has always been cordial," the Rev. Charles L. Collins replied to Sugar Bowl tournament officials, "and we hope the House Bill No. 1412 will be revised so as to permit our return to New Orleans."

Kentucky alone indicated that it intended to play in the tournament in New Orleans, assuming there was still going to be one. With the tournament field down to just the Wildcats, authorities in Louisiana nevertheless vowed to press forward. Referring to the three Catholic programs that had withdrawn, one state senator asserted that regardless "of what these institutions may have to say, I think the people of Louisiana still want segregated athletics."

Sensing an unprecedented competitive opportunity, the state of Kentucky moved quickly to organize a rival basketball tournament for the same dates as the Sugar Bowl event. The Louisville metro area now boasted a newly constructed 18,000-seat venue, Freedom Hall, and organizers signed up Dayton and Saint Louis for the inaugural Bluegrass Holiday Invitational. (Notre Dame, meanwhile, wriggled its way into the annual holiday tournament at Madison Square Garden.) Seeking two more teams for the new tournament's bracket, Kentucky's governor, A. B. "Happy" Chandler, sent telegrams to both the University of Kentucky and the University of Louisville encouraging them to participate. The Cardinals said yes. UK, however, still maintained it had to honor its contract at the Sugar Bowl.

In New Orleans, tournament officials had managed to scrape together three more teams when many observers had assumed the event would simply be discontinued. UK ended up winning the 1956 tournament, in a field that also included Houston, Virginia Tech, and Alabama. During those same two days, the Bluegrass Holiday tournament was played in Louisville. The host team took home the title, defeating Dayton 61–53 in the finals of an event where Saint Louis and Duquesne had played as well.

The dueling tournaments in New Orleans and Louisville signified the new landscape in the sport. College basketball was becoming bifurcated between a small number of programs that would agree to play in a state with a ban on interracial sports and a much larger population of teams that would refuse to do so. This state of affairs would outlive the Louisiana law that brought the question to the fore, and it would have a direct impact on which teams played in the NCAA tournament from 1959 to 1962. This dynamic even possessed a fair degree of predictive power. Of the programs that played in the 1956 Sugar Bowl tournament, three would not put a Black player on the floor in varsity men's basketball until 1969 at the earliest. Conversely, Houston would, wisely, recruit Elvin Hayes and Don Chaney, both of whom would debut as sophomores in 1965.

As for the three Catholic programs that withdrew from the 1956 Sugar Bowl tournament, their rosters in 1955–56 looked more like Kentucky's and less like San Francisco's, Duquesne's, or UCLA's in the mid-1950s. With the exception of one reserve who left the team early in the 1947–48 season, Dayton had been all-white for the entirety of the program's history to that point. Notre Dame and Saint Louis were at least adding Tommy Hawkins and Cal Burnett, respectively, as sophomores to their varsity teams for the 1956–57 season.

Hawkins would go on to have an outstanding career, leading the

Fighting Irish in scoring three straight years and earning second-team All-American honors in 1959. Yet when he visited a local pizza restaurant in South Bend with a white date, he was refused service. Hawkins would later remember that Notre Dame's president, the Rev. Theodore Hesburgh, issued an appeal urging all students, faculty, and staff to take their business elsewhere until Hawkins and his date had received a public apology. When none was immediately forthcoming, Hawkins recalled that he received a visit from a white friend, Fighting Irish football star Paul Hornung. "He said, 'Hawk, get your coat,'" Hawkins later related. "'We're going down to the pizza parlor to get this apology so that we can get back to all of that Italian food.'" Even at programs that were opening their doors, it was typical for pioneers of Hawkins's era to encounter obstacles that went beyond not being allowed to take the floor in a New Orleans tournament.

When holiday tournament time rolled around in December of 1956, this new polarized normal was very much in evidence. Mississippi State was ordered home from the Evansville Invitational in Evansville, Indiana, when MSU's athletic director, Dudy Noble, learned that his team had just won a game against a Denver program with Black players Rocephus Sligh and Bill Peay on its roster. If Mississippi State had remained in the tournament, Babe McCarthy's team would have next faced Evansville and its African American standout, Jim Smallins. That game never happened. MSU left Evansville, having posted a 1–0 record in what was meant to have been a four-team bracket. The next day, Ole Miss withdrew from the All-American City tournament in Owensboro, Kentucky, due to the presence of Stanley Hill in Iona's rotation. Bonnie Graham announced that his team was packing its bags and heading back to Oxford, Mississippi.

The withdrawals of Mississippi State and Ole Miss from invitational tournaments held during the last week of 1956 represented both a strategic refinement and a political escalation in the wake of Louisiana's ban on interracial competition. Even Louisiana's law had been silent on the question of opponents faced by local teams outside the state. Now, leaders in the state of Mississippi were doing Louisiana one better. This ban on interracial competition would not be limited to a prohibition within any one state's borders. It would instead travel with Mississippi State and Ole Miss wherever their teams roamed. Most crucially, this refusal to play against African Americans was never codified into law or even a university policy. It was, Mississippi authorities said repeatedly, an unwritten law, a custom, a rule, a tradition, and a "Southern way of life." It was, in effect, anything but an actual statute that could be challenged and, doubtless, overturned, just as Louisiana's law was destined to be. Most of all, the unwritten law was effective. After defeating Denver on December 28, 1956, Mississippi State would not face another Black opposing player in men's basketball until March 15, 1963.

In retellings of these 1950s-era controversies, Catholic programs tend to be portrayed in a relatively flattering light. The facts of the matter did indeed reflect credit upon the programs at times. Stanley Hill really was wearing Iona's uniform in Owensboro, Kentucky. Three heavyweight Catholic programs did in fact withdraw from the Sugar Bowl tournament. The praise and critiques voiced at the time extended beyond these particular news pegs, however. The Evansville Invitational and All-American City tournaments were hosted by Evansville College (later the University of Evansville) and by Kentucky Wesleyan, respectively. Both schools were affiliated with the United Methodist Church. Both were located along the Ohio River, and both were hosting teams with Black players in 1956. Smallins, a local product from Lincoln High School, had broken the color line in 1955–56 at Evansville.

That was more than could be said for the likes of Boston College, which was also playing at the Evansville Invitational that year, or for Georgetown, which was over at the All-American City tournament in Owensboro. BC's first African American player, John Austin, would make his varsity debut under head coach Bob Cousy in 1963–64. Bernard White would achieve that same distinction for the Hoyas in 1966–67. Catholic programs could indeed appear inclusive in the 1950s. So, too, could the Methodists.

Beyond the withdrawals and headlines at the two 1956 tournaments, there was also some basketball played. Host school Kentucky Wesleyan hammered Iona by 34, which, in part, reflected the growing pains of one of the nation's youngest Catholic programs. Iona School had been founded in 1916 as a high school in New Rochelle, New York. In 1940, the Christian Brothers received approval from Archbishop Francis J. Spellman to establish a college as well. Iona's men's basketball team began playing almost as soon as the college itself was founded, but the Gaels' modern history effectively began with the hiring of Jim McDermott as coach in 1947. McDermott was to stay in that position for 26 seasons, and, indeed, just two years would separate his tenure from that of a successor in New Rochelle named Jim Valvano. When organizers at the 1956 All-American City tournament asked McDermott if he might consider benching Hill for one game against Ole Miss, the coach responded with a vehement—and, by some accounts, profane—no. He was still telling this tale at age 90 when, in a remarkable instance of basketball karma, Ole Miss was bracketed to play Iona in the 2001 NCAA tournament's round of 64. Hill and his wife attended the game at Kemper Arena in Kansas City, as guests of the University of Mississippi, and watched the first half seated with Ole Miss chancellor Robert Khayat. The Rebels advanced, 72–70.

While Hill had been shunned by an opposing team in 1956, a basketball master who emerged a few years earlier had struggled to even find a space where he would be allowed to play the sport.

There is no biography of a basketball legend quite like the one offered by Elgin Baylor. While Bill Russell was a late bloomer and a mediocre West Coast high school player who nevertheless received a scholarship from a major basketball program on his doorstep, Baylor as a teenager was hailed as "the greatest high school player of all time" by the white newspaper of record in his East Coast metropolis. Yet, somehow, he was reduced to taking a scholarship in a different sport entirely from an Idaho college with 450 students.

Baylor would eventually wear the uniform of a Jesuit program in an NCAA title game, but reaching that point would require persistence.

In his case, the barriers to entry in the sport of basketball were literal. The gate at the playground around the corner from his row house in southeast Washington, DC, was open to whites during the day and then locked to keep out African Americans at night. In Baylor's telling, he didn't even try to play basketball until he was about 14, and, when he did, he often had to use a tennis ball or a volleyball.

When Baylor did manage to get onto the court as a high school player, however, he was an instant sensation. He played for a segregated high school, Spingarn, in the last year, 1953–54, that Washington, DC, still had officially segregated high schools. Spingarn somehow landed a game against perennial Catholic power Archbishop Carroll, and the opposing coach was just as effusive after his team lost to Baylor as any awestruck fan. "He is without a doubt the best high school player I've ever seen," Carroll coach Bob Dwyer marveled. "I've been coaching basketball for 18 years. And I never saw a high school player that could touch him—I mean even *touch* him."

Clearly, players Baylor's own age weren't enough of a challenge. Instead, some of his most legendary exploits occurred alongside and against older players on a storied semipro club, the Stonewalls. Baylor and his Stonewalls teammates were once matched in an exhibition against an all-white team that included several players from the University of Maryland's varsity roster. This team of unofficial Terrapins was led by future five-time NBA All-Star Gene Shue. The Stonewalls won behind 38 points from Baylor.

Despite Baylor's subsequent reputation as an overlooked DC high school titan, a player of his caliber was predestined to attract a wave of interest from college coaches. "I've got the best high school basketball player in the world," Seton Hall's Honey Russell told the *Washington Post*, "a kid from Washington." A tipster's column in Baltimore's *Evening Sun* likewise devoted one of its short blurbs to the budding legend in the District: "Ten colleges, plus Boston Celtics and Globetrotters eyeing 6-foot-6-inch Elgin Baylor, high-school cage star in Washington with a 39.6 average." Baylor was even pictured in *Jet* magazine, but in spite of the accolades, Duquesne's Dudey Moore said that "nobody would touch" Spingarn's star due to poor grades. In later years, Baylor bristled at this narrative, insisting he "never got a grade below a C." The real obstacle, he would say, was that "white scouts never came to our games."

For whatever reason, Baylor was open to listening to a friend's unconventional idea. Warren Williams knew someone from his neighborhood who was touring the West as a member of the opposing team for the Harlem Globetrotters. Through this acquaintance, Williams learned that the College of Idaho was offering football scholarships. Upon reaching Caldwell, Idaho, Baylor stepped into the gym one time and showed coach Sam Vokes all he needed to see to know that the new arrival belonged on the basketball team. Baylor's impact on the College of Idaho's basketball program in 1954–55 was as seismic as it was predictable. When he returned to Caldwell in 2017 for his first visit since his student days, he would be called "arguably the greatest athlete in C of I history." That may have been putting it mildly.

During this time, Al Brightman was coaching Seattle University to what would eventually be four straight appearances in the NCAA tournament. Brightman's teams played at a fast pace, and high-scoring John O'Brien had been named first-team All-American alongside Tom Gola and Walter Dukes in 1953. The Seattle coach moved on Baylor early, and an SU booster arranged for the College of Idaho star to be flown in on a private plane for a visit. Baylor agreed to play for Seattle, but he would have to sit out the 1955–56 season, a year in which he played for the best AAU team a Seattle Ford dealer ever had. It turned out, however, that by the end of that season SU's coach would be gone.

When Brightman announced suddenly that he was stepping down, there was a good deal of discussion about the coach's final game. Brightman's team had been at the same 1956 NCAA regional in Corvallis, Oregon, as San Francisco, UCLA, and Utah. After the Dons and the Utes won on the first night, Seattle faced the Bruins in a regional third-place game. Brightman had heated words with John Wooden during the contest (which UCLA won easily) and even, according to one account, approached the future icon after the game and challenged him to a fight. Whether or not that's true, the two coaches were nose to nose at one point during the game, and they were separated by Brightman's boss and athletic director, the Rev. Robert Rebhahn. Three days later, Brightman was gone, and someone else would be handed the opportunity to coach Baylor at the top level of college basketball. That someone was John Castellani, who arrived in Seattle at the age of 29 after five years as an assistant on John Jordan's staff at Notre Dame.

Baylor was a phenomenon in his first major college season. He averaged 30 a game while leading a team, known in some quarters as "Baylor Tech," to a 22–2 regular-season record and a top-five ranking nationally. Like San Francisco two years earlier, Seattle won the All-College tournament in Oklahoma City. Castellani's team defeated host Oklahoma City University in overtime in the title game, a marathon in which SU's two main scorers, Baylor and Dick Stricklin, fouled out, along with teammate Thornton Humphries. "We fouled out everybody on their team," Oklahoma City coach Abe Lemons said later. "Baylor, all of them. They put in a couple of priests and beat us in the last second." By January 1957, when Seattle dismantled Gonzaga 106–75 in Spokane, it was said that Baylor "can do things with a basketball which the late Dr. Naismith probably never could have conceived of when he nailed up his first peach basket." The NIT locked up Seattle as the first team in the field in early February, and SU carried the top seed into the tournament only to fall to St. Bonaventure by 17 in the quarterfinals.

Nonetheless, Baylor stayed over in New York to appear on *The Ed Sullivan Show* with the rest of the *Look* magazine All-American team. For the first time, *Look* had turned over responsibility for selecting its team to the newly formed US Basketball Writers Association. Just two sophomores were selected to the 10-player team, Baylor and Wilt Chamberlain. The two rising juniors would face off against each other that summer in a series of legendary playground contests on Baylor's home turf in Washington, DC.

At 6 foot 5, Seattle's star pointed the way toward future volume scorers like Tom Stith or Austin Carr, even as he rebounded like Walter Dukes or Bill Russell. Baylor accounted for as high a percentage of his team's shot attempts as Si Green did at Duquesne as a senior, but Seattle's featured scorer shot 51 percent from the field in 1957–58, a season in which Division I was making just 38 percent of its attempts. If we could ever glimpse trustworthy performance statistics for what Baylor did at SU, particularly in his second season, his work would likely go down as an extraordinary combination of volume and efficiency. At the same time, Baylor was also a dominant rebounder. He personally pulled down better than 23 percent of the available rebounds in all the games over his two-season Seattle career, equivalent to the figure that Russell posted in his senior season. Unfortunately, we don't know how many minutes either player recorded, and Russell was indeed the superior college rebounder overall. Nevertheless, to even be in the same conversation with the 6-foot-10 legend is itself remarkable. Baylor was unique.

Seattle started Baylor's second season slowly, losing at Oregon State and then collapsing in the final eight minutes of a loss to San Francisco in the second annual Bluegrass Invitational. The trip to Louisville did, however, see Baylor amass 29 rebounds in one half in the team's Bluegrass third-place win over Army. After a 1–2 showing at Madison Square Garden's holiday tournament, SU was just 3–3. Baylor and his teammates would not lose again during the rest of the 1957–58 regular season, a run of success against Pacific Northwest opponents that netted Castellani's team a No. 18 ranking entering the NCAA tournament.

Baylor sat atop the national scoring leaderboard for much of the season, averaging better than 32 a game. In one legendary performance, the junior scored 60 to lead his team back from a 79–60 deficit to a 94–91 win over Portland. "John, we almost had you," Portland coach Al Negratti told Castellani during the postgame handshake. "If we could have held Baylor to 54 points, we'd have won."

Castellani's group opened the NCAA tournament in Berkeley, where Seattle rolled over Wyoming by 37 points. That set up a meeting across the bay in the regional semifinals with San Francisco at the Cow

Palace. The Dons were 24–1 and ranked No. 4 in the nation. Woolpert's team had defeated SU twice in two seasons with Baylor in the lineup, and now USF was playing at home, more or less, and aiming for what was widely expected to be a fourth consecutive West regional title. Seattle's Frank Saunders had suffered a jaw injury against Wyoming and was out of action against the Dons, while teammate Jim Harney was already injured and would play sparingly against San Francisco. Yet, despite being shorthanded against a favored opponent, Castellani's team got just enough from two of its players: Indiana transfer "Sweet" Charlie Brown came through with 13 points and helped set the stage for Baylor's heroics.

With the ball in his hands in the final moments and the score tied, Baylor rose up from 30 feet and drained the game-winner with two seconds remaining. For the evening, SU's star had scored 35 points. The public address announcer at the Cow Palace was so stunned that he announced the final result to the crowd as "Baylor 69, USF 67."

Seattle needed more heroics in the regional final the next night against another local opponent, Cal. This time it was Brown who came through in crunch time, tying the game with a 10-footer at the end of regulation and then doing his best Baylor imitation and winning the contest with eight seconds left in overtime by connecting on "a 30-foot scorcher." SU's reward was a Final Four pairing at Freedom Hall in Louisville with still another heavily favored opponent. Kansas State had wrested its conference's automatic bid away from Wilt Chamberlain and Kansas, and in the tournament the Wildcats had prevailed in over-time against scoring sensation Oscar Robertson and Cincinnati. But Tex Winter's men never knew what hit them when they ran into Baylor. Seattle outscored the Wildcats 36–19 in the second half and won by 22 behind Baylor's 23–22 double-double.

That March, the possibility of yet another Catholic double triumph at the National Invitation and NCAA tournaments was still alive. Actually, the 1958 NIT honors were already locked up. On the same evening Seattle played for a title in Louisville, the NIT final paired Dayton against Xavier University. The Musketeers were now led by

Jim McCafferty, who had left Loyola New Orleans after five seasons and happily accepted a job with a sister Jesuit program in the Midwest. In the estimation of McCafferty, his new geographic home offered a version of the sport that was "much, much better than basketball in the South." While Xavier may not even have been the best team in its own city, the Musketeers put their 0–2 mark against the University of Cincinnati behind them and defeated Dayton 78–74 in overtime to capture the NIT title. XU's Hank Stein led all scorers, with 23 points, and earned rave reviews from the New York press as a "fiery thatched sharpshooter." A Seattle win at the NCAA that same evening would complete a national tournament Jesuit sweep.

It would not play out that way. The smashing victory against Kansas State that constituted arguably the greatest win in the SU program's history would also fairly seal the team's fate in the national title game. Baylor bruised or possibly even cracked a rib in the semifinal, and his effectiveness was limited the following night against Kentucky. This was not Rupp's usual juggernaut of star players, and in fact he termed his 1958 group a bunch of "fiddlers, not violinists," in tribute to a UK roster that could claim just one All-SEC performer (Johnny Cox). Still, Rupp's "fiddling five" got the job done against Seattle, taking the ball straight at the injured Baylor and hanging three fouls on him in the first 10 minutes. When Castellani switched to a zone to protect Baylor, the Wildcats erupted for 48 points in the second half. Kentucky won 84–72, though Baylor was named the tournament's most outstanding player.

At the age of 31, Castellani had just coached his last college game. A mere 30 days after the national final, he resigned when the NCAA hit the Seattle program with a two-year postseason ban. Investigators in Kansas City charged that Castellani had covered the airfare for recruits Ben Warley and George Finley in order to meet with them in a neutral location. On the same day that Castellani resigned, Baylor was taken with the No. 1 overall pick in the NBA draft by the Minneapolis Lakers. Though he had one year of eligibility remaining if he chose to use it, Baylor eventually decided to go pro. In his second season, he was joined in Minneapolis by Tommy Hawkins from Notre Dame and, briefly, by John Castellani. The Lakers gave the ex-Seattle coach a shot, only to sack him after an 11–25 start.

"When I got fired by the Lakers," Castellani would recall with some heat 55 years later, "I vowed that nobody—*nobody*—would ever tell me they didn't want me anymore." The Connecticut native bid farewell to basketball, took his savings from his stint with the NBA, and put himself through Marquette's law school. Upon graduation, Castellani settled down in Milwaukee and practiced law for the next five decades while turning down most interview requests. He initially refused to be interviewed in 2015 by the *Milwaukee Journal Sentinel*, then reconsidered only because he wanted to make his voice heard on Wisconsin's run to a second consecutive Final Four. "His team does four things better than anybody," the then 88-year-old Castellani said of Bo Ryan's Badgers. "They don't foul, they don't turn the ball over, they make their free throws, and the shooters get to their spots." The lawyer still had a coach's eye. Castellani also happens to have been pushed out of basketball and into the law not long before the law came back into basketball in force.

In 1959, St. John's earned its first NIT title since the days of Bill Kotsores and Hy Gotkin. The winning coach in both tournaments was Joe Lapchick. After eight full years at the helm of the New York Knicks, Lapchick left the NBA just short of the end of the 1955–56 season. He cited health reasons, but Lapchick was back coaching St. John's the following season. As of 1958–59, the head coach had a 33-year-old assistant on his staff named Lou Carnesecca. The overtime win in the title game against Bradley was powered by sophomore Tony Jackson's 21–27 double-double. Though listed at only 6 foot 4, Jackson would average 21 points and 14 rebounds over his three-year career and earn two second-team All-American selections. Lapchick would stay through the 1964–65 season and then hand the reins over to Carnesecca.

The NIT at the dawn of the 1960s was enjoying what would turn out to be a brief but unmistakable resurgence. There were two main factors driving this trend: Catholic programs and Bradley. Catholic independents were still culturally inclined toward the NIT, though not uniformly so, as seen in 1961 NCAA tournament bids accepted by St. Bonaventure, Xavier, Marquette, and Seattle. Just prior to that 1961 tournament season, however, programs like St. Bonaventure, Saint Louis, Providence, Holy Cross, Villanova, and St. John's would contribute to an impressive run in which the NIT would put a combined total of 12 ranked teams into its brackets in the 1959 and 1960 tournaments.

Ranked No. 4 in the final AP poll in both years was Bradley, arguably one of the nation's strongest and most consistent programs under Chuck Orsborn in the late 1950s and early 1960s. Nevertheless, the Braves never once appeared in an NCAA tournament in the Orsborn era, in part because Missouri Valley rival Cincinnati was also at the peak of its power. The Bearcats joined the conference at the start of the 1957–58 season, and UC proceeded to earn the MVC's automatic bid for the NCAA tournament in each of the next six years. The NIT benefited measurably from the excellence of the Missouri Valley's second-best teams over this span, a dynamic that could have worked in the tournament's favor had leagues like the ACC, Big Ten, and SEC likewise permitted their also-rans to play at Madison Square Garden. Instead, the conferences continued to steer clear of the NIT entirely. Events in the early 1960s would only reinforce this tendency on the part of the major conferences.

On the morning of March 17, 1961, Seton Hall's Al Senavitis was sitting in class when he received a note asking him to report to the chapel immediately. Senavitis was a junior and the third-leading scorer for a Pirates team that had just finished a good, if undistinguished, 15–9 season. Arriving in the chapel, he found the entire basketball team, minus two of his teammates. Decades later, Senavitis would remember what happened next:

> Father [John] Horgan was trying to tell us something, but his voice cracked and tears came to his eyes, so he just turned on the radio. The 11 o'clock news was on. I still remember

the exact station—WABC-77. It was all there. A basketball scandal. Point shaving. Seton Hall players involved. Art Hicks and Hank Gunter picked up by the New York District Attorney's office...

College basketball's second great point-shaving scandal had begun. Once again, New York district attorney Frank Hogan's office took center stage.

Seton Hall players Hank Gunter and Art Hicks stood accused of accepting $1,000 each to shave points against Dayton in a game played at Madison Square Garden in February 1961. The Pirates lost 112–77. At a Saint Patrick's Day dinner held the very night the news broke, Seton Hall's president, Monsignor John J. Daugherty, issued a plea for mercy for the players. "These young men are not to be condemned. They are to be treated with compassion." Richie Regan, now Pirates head coach, said that if any of his players had shaved points, "I'll stand behind them, even though they let me down and let the school down." The news made headlines the same weekend that Cincinnati, Ohio State, Utah, and Saint Joseph's were advancing to the 1961 Final Four.

This latest scandal stemmed from the arrest of New York gambler Aaron Wagman in September 1960, after he had attempted to bribe a University of Florida football player. Wagman was kept under close surveillance when he was released on bail, and over the next six months he enabled investigators to map out a far-flung network of point shaving in basketball. Unlike fixers in 1951, Wagman and a fellow gambler, Joe Hacken, allowed players to choose which games they would manipulate. That way, the gamblers reasoned, they could count on a sincere and ultimately effective effort by the players to alter the outcomes. Contrary to accusations that the district attorney had timed his announcement for maximum publicity, investigators reportedly felt their hand was forced when they learned that Wagman had applied for a passport.

Wagman and Hacken were independent hustlers and, occasionally, even rivals, but both operated more or less at the pleasure of lawyer and "master fixer" Jack Molinas. A former Columbia star, Molinas had been kicked out of the NBA as a rookie in 1954 for betting on his own games. Now, in 1961, accusations of point shaving quickly spread beyond Seton Hall, which would be mocked by fans on the road throughout 1961–62 as "Cheatin' Hall." La Salle's name also emerged early in the investigation, and in due course it was charged that Ed Bowler too had been in on the fix. (Bowler was a role player on a team whose highly touted leading scorer, Bill Raftery, averaged 18 points a game as a sophomore.) In addition, players Mike Parenti and William Chrystal had allegedly manipulated games at St. John's back in 1956–57. Four years later, the Johnnies' Tony Jackson would be criticized not for shaving points but for failing to report that he had been approached by gamblers. The scandal would eventually touch more than two dozen programs nationally, including NC State, Connecticut, and Columbia.

Even as the indictments, suspicions, and rumors continued to mount, there was still a Final Four to be played at Municipal Auditorium in Kansas City. Saint Joseph's had surprised many observers by reaching the national semifinals. All season long, it had been assumed that a different Catholic program from the East might be taking that spot. St. Bonaventure had spent the balance of the 1960–61 season ranked No. 2 in the polls behind undefeated Ohio State, the reigning national champion. The Bonnies had battled Fred Taylor's Buckeyes for the entire 40 minutes on New Year's Eve at Madison Square Garden only to lose 84–82. St. Bonaventure's Tom Stith had led all scorers, with 35 points, and throughout the rest of the season, fans in Olean, New York, had counted the days until their team would get another shot at OSU. In late February, with the Bonnies still having lost just the one game to the Buckeyes, a banner appeared on the St. Bonaventure campus: NCAA AND OHIO STATE.

The Bonnies did not lose a home game between 1948 and 1961, a run of 99 consecutive wins. As the streak continued and the victories accumulated, opposing teams began to fear St. Bonaventure's "snake pit" at Olean Armory and indeed avoided scheduling games there if at all possible. All this time, the Bonnies never once appeared in an NCAA tournament. Eddie Donovan's team had looked tremendous in bouncing Elgin Baylor and Seattle out of the 1957 NIT quarterfinals, but, over the course of six postseason appearances at Madison Square Garden between 1951 and 1960, St. Bonaventure never reached a National Invitation final. The program therefore occupied a spot just outside the national spotlight—respected for its incredible streak at home yet never quite breaking through as a primary focus of attention.

That changed in 1961, even as the Bonnies' incredible streak at last ended, with a 10-point loss at home late in the season to Niagara. Stith was putting the finishing touches on a second consecutive season that would earn him honors as a first-team All-American. The senior averaged 30 a game, but St. Bonaventure never got its second shot at Ohio State. Instead, the Bonnies bowed out against Wake Forest 78–73 in the regional semifinals of the team's first NCAA tournament. Even before the loss, both Stith and his coach had wondered why the senior had lost 15 pounds over the course of the season. The answer came when the star was selected with the second overall pick by the Knicks and given a complete physical: Stith was suffering from pulmonary tuberculosis. He made a complete recovery, but, except for a brief stint with the Knicks in 1962–63, his future would be in scouting basketball rather than playing it.

Instead of St. Bonaventure, it would be Saint Joseph's advancing to the 1961 Final Four. Jack Ramsay's 20–4 team was ranked No. 17, having won its last 13 games over a period of nearly two months. This would be the third consecutive appearance at the NCAA East regional in Charlotte Coliseum for St. Joe's and its 6-foot-6 leading scorer, Jack Egan. The Hawks had previously lost their first games to West Virginia, led by star player Jerry West, in 1959 and to Duke in 1960, by a combined total of five points. Finally, on its third try, the team broke what even the Raleigh *News & Observer* called a "Charlotte jinx." When Saint Joseph's recorded a five-point win over Princeton, the visitors from Philadelphia were next bracketed with relative home team Wake Forest in the regional final. Before a "stunned crowd" at the Coliseum, Ramsay's men opened up a 23-point lead over Len Chappell, Billy Packer, and the rest of the Demon Deacons on the way to securing a 96–86 victory. Frank Majewski earned particular praise for the defense he played in limiting Wake's second-leading scorer on the season, Packer, to just four points.

The Hawks' triumph at the 1961 East regional occurred the same weekend that the news broke regarding point shaving at Seton Hall. In Philadelphia, members of the Big 5 breathed a public sigh of relief that at least the Palestra was being monitored closely. Plainclothesmen had been assigned to all games at the venue, according to press reports in the days that followed, and any gamblers thus discovered were escorted to the ticket office for a refund prior to leaving the premises. "I've never talked to my players about it," Ramsay said with regard to point shaving. "I never thought it was necessary. I've assumed the kids have integrity and know right from wrong. But in view of what's happened in New York, perhaps I should make a point in warning my boys in the future." The next day, Ramsay put Saint Joseph's through its final practice in Philadelphia before the team boarded a plane for the Final Four in Kansas City. The school's faculty athletic moderator, the Rev. Joseph M. Geib, watched the practice along with the press. "Everybody looks good but Majewski," Geib told the writers. "I don't know where his mind is, but it certainly isn't here."

Paul Westhead was a reserve on that St. Joe's team, and Ramsay, as both coach and athletic director, talked a good game all week about having no fear of Ohio State. It was true the Buckeyes had navigated some close calls on their way to an undefeated record. None of that mattered, however, when Saint Joseph's met OSU in Kansas City, as Ohio State easily brushed the Hawks aside in a 95–69 blowout. When the St. Joe's win over Utah in the third-place game went to four overtimes, the Hawks and the Utes equaled the mark that had been set by Canisius and NC State back in 1956 for playing the longest NCAA tournament game in history. The two teams also succeeded in angering Ohio State and Cincinnati, both of whom had to wait for the endless third-place game to end before they could play for the national championship. The Bearcats prevailed in overtime, winning the first of what would be two consecutive national championships.

When Wagman and Hacken were arraigned the same week that the teams for the 1961 Final Four were determined, NCAA executive director Walter Byers was reportedly assured by prosecutors that none of the semifinalists had been implicated in the scandal. But either that was a misstatement on the part of authorities, or Byers was simply talking to the wrong sources. Ray Cave of *Sports Illustrated* had better information. He covered the week leading up to the Final Four with the understanding that the team he was assigned to had, in fact, altered games in exchange for cash. Cave was correct, and the truth was made public one month later, on April 27: Jack Egan, Vince Kempton, and Frank Majewski had been in on the fix at Saint Joseph's. "If a bomb had been dropped on Alumni Memorial Hall," the *Philadelphia Inquirer* observed, "it would not have caused greater shock on the Saint Joseph's College campus than the news that three Hawk basketball heroes had been expelled for involvement in the point shaving scandals."

Majewski had been Wagman's initial point of contact, and the senior had then enlisted the participation of Egan and Kempton. The three players were paid $750 each to guarantee that the Hawks won by less than three or lost to Dayton. The Flyers won 67–65. A payment of $1,000 was then made to each of the three on the condition that St. Joe's win the Seton Hall game by less than 10. The Hawks won 72–71. In addition, another $1,000 was fronted to each player to assure that Saint Joseph's would lose to Xavier by at least 11 points. The Musketeers won 87–75. Egan, at age 21, was the father of two children. "I needed the money," he said. Kempton had essentially the same backstory. "Whoever contacted me," he said, "knew I could use the money."

Ramsay himself had played basketball at Saint Joseph's in the 1940s. At a press conference held by the school, the now 36-year-old broke down and wept as the president, the Rev. J. Joseph Bluett, turned and addressed the coach directly: "Jack, may I say this to you with all the sincerity of my heart. If you couldn't save these boys, nobody in the world could have saved them. My faith and confidence in you is greater, if possible, than it ever was."

In the next five seasons, Ramsay would take St. Joe's to four more NCAA tournaments. His last two teams in the mid-1960s were led by Matt Guokas and Cliff Anderson and were consistently ranked in the top 10 nationally. Even so, the Hawks lost in the regional semifinals to equally elite opponents in both 1965 and 1966, first to Providence and then, by two points, to Duke. Ramsay left Saint Joseph's in 1966 to become the general manager of the Philadelphia 76ers. He would make his name as head coach of the NBA champion Portland Trail Blazers team, which featured Bill Walton, in 1977.

As in 1951, the fallout from the second point-shaving scandal was felt over a period of months. In May 1961, the repercussions ended the college careers of two of the most celebrated players ever to come out of New York City, Connie Hawkins and Roger Brown. The two friends had starred for rival Brooklyn high schools, and both players were college freshmen in the spring of 1961. Hawkins was at Iowa, and Brown was at Dayton. They had been befriended in high school by Molinas personally, and the two stars could on occasion be seen together as they drove their dates around in the attorney's car. Possibly, the two players were being groomed to eventually recruit others for use by Molinas and by Hacken. That alone was enough to earn Brown a directive from authorities to come to New York and tell investigators everything he knew. Years before Miranda rights, the 18-year-old Brown was confined to a Manhattan hotel room and interrogated for four days with no lawyer, family member, or companion present. Brown's testimony before a grand jury was both contradictory and, plainly, coerced. In any event, freshmen in 1961 could not shave points. They weren't playing varsity basketball. Nevertheless, Hawkins and Brown were both summarily expelled from their schools, banished from any further NCAA competition, and effectively blacklisted by the NBA, along with all players implicated in the scandal of 1961.

The story of Hawkins's subsequent career would be told more often through the years, because he did play in the NBA eventually.

Brown chose a different path. He elected to remain in the city of Dayton, where he was taken in by the local Black community. Brown worked at a General Motors plant, dominated AAU basketball, and shone in occasional pickup games against current and former University of Cincinnati players, including Oscar Robertson, now playing professionally. The NBA star was impressed, and Brown was named to an AAU All-American team that would play an exhibition against the Soviet Union in 1962 at Madison Square Garden. He was forced to withdraw from the team, however, after a gratuitous and waspish bit of pearl-clutching appeared in *Sports Illustrated*'s Scorecard column. By 1964, the general manager of the Cincinnati Royals was publicly lobbying the NBA front office to lift its blacklisting of Brown. That same year, Brown, as possibly the top AAU player in the nation, was also in line for a spot on the US Olympic team. Neither opportunity materialized. Brown continued working for GM in Dayton, married, and started a family.

When a group of Indianapolis businessmen launched the Pacers franchise in 1967 as part of the new American Basketball Association, the team's first general manager attempted to lure local hero Robertson away from the NBA. Instead, Robertson advised the Pacers to grab the 6-foot-5 Brown. He became known as "the Rajah," and from day one he shared leading-scorer honors with Freddie Lewis, and with both Lewis and Mel Daniels as of the Pacers' second year. Even better, Brown shook off the rust and became markedly more efficient over his first three seasons. By the time the Pacers won their first ABA title in 1970, he was plainly one of the top players in either professional league. The ABA throughout its existence had a three-point line, giving Brown's statistics a clarity today that's lacking for NBA or college greats of the same era. His figure for win shares in the 1969–70 regular season is still the highest number posted by any player in Pacers history.

In the last three games of the 1970 championship series against the Los Angeles Stars, Brown scored 53, 39, and 45 points while shooting 58 percent from the floor. He even provided a glimpse of basketball's future by draining seven three-pointers in the final game. Stars head coach and NBA mainstay Bill Sharman would later call it the greatest playoff performance he ever saw in 26 years as a professional player and coach. In all, Brown would play eight seasons in the ABA and win three titles with the Pacers. Like Hawkins, he sued the NBA and ultimately forced the league to reach a settlement out of court. Unlike Hawkins, Brown refused to play in the NBA even when he was formally cleared to do so by the league.

Aside from the African American community of the city of Dayton, few parties to this narrative could look back on it without shame. The New York district attorney's office, the Catholic University of Dayton, the NCAA, the NBA, and the press all failed Roger Brown. Justice came too late for the legend, who passed away in 1997 due to cancer. But proper recognition, at least, did arrive eventually in three respects. The year Brown died, he was named as one of seven unanimous selections to the all-time All-ABA team, alongside the likes of Julius Erving and George Gervin. In 2013, he was enshrined in the Naismith Hall of Fame. Finally, in 2019, UD "humbly yet proudly" established a scholar's residency in Roger Brown's name. "This is long overdue," the university's president, Eric Spina, said in announcing the program, "and is intended to begin to make things right."

Perhaps the most remarkable aspect of the 1961 point-shaving scandal is that, despite being every bit as devastating and destructive as the 1951 affair had been to the players involved, the later episode had nowhere near the same impact on the sport itself. In 1951, columnists assessed whether college basketball was finished as a revenue sport. Few if any responsible observers wondered whether that was the case in 1961; college basketball was far more established both as a business and as a cultural touchstone, and, of course, the sport had already demonstrated that it could indeed survive a major point-shaving scandal. In the coming years, the game would continue to grow, even as the regional polarization that had become so evident in the 1950s would be highlighted as never before by a Catholic national champion and by one of its opponents in the 1963 NCAA tournament.

9.

Loyola Chicago
and Milestones

From 1924 until 1941, Loyola University in Chicago hosted an annual 32-team championship for Catholic high schools called the National Catholic Interscholastic Basketball Tournament. The cumbersome title was intended as a reply, for there was already a National Interscholastic Basketball Tournament. Hosted annually by the University of Chicago, the NIBT excluded Catholic high schools. Fortunately for Loyola, both the unwieldy name (a mouthful even when reduced to NCIBT) and the need to wave the Catholic flag in the face of a competing local event were taken care of nicely when the tournament became known colloquially as the Cardinal's Cup Classic. Each year, the nominal Catholic high school national champion would receive a first-place trophy donated by George Cardinal Mundelein, archbishop of Chicago. One player who competed for the Cardinal's Cup in the early 1930s was George Ireland, from Campion Academy in Prairie du Chien, Wisconsin. Among the opponents Ireland faced was future DePaul coach Ray Meyer, from St. Patrick Academy in Chicago.

Ireland went on to play at Notre Dame, culminating in a highly successful senior season in 1935–36 under George Keogan. Alongside

Meyer, as well as sophomore stars Johnny Moir and "giant" 6-foot-5 Paul Nowak, Ireland and the Fighting Irish won a mythical national title three years before the creation of the NCAA tournament. Upon graduation, Ireland took the coaching job at Marmion Military Academy, a high school in suburban Chicago. He was now married to Nowak's sister, Gert, and he stayed at Marmion for 15 years, coaching nearly 350 games. Still, when he was hired by Loyola's athletic director, the Rev. Richard Tischler, in 1951, Ireland was just 37 years old.

Ireland caught Loyola at a moment when reporters were asking Tischler if the school was planning to drop basketball entirely. The Korean War–era military draft was a strong headwind for many college sports programs, and, anyway, the Ramblers had already done away with football back in 1930. A backdrop like that may have made things tense for the new basketball coach, particularly since, after an encouraging 17–8 debut in 1951–52, wins were elusive for Ireland on the lakefront. "When I first came to Loyola in 1951, I inherited a good team," the coach would explain a decade later. "But they all graduated in 1952, and I found there hadn't been much recruiting for several seasons. The administration told me, 'Do the best you can with what you have.' But we didn't have much." The Ramblers were just 89–98 over the next eight years.

Loyola's fortunes improved at last when Jerry Harkness joined the varsity for the 1960–61 season. Though less celebrated than New York City contemporaries like Connie Hawkins and Roger Brown, Harkness was a product of that same competitive basketball crucible and had played against both stars. He had intended to enroll at Texas State, but the recruit was forced to make a new plan when a fire on January 11, 1959, destroyed the school's athletic dormitory. Instead, Harkness chose Loyola and ended up being handed the keys to Ireland's offense from day one. In his first season, the sophomore averaged 23 a game and shot 50 percent from the field as the Ramblers very nearly earned the program its first-ever NCAA bid. While Ireland's team was just 14–8, the coach entered the season finale against Xavier at Chicago Stadium knowing that a win would land the Ramblers in the NCAA's

24-team field. Ireland knew this because he'd received a phone call from a member of the selection committee, West Virginia athletic director Red Brown. In this Midwestern Jesuit showdown, however, Jim McCafferty and the Xavier Musketeers recorded a 94–85 victory.

That defeat would mark the last time any Loyola player then on campus, including the freshmen, would not proceed to either the National Invitation or NCAA tournament. Help was on the way for the Ramblers, in the form of a freshman team that was winning games and attracting notice. Les Hunter, Vic Rouse, John Egan, and Ron Miller would all be eligible as varsity players in 1961–62. Miller was another New York City product, while Egan was a graduate of St. Rita High School in Chicago. Hunter and Rouse had been teammates at Pearl High in Nashville. (Hunter grew up near Vanderbilt's campus and hoped someday to play for the Commodores, but Vandy was still a few years away from breaking the SEC's color line, with Pearl High graduate Perry Wallace.) The pair of 6-foot-7 friends wanted to play together in college and, while Notre Dame offered Hunter a scholarship, the Ramblers recruited them both. This infusion of new talent alongside Harkness resulted in far and away the strongest team of Ireland's tenure to that point. In December 1961, Miller was a reserve and senior Mike Gavin started alongside Harkness, Hunter, Rouse, and Egan. The Ramblers were hammered by 20 in a road game against reigning national runner-up Ohio State, and Loyola also lost by three early in January 1962 at Marquette. Aside from those defeats, the Ramblers rolled to a 16–2 record.

In late February, Loyola accepted a bid as one of the top four seeds in the 1962 NIT. Ireland had the option of playing in that year's NCAA tournament, but he said he preferred the NIT because it would result in his players missing fewer classes. The coach also acknowledged, however, that it would be easier to win the event at Madison Square Garden than it would be to capture the NCAA title. This would be the program's first postseason appearance since the ill-starred 1949 NIT, and it did not go as well as Ireland had wished. Loyola not only lost in the semifinals, but the Ramblers allowed Dayton to explode for

57 points in the second half of a 98–82 collapse. The Flyers would go on to defeat St. John's in the finals, behind 24 points from Bill Chmielewski, a victory that marked UD's first-ever NIT title. Prior to that year, Tom Blackburn had taken nine Dayton teams to the National Invitation Tournament and had reached the finals no fewer than five times, yet this was the program's inaugural championship at Madison Square Garden. Soon after the final horn, the chimes at Sacred Heart Catholic Church on the corner of Fourth and Wilkinson in Dayton pealed with joy that had been pent up for too long.

As for Loyola, Ireland apparently decided the future was now. In the 95–84 win over Duquesne in the third-place game, the coach benched Gavin and started Miller. The sophomore promptly responded with a 20-point performance in his hometown. Harkness, Hunter, Rouse, and Miller took the floor alongside Chicago Catholic League veteran Egan, making it the first time Loyola Chicago had started four Black players. This was not a first in "major" college basketball. It wasn't even unique among teams in action that night. No sooner had the Ramblers defeated the Dukes at the Garden than, at Freedom Hall in Louisville, Cincinnati would start Paul Hogue, Tom Thacker, George Wilson, and Tony Yates in the Bearcats' 71–59 win in the NCAA national title game over Ohio State.

The rotation Ireland had put together so painstakingly over the course of many frustrating years was ranked No. 4 in the nation in the first AP poll of the 1962–63 season. No Loyola starter was taller than 6 foot 7, so the Ramblers did not appear to owe their success to dominance at the rim. Even though reliable performance measures for players and teams from the era are limited, we can make an educated guess on the question of what made this rotation so good. One feature that stands out is that the Ramblers didn't shoot all that much better from the field than did their opponents that season, at least not to the extent that would be expected while outscoring the opposition by 24 points per contest. While turnover numbers from decades ago are close to non-existent, it's likely Loyola was in fact taking excellent care of the ball while also recording a fair number of takeaways with its vaunted press defense. Individually, Harkness and Hunter both shot a hair above 50 percent from the floor. Their teammates were markedly less accurate, leaving us to infer that these two in particular were able to create, or were afforded, good looks at the rim.

Even though we can't measure it precisely years later, it's clear enough that Loyola played at an exceptionally fast pace. "We probably have the most simplified offense in the country," Ireland said that season. "We have a pattern, we move it and don't take too long to get a shot off. Our boys like to shoot." When the Ramblers arrived in Oklahoma City for the All-College tournament at the end of December 1962, the team was 7–0 and averaging 108 points a game. In Oklahoma City, Hunter had a spectacular tournament. He recorded a 34–14 double-double on 13-of-19 shooting from the floor in the title-game win over Wyoming. Hunter had already earned a comparison to Bill Russell from the same *Oklahoman* newspaper that had gazed in wonder at the newly emerging San Francisco star on the same floor eight years earlier. The victory over the Cowboys, however, would be remembered less for Hunter's excellence than for what happened after Egan was thrown out of the game.

With 7:45 left to go in the contest, Egan got into a bruising tie-up on the floor with Wyoming's Bob Hanson. When the players were brought together for a jump ball, referee Joe Conway, "a showboat" in Egan's recollection, demanded that the two opponents verbally acknowledge their transgressions. "Number 11," Conway said to Egan, "I don't want any more of this, understand?" But Egan refused to give the referee the satisfaction. "Throw the ball up," he replied. "Just throw the ball up, will you?" Egan was promptly ejected, whereupon Ireland put Pablo Robertson into the game. A sophomore from New York City, Robertson was on the floor with Harkness, Hunter, Rouse, and Miller. If it hadn't happened before in "major" college basketball history, the first was recorded here. Five Black players represented Loyola Chicago on the court at Oklahoma City's Municipal Auditorium on December 29, 1962.

Despite his pivotal role in creating the signature moment, Robertson didn't last long with the team. At the beginning of February, he was, in the words of the *Chicago Tribune*, "dropped from the university because of scholastic deficiency." Egan would later say his teammate earned four Fs and a D, and concluded the problem was that he had devoted too much time and effort to just that one class. Robertson would go on to lasting fame as a 5-foot-7 crowd favorite with the Harlem Globetrotters and, no less, as a cartoon character on Hanna-Barbera's *Harlem Globetrotters* show in the early 1970s.

Loyola was now down to nine eligible players, with the larger challenge being that Ireland, in effect, trusted just five of them. When the Ramblers required overtime to defeat Marquette 92–90 at Chicago Stadium in February 1963, four starters played all 45 minutes. Ireland's "ironmen" ran their record to 21–0 and were ranked No. 2 in the nation, but the perfect record came crashing down at Bowling Green just days later. Led by rebound king Nate Thurmond, the Falcons scored the game's first nine points and were never seriously threatened after that in what became a 92–75 win. The Ramblers nearly lost twice in one week but managed to pull out a four-point victory at Houston despite being showered with popcorn, ice, and racial epithets. Harkness later recalled Cougars head coach Guy Lewis apologizing to the visitors after the game, a contest played a mere 18 months before Elvin Hayes and Don Chaney would arrive as UH freshmen. Loyola also lost its regular-season finale at Chicago Stadium to Wichita State 73–72, enabling the Shockers to one day boast to grandchildren of how they defeated both the 29–2 Ramblers and 26–2 Cincinnati in 1962–63. Hunter and Rouse both fouled out with more than five minutes remaining against Wichita, highlighting concerns regarding the team's depth heading into the NCAA tournament.

Ireland had accepted the program's first-ever NCAA bid on February 18 in the aftermath of the loss at Bowling Green. Despite a suggestion from the *Tribune* that it might be "wiser" for a team with such a thin rotation to return to Madison Square Garden for a second consecutive year, the Ramblers wanted a shot at reigning champion

Cincinnati. The top-ranked Bearcats weren't on Loyola's schedule, yet Ireland had devoted precious staff hours to scouting UC as early as December. That act alone signaled a preexisting intention to play in the NCAA tournament. As an independent program, the Ramblers had to win a preliminary game in order to reach the regional semi-finals in East Lansing, Michigan. The preliminary contest took the form of a 111–42 victory over Tennessee Tech at McGaw Hall on the Northwestern campus. The blowout represented the largest margin of victory ever recorded in the NCAA tournament, and it was witnessed in person by Mississippi State head coach Babe McCarthy. The MSU coach was in Evanston to scout the game, and he came away amazed by Loyola. "Nobody can beat a team like that," he said. Nevertheless, his players would try to do just that in four days, assuming they were, in fact, allowed to play the game.

Mississippi State had made national news in 1956 by withdrawing from the Evansville Invitational tournament to avoid facing an opponent with a Black player. What was less clear at the time, however, was that this issue would come up repeatedly with regard to this program in particular. For years, MSU would extend every geographically insular effort in scheduling to make this question a moot point. Yet from the perspective of authorities in the state of Mississippi, the problem was that the basketball team was just too good. Mississippi State won SEC titles in 1959, 1961, and 1962. But in each of those years, the so-called unwritten law of the South forced MSU to stay home rather than play in an NCAA tournament that included Black players.

The fourth controversy over NCAA tournament participation in five seasons at Mississippi State began in earnest on February 25, 1963, when the Bulldogs defeated the Tulane Green Wave to clinch at least a share of the SEC title. This latest enactment of what had become a February and March ritual in Mississippi would prove to be the most contentious version of the struggle to date. Babe McCarthy was determined to go to the NCAA tournament after sitting at home with three conference championships. MSU's rotation featured four seniors: Leland Mitchell, Red Stroud, Joe Dan Gold, and Bobby Shows. Sentiment ran high that the players who had now earned their third conference title should be allowed to play at last for a national championship. Finally, the traditional slippery-slope argument against participation apparently no longer applied with regard to higher education in the state. Backed by hundreds of federal marshals, FBI agents, and deputized officers, James Meredith had enrolled as the first African American student at Ole Miss in October 1962. The "unwritten law" against the state's teams playing African American opponents, dating from the mid-1950s, was an attempt to stave off precisely this outcome. What would happen to the unwritten law now?

Following his team's win over Tulane, McCarthy made a statewide appeal on live radio. "It makes my heart sick," the coach exclaimed in his postgame interview, "to think that these players, who just clinched no worse than a tie for their third straight Southeastern Conference championship, will have to put away their uniforms and not compete in the NCAA tournament...This is all I can say, but I think everyone knows how I feel." Later that week, MSU's president, Dean Colvard, released an artfully phrased statement: "I have decided that unless hindered by competent authority I shall send our basketball team to the NCAA competition."

Colvard's wording was skillful, but his timing was perhaps ill-advised. The president had made his declaration nearly two weeks before a Mississippi State team would, if allowed, take the floor in the NCAA tournament. That afforded ample time for opponents of participation to make their voices heard. One member of the state's board of trustees for higher education, M. M. Roberts, stated that Mississippi State's participation in the 1963 NCAA tournament constituted "the greatest challenge to our way of life since Reconstruction." The Jackson *Clarion-Ledger* published a six-column photo of Loyola's starting five on the front page of the sports section over the caption: POSSIBLE FOE FOR BULLDOGS IN NCAA.

Billy Mitts, a Mississippi state senator, joined forces with a former senator named B. W. Lawson and sought an injunction that would bar the team from leaving the state. Mitts and Lawson secured their injunction from Hinds County chancellor L. B. Porter, the same magistrate who had given Governor Ross Barnett an ultimately futile court order the previous fall to prevent Meredith from enrolling at Ole Miss. This 11th-hour "temporary" injunction was intended to tie up Mississippi State in just enough jurisprudence to miss the games.

Instead, when Hinds County sheriffs attempted to serve papers on Colvard, McCarthy, Mississippi State athletic director Wade Walker, or anyone else in authority, no one could be found. All of the above had fled the state the moment they were tipped off about the injunction. McCarthy and Walker took a car to Memphis and from there flew to Nashville. Colvard drove to Birmingham and checked into a motel under an assumed name. As for the team, the players were in hiding on the Mississippi State campus, along with assistant coach Jerry Simmons. A group of reserves and freshmen had gone to the airfield to impersonate the varsity and, if necessary, serve as "expendables" for any interdiction by law enforcement. But when the decoys discovered the coast was clear, trainer Werner Luchsinger phoned Simmons and told him to rush the varsity players to the plane. As the flight cleared Mississippi airspace, one of the players said, "Now I know how those East Berliners feel when they make it past the wall." The Bulldogs were on their way to play Loyola Chicago in East Lansing, Michigan.

When Jerry Harkness shook hands with Joe Dan Gold before the regional semifinal at Jenison Field House on the campus of Michigan State, the photographers in attendance all snapped their shutters in unison. More than the game itself, the handshake was and would be remembered as the defining moment of March 15, 1963. There were a few Mississippi State fans on hand, and the "sound of cowbells, stamped with Confederate flags and wielded by a knot of State students who had driven north for the tournament, filled the field house."

McCarthy had resolved not to let Loyola run wild, and, in the words of one reporter on press row, MSU's "famed stall offense, employed early in the fray, gave the crowd mixed emotions." The Bulldogs recorded the game's first seven points but would be outscored by 17 the rest of the way in what became a 61–51 victory for the Ramblers. Mitchell was the lone effective rebounder on this day for undersized MSU. When he fouled out with 6:47 remaining, it meant that Rouse was free to put the finishing touches on his 16–19 double-double. Asked if Loyola's superiority on the boards had made the difference in the contest, Ireland responded characteristically, "It sure as hell helped." The Ramblers then faced Illinois in the regional finals for what the *Tribune* excitedly called the championship "of the Mideast regional and that of the state of Illinois." Loyola won both titles convincingly with a 79–64 victory that wasn't as close as the final score suggested. The Fighting Illini committed at least 20 turnovers and at one point trailed 75–47. Harkness had been named a first-team All-American, and he very much looked the part, ringing up 33 points.

In addition to crowning a national champion, the 1963 Final Four in Louisville was a celebration of the 25th NCAA tournament. This would also be the first title game since 1954 to be televised nationally—or at least available nationally. The game would be syndicated by Sports Network, Inc., which estimated that 94 percent of the nation's TV sets would have access to the broadcast. This, of course, assumed a local station received by that set had chosen to buy the game. Loyola Chicago, defending champion Cincinnati, Duke, and Oregon State were vying to play in that national final, and in the semifinals the Ramblers would face an opponent with whom they appeared to share a good deal in common. Duke was also making its first-ever appearance in a Final Four. Led by Art Heyman and Jeff Mullins, the Blue Devils also loved to run. They, too, were ranked nationally in the top three, and head coach Vic Bubas was asked repeatedly that week if he was really going to run against the highest-scoring offense in the nation. A shoot-out was eagerly anticipated.

Ireland had watched film of one Duke game, and, before the regional final against Illinois, he and Fighting Illini coach Harry Combes had agreed to split the cost of obtaining a scouting report on the winner of the Blue Devils' region. Many years later, Ireland would additionally claim to have received a scouting report on Duke from Dean Smith at the direction of Frank McGuire. Smith had been hired as an assistant by North Carolina head coach McGuire in 1958. By March 1963, Smith had finished his second season as head coach of the Tar Heels, while McGuire, possibly to Smith's chagrin, was again living in Chapel Hill.

Ireland and McGuire were contemporaries, and the latter was taking a break from the sport after having coached the NBA's Warriors in 1961–62. When he elected not to follow the franchise in its relocation from Philadelphia to San Francisco, McGuire became one of the earliest objects of intense media speculation with respect to what would later be called the coaching carousel. For two years, he mulled his options, supported all the while by the settlement he'd received from the Warriors. McGuire's name was linked to openings or potential openings with the Detroit Pistons, at the University of Maryland, and even, when Smith went 8–9 in his first season, at UNC. In the meantime, according to Ireland's recollection in the 1990s, McGuire reached out to help an old friend whose team had been bracketed with North Carolina's ACC rival at the 1963 Final Four.

The Ramblers certainly played like they had received an excellent scouting report. Loyola jumped out to a 20–5 lead and maintained that margin for much of the evening. When Duke drew to within 74–71 with 4:20 left, it looked as though Ireland's total reliance on his starting five had been exposed as a weakness. On the contrary, the coach said afterward. The game to that point had been played at a slower pace than his team was accustomed to, and so, he maintained, his players were rested and primed for a big finish. The Ramblers lent support to that narrative by fairly exploding the rest of the way and recording a 94–75 victory. Hunter had still another remarkable outing, recording a 29–18 double-double and leaving quite an impression on one Tobacco Road writer by getting "his elbows above the rims when he goes after an offensive rebound." Ireland's men would play for the national title against Cincinnati, which had easily dismissed Oregon State by 34 points.

If the first task of any defense is to take away the opponent's best player, Cincinnati should have won going away. Harkness was held scoreless from the field for the first 35 minutes, as Ed Jucker's team treated the nationally syndicated television audience to a masterful display of pressure defense. UC led at the intermission 29–21, and by early in the second half the Ramblers trailed the best defense in the country by 15. But, for one of the few times in the past 50-some games, fouls were becoming a problem for Cincinnati. The box score would show that on the evening an equal number of whistles had been blown against the Ramblers, but three starters picking up four fouls was foreign territory for the Bearcats. After Thacker's fourth sent him to the bench with six minutes left, UC went into a stall, with the score 48–41. By the time Harkness scored in the lane with 2:45 remaining to bring the Ramblers within two, Ron Bonham was choosing to merely hold his position with his arms at his side, rather than risk being called for a foul.

Cincinnati was still up 53–52 when Loyola was forced to foul with 12 seconds left on the clock. The Ramblers had elected to foul Larry Shingleton and send him to the line, a place where the senior had been just 26 times in 27 previous games. Shingleton made the first free throw and, after an icing time-out by Ireland, missed the second. In a sequence Loyola had run countless times before, Hunter zipped an outlet pass up ahead to Miller at midcourt. This time, however, the junior's catch on the run was less than clean, and UC loyalists would insist forever after that there should have been a call then and there for traveling. When no whistle sounded, Miller hit the streaking Harkness for the tying basket in the closing seconds of regulation.

After each team added four points in overtime, Ireland called time-out with 1:49 left. For one of the few times, if not the only time, in the last two years, the plan coming out of the huddle was for Loyola to hold the ball. As the clock went down under 10 seconds, Harkness would then try for the game-winner. Instead, Egan was tied up by Shingleton with more than a minute remaining. The diminutive Rambler controlled the ensuing jump ball, a feat which would loom large in subsequent Loyola mythology despite the fact that the opposing player in this instance was, like Egan, 5 foot 10. (As Egan would say decades later with reference to both the myth and to Shingleton, "He gets taller every year.") It would be up to Harkness after all, but as he rose for his shot on the left wing, he was closely defended by Bonham. In midair, Harkness elected instead to pass off to Hunter in the lane. When Hunter's 10-footer rimmed out to the right, Rouse was there for the putback as time expired. "I've played with Les for a long time," Rouse said afterward in explaining his perfect position and timing. Loyola Chicago had won the national championship over Cincinnati, 60–58.

No one could accuse the Ramblers of not earning their title. In prevailing against Mississippi State, Illinois, Duke, and Cincinnati, Ireland's men had defeated the Nos. 6-, 8-, 2-, and 1-ranked opponents in the nation. Winning the 45-minute duel at the end of that sequence had entailed five starters relying upon stamina and shot volume once again. Ireland did not make one substitution. On a night when Loyola's offense converted just 23 of its 84 shots, the key number was the 84. The Bearcats attempted a mere 45. And the Ramblers committed just three turnovers, while UC gave the ball away 16 times.

Loyola's combination of terrible shooting and near-zero turnovers would prove to be the polar opposite of the winning recipe used by another Catholic team against another top-ranked defending national champion in another legendary NCAA title game played in another arena in the state of Kentucky 22 years later.

The Ramblers were thought to have an excellent shot at winning a second consecutive title because every starter would be back except Harkness. Cincinnati itself had won two championships and played in three consecutive national finals only after Oscar Robertson's departure. If the Bearcats could thrive without Robertson, who was to say Loyola wouldn't do the same without Harkness? Ireland's team entered the following season ranked No. 1 and won its first six games, but, interestingly, what took a hit without Harkness on the court appeared to be the defense. The Ramblers closed the season 22–6 after losing by four in the regional semifinals to a Michigan team led by sophomore Cazzie Russell, a Chicagoan.

It's conceivable that Ireland's second-best team came not the year before or the year after the national title but in 1966 instead. That was when Billy Smith, Corky Bell, Jim Coleman, and Doug Wardlaw powered the Ramblers to a 22–2 record and a No. 3 ranking before being smashed 105–86 by Western Kentucky in the NCAA's preliminary round.

In all, the coach would work the sidelines at Loyola for almost 25 years before stepping down in the middle of the 1974–75 season due to health reasons. He continued in his role as athletic director until 1978, and passed away 72 hours after the September 11 attacks in 2001 at the age of 88. The coach so frequently praised for opening doors to African Americans in advance of many of his peers was not as often described as particularly warm. "George didn't see color," Egan said at Ireland's funeral. "He hated us all the same." Yet it's telling that his players showed up to offer their eulogies for the coach after having stayed in contact with him and with each other for so long.

A few years before Ireland's passing, at some point in the 1990s, Cincinnati's Tony Yates ran into Loyola's Ron Miller by chance.

"Ron," Yates said to Miller, "how are you?"

"Good to see you," Miller responded.

Yates replied, "You know you walked."

From the safe distance of many intervening years and while wearing a championship ring, Miller would volunteer this much: "When I look at the film, I traveled." The 1963 title game thus affords every element required to be ranked as a classic. The two best teams in the country had met. History was at stake: Cincinnati was trying to become the first program ever to win three consecutive national titles. An amazing comeback occurred. A controversy arose that has been argued over ever since. (Contacted 50 years after the fact, Tom Thacker was still aggrieved. "We should have won the championship three times, but we got sidetracked by a couple of Chicago officials.") The contest went to overtime. The outcome was decided by a game-winning shot in the final seconds. The 1963 title game *was* a classic.

It is, however, a classic that has been eclipsed. A different game Loyola played that month is now marked with a plaque where the contest occurred. The plaque was unveiled outside Jenison Field House at Michigan State in December 2012 to commemorate the Mississippi State game as part of the 50th anniversary celebrations of the Ramblers' championship season. Well before the anniversary, the 1963 meeting between the two programs had acquired a name. It was called the Game of Change.

Instead of true cause-and-effect, the Game of Change's most enduring legacy may be something as ephemeral as the sport itself—namely, Rich Clarkson's photograph of Harkness shaking hands at center court with Gold. Not to be confused with a different picture of a different handshake featuring Rouse at the center jump at the start of the game, Clarkson's image of Harkness and Gold meeting as captains distilled the historic moment while adding to it. When Harkness attended Gold's funeral in Kentucky in 2011, he found that the family had mounted a large print of the Clarkson photograph in a prominent position. The photo has become a secular icon.

While societal uplift is an impossible task to place upon any mere sporting event, "Game of Change" is a serviceable enough label for a contest the Chicago *Defender* in 1963 termed "the most talked-about, and awaited, basketball game in the history of the NCAA." What Clarkson captured in his lens was not a sweeping moment of revolutionary change but a vivid and singular milestone on a journey spanning generations.

10.

McGuire and Marquette

When Loyola Chicago reached the 1963 Final Four, Ramblers assistant coach Bill Shay distributed eight tickets to his friends from Maguire's, a tavern in suburban Forest Park, Illinois. The bar was a popular destination for Chicago-area high school coaches and, eventually, for college coaching staffs. As basketball types from different high schools and colleges rubbed elbows with each other over the years at the watering hole, they began to refer to themselves as fellow colleagues from "Maguire University." Encouraged by Loyola's run, a contingent claiming to represent Maguire U began attending the Final Four annually.

On a whim, the Maguire University name was submitted to the NCAA in 1972 for inclusion in its National Directory of College Athletics, referred to as the Blue Book. Instrumental in this process was one-time DePaul assistant coach Bob Luksta. In filling out the application, Luksta and his fellow conspirators listed Maguire's president as Mel Connolly, a truck driver friend, who was now presented to the NCAA as Dr. Mel Connolly. The director of women's physical education was Gert Ireland, the wife of Loyola coach George Ireland. School colors were listed as green and white, and the basketball team, the Jollymen, played home games at Lawless Fieldhouse. Sure enough, Maguire University, at 7215 West Madison in Forest Park, was listed as an NCAA institution in good standing in the next edition of the Blue Book. The actual Maguire's phone number was printed in the national directory, and soon the bartenders were receiving calls from coaches around the country looking to schedule games with the Jollymen. In a masterpiece of understatement, Luksta would observe in 2018 that you "couldn't get away with that today with the internet and computers and everything."

Would Maguire University have earned its fleeting NCAA membership if Luksta in 1972, instead of being a former DePaul assistant coach and ex–head coach at Loyola New Orleans, had been the head coach at Marquette? It nearly happened.

In 1964, one year after Loyola Chicago's national title, the Ramblers' fellow Jesuit program on the shores of Lake Michigan made a coaching change. Ed Hickey was let go at Marquette. "I'm not ready or prepared for retirement," Hickey told the press at the time, but things looked rather different to Marquette's president, the Rev. William F. Kelley. "In the volatile and whimsical realm of athletics," Kelley announced, "sometimes a change of personnel or direction is required." The school president noted that this step had been recommended by his athletic board months before, in the midst of a 5–21 season. While Marquette had gone 20–9 in 1963 and reached the NIT semifinals, the team's record the following year qualified as MU's worst performance in men's basketball since 1941. The team's struggles appeared to date from Hickey's decision to dismiss four players for missing curfew on New Year's Eve in Louisville. At the time, all of the players were reserves, though one of them, Jim Warras, had been a starter earlier in the season. More than any pure basketball impact, however, the swiftness and apparent relish with which Hickey canceled all four scholarships seemed to take the wind out of the entire team.

A little more than two months later, Hickey joined his four ex-players in being forced out at Marquette. The first names to surface as potential replacements were MU assistant Hank Raymonds and former Seattle head coach John Castellani, a recent graduate of Marquette's law school.

Out of a reported 50 applicants, three finalists eventually earned interviews: Raymonds, Luksta, and the longest of all long shots, Belmont Abbey head coach Al McGuire. At age 35, McGuire had not fared much better with his small Benedictine program in Belmont, North Carolina, in 1963–64 than Hickey had with his team in Milwaukee. When Marquette chose McGuire anyway, MU officials touted their new hire by stating that McGuire had compiled a 120–60 record at Belmont Abbey. That was correct, but what the Jesuits in Milwaukee glossed over was the fact that their new coach was coming off 7–21 and 6–18 seasons in his last two years. It was hardly the profile of a new coach who was going to win the press conference.

Nevertheless, McGuire got the job, thanks to two significant competitive advantages. First, he was, as would immediately become evident and would soon become legendary, a born salesman. Second, for a head coach at a tiny college in North Carolina, he was incredibly well-connected within the profession. McGuire was recommended for the position in Milwaukee by none other than Frank McGuire, who had himself just accepted the job as the next head coach at South Carolina.

Salesmanship had started early and necessarily for Marquette's new coach. After shooting 29.6 percent from the field over his junior and senior years on Frank McGuire's teams at St. John's, Al McGuire somehow landed a spot on an NBA roster in 1951. He played three seasons for the New York Knicks under Joe Lapchick, averaged four points a game, and earned praise for his defense. Many years later, when McGuire had long been celebrated as both a coach and an analyst, he would invariably say of himself as a player, "I stayed in the league three years by diving over press tables and starting fights." As a member of the Knicks, he garnered a nickname that referenced both his Queens upbringing as the son of a tavern keeper and his temperament. In the eyes of New York's Cold War–era tabloids, McGuire was the "Rockaway pepperpot."

If Frank McGuire or Lapchick hadn't been able to provide sufficient backing to impress the decision makers at Marquette in 1964, Al McGuire could also have turned to Doggie Julian. The coach who'd led Holy Cross to the 1947 national title had acted on the recommendation of Lapchick and hired McGuire as the freshman coach at Dartmouth in 1954. McGuire coached Dave Gavitt in Hanover, once complimenting his freshman during a game by saying, "Nice play, George." ("He never remembered anyone's name," according to Gavitt.) Finally, if all of the above connections weren't enough to get McGuire his next job beyond Belmont Abbey, there was always the family tie. McGuire's older brother, Dick McGuire, was not only a legendary guard both at St. John's and in the NBA, as of 1965 he was also serving variously as the Knicks' head coach and as the franchise's chief scout. Telling high school recruits about your brother the NBA coach or scout would prove to be an effective pitch for Marquette's next coach. Al McGuire's network was one and the same with any listing of East Coast basketball's leading lights, both professional and collegiate. His references and his presence were irresistible to Marquette.

McGuire moved quickly to persuade Raymonds to stay on as an assistant, and to reinstate one of the players Hickey had banished. But the largest win of his first year was signing George Thompson out of Erasmus Hall High School in Brooklyn. "We regard him as the number two player behind [Lew] Alcindor in the New York area," McGuire crowed in May 1965, referring to the player who later changed his name to Kareem Abdul-Jabbar. Indeed, Thompson would prove to be the coach's first NBA player. Early in McGuire's tenure, Marquette also introduced its "scrambled eggs" unit, a five-player platoon that would come off the bench with an eye toward changing a game's momentum through disruptive and even chaotic defense. When Thompson became eligible as a sophomore, MU advanced to the title game of the 1967 NIT before losing in the finals to future NBA great Walt Frazier and Southern Illinois. Marquette would play in either the NCAA tournament or the NIT in every remaining year of the McGuire era.

On October 30, 1965, a letter bearing a postmark from Hazleton, Pennsylvania, was mailed to Notre Dame head football coach Ara Parseghian. "Knowing that you have little time to waste," the note began, "I don't expect you to answer my letter in the near future, but I would appreciate a short reply after the season, if your busy schedule permits." The writer continued: "Eventually, I'd like to coach on the college level. My big dream is to coach basketball at Notre Dame." The letter was signed by the 24-year-old head coach at St. Gabriel's High School in Hazleton, Dick Phelps.

Richard Phelps owed his nickname, Digger, to his father's line of work (funerals), and he would wait years before receiving a response from South Bend. When Phelps sent his letter, Johnny Dee was 42 years old and earning positive press as he prepared for his second season as head coach of the Fighting Irish. During Dee's seven years at Notre Dame, he built a recruiting pipeline to the greater Washington, DC, area that would pay dividends for many seasons to come. The cream of the DC-to-South Bend crop was Austin Carr, a transcendent talent from Mackin Catholic who, along with Artis Gilmore, Curtis Rowe, and Howard Porter, was one of the most highly sought recruits nationally in 1967. Dee managed to win that battle, and Carr, in a remarkable career from 1968 to 1971, would manage to outperform his advance billing.

Notre Dame would need players of Carr's caliber to keep pace in what was shaping up as an increasingly competitive Catholic basketball landscape in the Midwest. After years as the ultimate example of an independent program that seemingly ignored the NCAA tournament entirely in favor of the NIT, Dayton felt the winds of change blowing its way in the mid-1960s. Tom Blackburn retired as coach, and Don Donoher, like McGuire and Dee, took the reins of his new program as of the 1964–65 season. One difference between Donoher and his predecessor became apparent that first year, when UD accepted an invitation to play in the 1965 NCAA tournament. It was just the second such appearance in Dayton's history and, indeed, the first since the NCAA adopted its rule in the early 1950s mandating that teams appear in only one postseason tournament.

Rather than journeying to the Big Apple, fans of the Flyers traveled to Lexington, Kentucky, in 1965, and to Iowa City, Iowa, in 1966. In those locales, UD was paired in both years in the regional semifinals with the reigning No. 1 team in the nation—first, Michigan, and then Kentucky.

Dayton lost both games, but by the time the 1967 NCAA tournament rolled around, Donoher's luck was improving with respect to the brackets. This time, the Flyers didn't run up against the No. 1 team until the national championship game. To make it that far, UD won overtime contests against Western Kentucky and Virginia Tech, as well as a one-point game against Tennessee. This good fortune was expected by some observers to finally run out in the national semifinal against a North Carolina team making its first NCAA tournament appearance under Dean Smith. Instead, Dayton's Don May tucked a Miraculous Medal into his uniform, converted 13 straight shots from the field, and scored 34 points to lead his team to a 14-point win over the Tar Heels. That was as far as momentum and devotionals could carry the Flyers, however, in a tournament that also included Lew Alcindor. UCLA at least had the decency to put UD away early in the title game, building a 38–20 lead at the half and gliding to a 15-point victory and a perfect 30–0 season.

While Dayton was reaching new heights and Notre Dame was rejoicing at Carr choosing the Fighting Irish, Marquette was also thriving on the recruiting front. Having scored a big win with George Thompson, McGuire notched an even larger triumph in 1967 with the signing of Dean Meminger, also out of New York City. McGuire said that the 6-foot-1 Meminger was "quicker than 11:15 Mass at a seaside resort." The coach was recruiting his hometown like a master, and he was doing so with blunt candor and a complete lack of flattery. "I asked Al if he was going to stay at Marquette my four years," Meminger would later remember, "and he told me, 'Dean, you're born alone and you die alone.'"

McGuire's honest assessments weren't restricted to the elite recruits. A fellow first-year player at MU alongside Meminger was 210-pound newcomer Rick Majerus, who was excited to parlay his tireless effort and textbook screening as a walk-on with the freshman team into a shot at the varsity. McGuire had to inform Majerus that would not be happening, because the freshman was, in fact, the worst basketball player the coach had ever seen. Nonetheless, Majerus would join the MU staff as an assistant coach upon graduation in 1971.

Events would prove Meminger had posed an excellent question

when he asked McGuire if he would be around for the next four years. In March 1968, the Marquette administration learned that McGuire was negotiating to become the first head coach and general manager of a new Milwaukee NBA franchise that at the time was yet to be named. "As far as we are concerned," the school's executive vice president, the Rev. Raymond R. McCauley told a press conference, "Al McGuire is our coach now and he will be our coach next year." McGuire was just one year into a five-year contract and had already landed his team a spot in the 1968 NCAA tournament, his first ever as a coach and the program's first appearance in the event since 1961. McCauley thought that was where the coach's focus should be. "I do not understand why he continues to negotiate with the local NBA franchise owners or why he decided to publicize the matter," McCauley said to the press. Gradually, McGuire came to the conclusion that the Jesuits did indeed have him locked in and that he wasn't going anywhere. The coach stayed, though his surrender had a typical Al McGuire verbal edge. "The priests at Marquette take a vow of poverty, and they expect you to abide by it."

Marquette opened the NCAA tournament with a 72–71 win over Bowling Green in a game played at Kent State. The victory set up a collision with Kentucky in the regional semifinals on the Wildcats' home floor. Adolph Rupp's team was a six-point favorite, and McGuire tried to give his players a lift by predicting victory at a pregame press conference with all four coaches at the regional. That wasn't customary behavior from opposing coaches in Lexington, and it was reported in the Bluegrass State that Marquette "has a brash coach named Al McGuire who says—even though he hasn't scouted UK—that there's no reason why his team should lose."

Rupp remembered McGuire well. He had respected him as a player from the annual games UK and St. John's played in the late 1940s and early 1950s. Still, when McGuire said he didn't need to scout the Wildcats, Rupp couldn't help but respond, "Al, I know damn good and well you didn't scout Kentucky, because we finished our season before you were even invited." This time, the UK coach held all the cards. Ignited by 36 points from Dan Issel, the Wildcats pummeled Marquette

107–89. Rupp gave McGuire credit for the Wildcats' win, saying the Marquette coach had motivated UK's players. "He fired Issel up," Rupp said of the opposing coach. "I think McGuire helped us, because our boys can read too. It's very unfortunate, because everything they have said since they've come to town has been to antagonize us."

One year later, Marquette was again paired with Kentucky in the Mideast regional semifinals, though this time the game would be played in Madison, Wisconsin. Dean "The Dream" Meminger was a sophomore, George Thompson was a senior, and MU entered the contest with a 23–4 record and rated as a one-point favorite over the Wildcats. When Marquette won 81–74, McGuire called it "the biggest thing that has happened to me in my 28 years in basketball." The coach was apparently counting back to his first CYO game as a 12-year-old, but he would be less euphoric after the regional final. Instead of reaching the program's first-ever Final Four, Marquette lost to Purdue 75–73 on a Rick Mount jumper from the corner with two seconds left in overtime.

In just two years, a surprisingly intense NCAA Mideast regional rivalry had sprung up between MU and Kentucky. McGuire may have taken it as a matter of course that this was the path his team would follow every year. The NCAA had other plans. In 1970, Marquette was bracketed in the Midwest and not the Mideast regional. MU was ranked No. 8 in the AP poll when McGuire received the news that the NCAA had his team playing not in Dayton, Ohio, but in Fort Worth, Texas. The coach huddled with university officials in Milwaukee, considered the invitation, and, in the end, elected to turn down the NCAA and play in the NIT instead. Reports stated that the school's nine-member athletic council had engaged in three hours of "heated debate" over the question. In later years, it would become part of the McGuire legend that, during these feverish discussions over which tournament to choose, the coach had received a phone call. "Next I hear from the university president's office," McGuire would relate. "His assistant says, 'I think we should go to the NCAA.' I told him, 'Father, I don't hear confession and you don't coach this team.'"

We do know McGuire spent a good deal of time on the phone that evening, much of it with sportswriters. The next morning, McGuire's heated anti-NCAA invective was featured in sports sections all over the country. "What kind of joke is this? We knock ourselves out all season just to get another shot at Kentucky and then they [NCAA committee members] set you up as a patsy," he fumed. "I'm disgusted and disappointed." McGuire noted that he had four of the five starters back from a team that was one shot away from making the 1969 Final Four. "I wanted to go to the NCAA tournament, and we deserve to be in Dayton on March 7. But we were [screwed] by the so-called ethical people of the NCAA...They worry more about whether you give an athlete a T-shirt rather than for their own ethics." McGuire's fury was real and, as always, stated in remarkable sound bites. If the NCAA was a lion, no one could twist the lion's tail quite like McGuire. A broad audience of sports fans with zero stake in Marquette's bracketing loved watching him do so. In this instance, however, the decision to forgo the NCAA tournament was both steeped in precedent and, in the specific case of MU in 1970, open to question.

Several programs had turned down NCAA bids in the 1960s. In addition to Mississippi State in 1961 and 1962 and Loyola Chicago in 1962, Army head coach Bob Knight famously said no to the NCAA in 1968 and took Mike Krzyzewski and the rest of the team a short distance downriver from West Point to the NIT. Still more applicable to Marquette's situation was the NCAA invite that Villanova turned down in 1965. Jack Kraft's program gave up the bid that year because the NCAA had proposed to send the Wildcats to the Mideast regional in Bowling Green, Kentucky, instead of putting them in the East region at the Palestra. Kraft said "no, thank you" in customary phrasing that was forgotten the next day, and Bill Melchionni, Jim Washington, and the rest of the Cats advanced to the finals of the 1965 NIT before falling to St. John's in Joe Lapchick's coaching swan song. Yet it's McGuire's iconic refusal that has stood out ever since. In comparison to the Army and Villanova precedents, McGuire's decision appears to have been motivated less by geography and more by pride and expectation.

Ironically, Marquette may have had a smoother path to the 1970

Final Four had McGuire accepted the bracket the NCAA was trying to give him. If MU had gone to the Mideast as McGuire was insisting, his team would have been competing not only against Kentucky but also with Iowa and with Artis Gilmore and Jacksonville. All three were among the strongest teams in the country that year in terms of schedule-adjusted scoring margin, and all three were, on paper, superior to Marquette. Indeed, Jacksonville would reach the national championship game before losing to UCLA. Conversely, the best team in the Midwest region statistically was New Mexico State. Lou Henson's Aggies were no pushover; they reached the Final Four that year, and NMSU was, in fact, a hair stronger numerically than Marquette. Nevertheless, it may have been an easier route for MU to navigate than what looked like a Mideast "bracket of death." We'll never know.

No sooner had university officials in Milwaukee announced their decision than MU was snapped up by the organizers of the 1970 NIT. Choosing to play at the National Invitation Tournament was, among other things, a public relations masterstroke. When the team arrived in New York and took up residence at an undisclosed hotel, McGuire was hunted down for an interview by famed ABC sportscaster Howard Cosell. Soon, however, it appeared that McGuire's moment in the media sun might prove short-lived. Having been paired with Massachusetts in the first round, Marquette found itself being carved to pieces in the game's opening minutes by one Minuteman in particular.

McGuire was both furious and mortified. Here he had raised Cain in turning down the NCAA on behalf of what he indignantly called his strongest team yet. Now, he was in danger of being eliminated from the NIT after the first game. McGuire called time-out and started screaming at his assistant coach, Hank Raymonds, "Who the hell is that kid out there?" Told that it was Julius Erving, a sophomore from New York, McGuire redirected his yelling to Meminger. "New York! New York! We get all the good players from New York. Dean, how come you didn't tell me about this Julius guy?" Fortunately for McGuire, Marquette rallied for a 62–55 win, then recorded victories by double-digit margins over Utah, Pete Maravich and LSU, and St. John's, to earn the NIT title and prove a point. MU won the tournament wearing navy-blue uniforms with bold horizontal gold stripes. The look became known as the "bumblebees," and the "psychedelic" uniforms were later banned by the NCAA as too distracting for opponents.

While the most intensely discussed Catholic program in the 1970 postseason was certainly Marquette, the strongest such team that March was St. Bonaventure. Larry Weise's group arrived at its regional NCAA final against Villanova sporting a 24–1 record and a No. 3 ranking in the AP poll. The Bonnies' only loss on the season had come by two points on the road to the Wildcats, and now fans of the Franciscans wanted, as their not-very-Franciscan signs put it, "revenge." Bob Lanier was a first-team All-American on his way to a Hall of Fame career, and he was working his wonders for, of all programs, the small school in Cattaraugus County, New York. In a sequence similar to the one Bill Russell had charted, Lanier had been relatively overlooked at Bennett High School in Buffalo as the center playing on a team of shooters. Weise pounced on the budding star in his own backyard. "What I sold was that his parents could come watch him play," the coach would one day recall.

Catholic college basketball in Western New York could claim its greatest-ever concentration of talent in 1970 with Lanier at St. Bonaventure and Calvin Murphy at Niagara. Twice named a first-team All-American, Murphy was a 5-foot-9 native of Norwalk, Connecticut, who set what was then a Division I record in December 1968 by scoring 68 points against Syracuse. The Hall of Famer is still the Purple Eagles' all-time leading scorer despite playing just three seasons for Frank Layden. As for Lanier, by the time he was a 6-foot-11 senior, he was being compared to Lew Alcindor. St. Bonaventure was thrashing Villanova in the second half of the regional final when Lanier collided with the Wildcats' Chris Ford and suffered a college-career-ending knee injury. The Bonnies finished up the 23-point win and advanced to the 1970 Final Four, but without their star, they lost 91–83 to Jacksonville. Gilmore and the Dolphins were then defeated in the national title game by UCLA, thus creating an ageless and enticing "what if" among the St. Bonaventure faithful. In a year where John Wooden didn't have Alcindor anymore and didn't have Bill Walton yet, what if Lanier had played?

With McGuire consistently adding elite talent to his Marquette roster, most of his teams over his first six or seven years could be labeled as his "best team yet." His 1971 rotation continued that tradition. Meminger was a senior, and 6-foot-11 Racine product Jim Chones was a sophomore. MU survived close games at home against Wisconsin and Notre Dame and an overtime at Madison Square Garden against a Fordham team coached by Digger Phelps to preserve a perfect 27–0 record. Entering the 1971 NCAA tournament, McGuire's team was ranked No. 2 in the country behind UCLA and had won 39 straight games, dating back to 1970. For a heady two weeks in late January, Marquette had even been ranked the No. 1 team in the country. There was a reason for this sudden opening atop the polls.

At Notre Dame that month, Coach Dee's pipeline of Washington, DC, talent had paid off in the most spectacular way imaginable when the Fighting Irish ended UCLA's 19-game win streak with an 89–82 victory in South Bend. Austin Carr brought the Bruins defense to its knees on his way to 46 points, a performance that earned him the ultimate compliment from Coach Wooden. "There is no one," he said when asked after the game what scorer could compare. In the Notre Dame locker room, Carr gave full credit to a manic home crowd who had posted, among other signs, EVEN THE POPE WOULDN'T PICK UCLA NO. 1. Carr had already scored 61 points on 57 percent shooting against Ohio in a 1970 NCAA preliminary-round game, and he had followed that up with a 52-point performance in a loss to Kentucky in the regional semifinals. Notre Dame would again bow out in the round of 16 in 1971, but not before its star had put up another 52 points, this time in an opening win over TCU. Including third-place contests, Carr averaged 41 points in seven career NCAA tournament games, making him the greatest scorer in tournament history.

For its part, Marquette remained undefeated all the way to the postseason. This time, "the postseason" would mean the 1971 NCAA tournament. There would be no controversy and no NIT this year, as McGuire was once again given his customary spot in the Mideast region. Having disposed of Miami of Ohio in an opening-round game at Notre Dame, Marquette was slated to play Ohio State in the regional semifinal on the campus of the University of Georgia. If McGuire had been told before the game against the Buckeyes that his next opponent would be Kentucky, he no doubt would have been pleased. Unfortunately for him, that game would be played to determine the third-place finisher. Marquette lost to OSU 60–59 after Meminger fouled out for the only time in his career. The coach's son, Allie McGuire, had made a layup at the buzzer to give the game its final score. After the loss, MU's players named the two referees from the Ohio State game to their "all-opponent team" for 1970–71. The season marked a painful missed opportunity for what, in retrospect, was perhaps one of the two or three strongest teams McGuire would ever have.

Fordham was playing in the round of 16 on the same day as Marquette. Even with the overtime loss to MU at the Garden, the Rams and their 29-year-old rookie head coach had put together what many considered to be the best season in the program's history. Given many of the same players who had gone 10–15 the season before, Phelps led his team into the 1971 NCAA tournament with a 24–2 record and a No. 10 ranking in the AP poll.

Following a 31-point win over Furman at Alumni Hall on the campus of St. John's, Phelps sounded confident in advance of his team's clash with Villanova and Howard Porter in the regional semifinal in Raleigh. "I think we can contain Porter," Phelps said while offering what bordered on a Joe Namath–style guarantee. "The semifinals in Houston [will] have UCLA, Kansas, Marquette, and Fordham." Instead, unranked Villanova defeated the Rams 85–75. Porter's 25 points may have taken a back seat to the 32 Charlie Yelverton scored for Fordham, but 57 percent shooting by Jack Kraft's team was too much to overcome for the Rams. The Wildcats had an even easier time in the next round, dispensing with Big 5 rival Penn by 43 points to reach the program's first national semifinal since 1939. The Villanova attack was built around Porter, a onetime high school phenomenon from Sarasota, Florida, who'd been scouted by former Nova standout and then assistant coach George Raveling.

Villanova's pairing with Western Kentucky in one semifinal raised eyebrows along press row at the Houston Astrodome. The game was called "a preview of next year's ABA playoffs," amid rumors that both Porter and Hilltoppers star Jim McDaniels had already signed professional contracts with the NBA's rival league. The Wildcats won a double-overtime thriller against WKU and then gave UCLA one of the few close championship games the Bruins experienced during their extraordinary run of 10 titles in 12 seasons. Wooden was even compelled to stall late in the first half to force the Wildcats out of their zone defense. Porter scored 25 points while guarding Sidney Wicks in Villanova's 68–62 loss, an effort that earned him the tournament's most outstanding player award.

Strangely, however, the traditional ceremony for the individual so honored was not held that year. It appeared the NCAA believed that Porter was ineligible to play. Indeed, it turned out he had signed with an agent on December 16, 1970, and Villanova would later vacate its wins from that date through its victory over Western Kentucky. Porter went on to a seven-year career in the NBA, then chose to retire rather than risk further danger to his health when a blood clot was found to have lodged in his lung. Tragically, he struggled with substance abuse in later years and died an untimely and violent death in 2007. When the Wildcats won national titles in 2016 and 2018, Porter would be lauded by former teammates as having brought about "the start of Villanova being recognized nationally."

In the aftermath of the 1970–71 season, officials at Notre Dame invited McGuire to speak to the team at its annual awards banquet. There was an agenda behind the invitation. Dee had told the administration that this would be his last season and that, at age 47, he wished to pursue opportunities outside basketball in his beloved Denver. When McGuire arrived in South Bend, he was asked by athletic director Moose Krause and sports information director Roger Valdiserri if he would like to be the next coach of the Fighting Irish. The Marquette coach said no, whereupon he was requested to offer his opinion as to the three best young coaches in the country. McGuire reportedly responded: Dean Smith, Bob Knight, and Digger Phelps. Notre Dame introduced Phelps as its next basketball coach on May 5. At the first opportunity, he asked Fighting Irish football coach Ara Parseghian if he still remembered the letter he'd received from Phelps six years earlier. The meticulously organized Parseghian not only remembered it, he instantly produced the letter and even its envelope. The correspondence had been catalogued in Parseghian's "crazy letters" file.

On February 18, 1972, at 1:45 in the morning, an unusual time for announcements from university presidents, Marquette's president, the Rev. John P. Raynor, released a statement. "Jim Chones telephoned Coach Al McGuire late Thursday night informing him that he had just signed a contract to play professional basketball with the New York Nets ... We at Marquette University wish Jim every success in his new venture."

Marquette was ranked No. 2 in the country when the 6-foot-11 Chones elected to cut short his junior year and play instead for head coach Lou Carnesecca with the ABA's Nets. This apparently sudden decision by Chones had in fact been both predicted and blessed a year earlier in one of McGuire's most famous quotes: "I looked in my re-frigerator and it was full. I looked in Jimmy's and it was empty." After its 20–0 start, MU went 4–2 the rest of the way. That record included a 16-point loss to Kentucky in the 1972 NCAA tournament round of 16. The UK victory was the last of Adolph Rupp's 876 wins, dating back to 1930. The following year, Marquette would lose to Indiana in Knight's first-ever NCAA tournament appearance as a coach.

By the 1973–74 season, McGuire had a roster stacked with future NBA players: Maurice Lucas, Earl Tatum, Lloyd Walton, and Bo Ellis, a freshman. (Freshman eligibility had been restored in 1972.) This was also the season in which an altercation between teammates gave rise to one of the most renowned McGuire stories of all. Typically, the coach functioned as the solitary active figure in parables of street-smart wit or cunning. These tables were turned to great effect when a second McGuire figure was added to the narrative.

In late 1973, a fight broke out at practice between Marcus Washington and Dave Delsman. Washington was a senior from Chicago, wrapping up a career as a three-year starter. Delsman was a 5-foot-11 reserve from Waukesha, Wisconsin, who would average three points a game at MU. Upon arriving at practice 45 minutes late in a three-piece suit, McGuire found Raymonds and Majerus struggling to pull Washington and Delsman apart. The head coach swiftly stepped between the two players and announced rather grandly that anyone who wanted to fight could come right ahead and start with him, McGuire, the former bartender from Rockaway Beach. Delsman promptly called his coach's bluff and punched McGuire with full force, staggering the 45-year-old. The fact that this was precisely what McGuire himself would have done as a player did not endear Delsman to his coach in the heat of the moment. "You SOB!" McGuire yelled, groggily swinging and missing in reply. Appalled at what he had just done, Delsman was certain his affiliation with the Marquette men's basketball program was at an end. Instead, McGuire told him the next day, "Dels, work on your free throws. It's over." The story would be written up at that year's Final Four by renowned New York columnist Jimmy Breslin, a lifelong friend of McGuire's older brother John.

While McGuire was engaging in fisticuffs with Delsman, Notre Dame was thriving in its third season under Phelps. The Fighting Irish were still benefiting from the Washington, DC, area connection forged by Dee and strengthened by his successor, as seen that season by the arrival of DeMatha Catholic High School legend Adrian Dantley. For his part, Phelps, in a characteristically brash and public gesture, had added UCLA to his team's 1973–74 schedule immediately upon arrival in South Bend in 1971. "We're gearing our program for the future," Phelps had said at the time. Now, the future had arrived. In January 1974, Notre Dame had Georgetown and UCLA coming to South Bend in consecutive games. No coach's reputation before or since has approached or, perhaps, ever could approach that of Wooden's in the mid-1970s. In advance of the game against the Hoyas that week, a Notre Dame faculty member remarked to Phelps, "Well, we've got the Jesuits Tuesday and God on Saturday."

For the balance of the Saturday game, it looked like "God" was going to will another win for the Bruins. Despite playing in a back brace, Bill Walton netted 24 points, and UCLA led by as many as 17. Then, uncharacteristically, the Bruins appeared rattled when it mattered most. The Fighting Irish closed on a 12–0 run to win 71–70. Gary Brokaw and John Shumate combined to put up 49 points for the victors. The go-ahead basket was scored from the corner by Dwight Clay, with 29 seconds remaining, thus giving the *Los Angeles Times* one of its better headlines of the decade: THE STREAK ENDS ON FEAT OF CLAY. The defeat ended the Bruins' record-setting 88-game win streak, which itself dated to the victory Carr and the Irish had recorded over Wooden in South Bend in 1971.

Phelps would quite rightly cherish this favorite topic of discussion for the next several decades. The coach had had his players prepare for the game by cutting down nets, and he'd even given a pregame talk to the press on how the Fighting Irish were about to win. "I'm hoping President Nixon will call and cancel our flight," Phelps said afterward when asked about the rematch at Pauley Pavilion in one week's time. "I hope we run out of gas before we go out there." The coach's trepidation was well-founded, and the Irish were, in fact, pounded 94–75 by the Bruins in Westwood. Nevertheless, history had been made in South Bend, and that fact would be remembered down through the years.

Notre Dame eventually lost by nine in the 1974 NCAA tournament to Michigan, which would next face Marquette in Tuscaloosa, Alabama. If Delsman hadn't earned his way back into his coach's good favor before, he no doubt did so with two key free throws late in Marquette's 72–70 regional final win over Campy Russell and the Wolverines. In MU's first-ever Final Four appearance, the team recorded a 13-point victory over Kansas in Greensboro, North Carolina, which qualified as one of the most overlooked national semifinals ever. David Thompson and NC State scored their historic double-overtime triumph over UCLA on the other side of that 1974 Final Four.

As it happens, the national title game was destined to stand out in its own right. With Marquette leading 28–27 late in the first half, McGuire earned two technical fouls within 53 seconds, which, in effect, put NC State ahead 37–28. He may well have had a point on both a charging foul whistled against Washington and on an Ellis block that was ruled goaltending. Still, NC State made every resulting free throw and scored baskets on both ensuing possessions when Coach Norm Sloan's team retained possession. "I would say I cost us the game," McGuire remarked after the Wolfpack prevailed 76–64.

When Kentucky thrashed his next team by 22 in the 1975 NCAA tournament, McGuire shrugged it off as a foreseeable result with a rotation that lacked height. The following year, Jerome Whitehead and Bernard Toone joined Tatum, Ellis, and Butch Lee. Marquette rolled to a 25–1 regular-season record, with its only loss coming in overtime at Minnesota. On paper, this was the best team McGuire would ever have at Marquette. Tatum, a senior, was both the team's featured scorer and its most accurate volume shooter, while Whitehead defended the rim and helped Marquette hold opponents under 43 percent shooting for the season. Unfortunately for McGuire, Indiana had a pretty fair team of its own that season, and the No. 1 and 2 teams in the AP poll met in the Mideast regional final of the 1976 NCAA tournament. MU played what the *Indianapolis Star* classified as a box-and-one against Scott May, and the Hoosiers gave Marquette an opening in the second half, when Knight's team committed turnovers on five straight possessions. But after trailing by three with a little more than a minute remaining, MU lost 65–56. Two more technical fouls were assessed on McGuire, cementing his pre-1977 reputation as a preeminent coach whose temper worked against him on the biggest stage.

Without Tatum in 1976–77, the offense suffered statistically even as MU's defense, still anchored by Whitehead, stayed strong. "I had seven or eight teams better than that" season's team, McGuire would later say. The coach triggered something close to universal shock when he announced on December 17, 1976, that he would step down after that season. Majerus would one day remember McGuire telling him simply that the head coach felt he was "getting older and the kids are staying the same age." Nor was the decision a contrived motivational ploy with regard to his current players, as that year's team would amply demonstrate by nearly missing the NCAA tournament entirely.

For the stretch run of McGuire's farewell season, the plan among Marquette boosters was to gather after every home game to celebrate the coach with a cash bar at Mader's, a German restaurant in downtown Milwaukee. As MU continued to suffer defeats at home in February of 1977, however, attendance at Mader's after each game steadily dwindled. In the end, few were on hand who weren't either employed by the university or related to the coach by blood. McGuire was hearing boos in the midst of what was supposed to have been an affectionate good-bye for a program that had won 81 straight at home between 1967 and 1973. The coach came to believe he'd made a fatal mistake by announcing his decision in advance. It appeared the season, in McGuire's words, was proving "you can't have a lame duck."

MU's outgoing coach lost the last three home games of his career, including a 64–63 defeat at the hands of Detroit. When reporters gathered for postgame remarks from McGuire, he told them the real newsmaker was his counterpart with the Titans. Detroit's 37-year-old head coach was indeed overjoyed by the victory, as duly reported by the press: "'All the way to the NCAA,' smiled Dick Vitale, brushing an uncontrollable lock of hair from his eyes. 'All the way to the NCAA.'" "Give Vitale the credit," McGuire said of his young colleague after the game. "I think he's charming to the profession. He's my kind of guy, but probably not the NCAA's type of guy."

McGuire speculated publicly and morosely that his last team was about to miss the NCAA tournament. Instead, he was notified at halftime of what became a one-point loss at Michigan that Marquette had been given a bid. MU was just 20–7 on the season, but McGuire chose to sound a confident note after the defeat in Ann Arbor. "We're capable of beating anybody," he vowed. "Look, I've got real players. We're not going into this tournament with two-handed dribblers and guys with their underwear hanging out of their pants." What was indeed hanging out, though, were Marquette's notorious uniforms. The jerseys were untucked by design, and MARQUETTE appeared not in the traditional spot above the numbers, but below them. The team's signature look, yet another lark of sartorial ebullience fated for prohibition by the NCAA, had been created by Ellis himself before the 1974–75 season. A fashion design major, Ellis was his team's second-leading scorer behind Lee in 1977.

Looking back years after the fact, McGuire would say that a heated altercation he had with Toone at halftime of an opening-round win over Cincinnati sparked his team in the postseason. "The whole room ignited to break us apart," he recalled, "and for some reason, right there, was a championship wristwatch." The wristwatch was no sure thing. Marquette defeated Kansas State 67–66 in the regional semifinals in Oklahoma City after McGuire was again whistled for a technical foul. McGuire unburdened himself of what might be called his grand remonstrance against the NCAA after the game. "I had one technical foul called on me all season," he pointed out, "but every time I come to an NCAA tournament, they start up the same crap again." McGuire said he merely had made the choking signal in communicating to his team, and he meant the opponent was faltering. But official Frank Buckiewiscz thought McGuire was referring to him, and MU had to rally from 10 points down in the last 11:56 to win. "This is why I'm getting out of the NCAA," McGuire barked. "I'm tired of this."

By outscoring Wake Forest 51–33 in the second half for an 82–68 win in the regional final, Marquette reached its second Final Four under McGuire. The coach would say of his next opponent—UNC Charlotte—that there are "100 schools in the country with names like" theirs, but there was nothing accidental or lucky about the 49ers' run to the national semifinals. Cedric "Cornbread" Maxwell was on the cusp of a 13-year NBA career, one that would begin with him being selected before any Marquette player in the 1977 draft. Charlotte had already defeated the nation's No. 1 team, Michigan, to make it to Atlanta, and the 49ers were just as tough against MU.

The game was tied at 49 with three seconds remaining on the clock when McGuire called time-out. Marquette would have to go the length of the floor, and the MU coach walked to the center of the court. "I wasn't there to do my Jimmy Durante act," he explained afterward. "I wanted to check the height of the clock." When play resumed, Lee fired a baseball pass to the far free-throw line, too high for Ellis to reach and too hot for Charlotte's Maxwell to intercept cleanly. Instead, Maxwell deflected the ball to MU's Whitehead. Maxwell recovered well enough to challenge Whitehead's halting attempt at a dunk, but the ball went off the board and in the basket as time expired. It was an odd bank shot, launched not at an angle but straight on from the front of the rim. It also appeared Whitehead may have committed basket interference as the ball came back off the board.

No signal was made on the play initially. Instead, officials huddled at the scorer's table. They were joined by a teeming mass of shouting coaches and players, as both teams made their cases. "I argued so hard about the clock, because I didn't want them to get around to Jerome's hand being in the cylinder," McGuire would volunteer years later. After a tense few moments, the basket was ruled good and Marquette advanced to the championship game against North Carolina. This time there would be no technical fouls. When the Tar Heels rallied from 12 down to tie the game at 45, Marquette faked a man-to-man defense before switching back into a zone. Dean Smith had his team pull the ball out into its four-corners offense.

McGuire's future broadcast partners Dick Enberg and Billy Packer were working the game for NBC, along with Curt Gowdy. When the Marquette coach directed his defense from the sideline during this crucial two-minute possession, he was compared to symphony conductor Leonard Bernstein. "A little more from the woodwinds, please," Enberg observed. The MU staff was convinced the game turned on this sequence with 12 minutes remaining. "It dried their sweat and they lost their momentum," McGuire later said of UNC in that moment. Ellis blocked Bruce Buckley's layup attempt with less than 10 minutes left, and Marquette shot 23-of-25 at the line to seal the 67–59 victory.

McGuire was in tears on the bench in the game's final seconds, while Raymonds draped his arm around the outgoing head coach. As the postgame celebration erupted on the court, McGuire shook hands with Smith and then ducked into the mostly deserted locker room at the Omni. "I'm not ashamed to cry," he explained. "I just want to cry alone." Like John Wooden in 1975 and like no other coach in history up to that time, Al McGuire won the national championship in his final career game. Like UCLA and no other program, Marquette finished in the AP top 15 every year from 1969 to 1977.

Even before he won a national championship, McGuire had reached the pinnacle of a profession that he insisted he didn't enjoy pursuing all that much. "I've never blown a whistle, looked at film, worked at a blackboard, or organized a practice in my life," he famously, if somewhat hyperbolically, claimed, adding, "I don't think any decent human being enjoys recruiting." His peers flocked to his speaking appearances, and when McGuire held forth on his approach in front of 500 coaches in 1976, Penn coach Chuck Daly whispered to a neighbor, "If the rest of us operated his way, we'd be out of business." McGuire himself could sound a similar note. "I'm jealous of guys like Dean Smith, Bobby Knight," he said. "I'm jealous of their dedication. I wish I had it. I admire the way their teams are dressed, the way their kids handle themselves. At the regionals last year, one of our kids came down to lunch barefoot. But I just don't like coaching that much to put the time in on a thing like that."

In addition to process and strategy, McGuire projected an image based on hard-earned wisdom and a perspective beyond basketball. Ironically, the image was identical in these two respects, at least, to that of the dominant coach of the era and McGuire's complete stylistic opposite, Wooden. "I always tried to make it clear that basketball is not the ultimate," Wooden stated. "It is of small importance in comparison to the total life we live." McGuire put it this way: "Winning is only important in surgery and wars." The Marquette coach was plainly beloved of sportswriters for his ability to mint memorable quotes on demand: gems about cracked sidewalks, the relationship between chili and waitresses' dirty ankles, and, of course, "You can always tell the Catholic schools by the length of the cheerleaders' skirts." Also: "A coach is like a mistress for the [university] administration. They act like they love you for a few rare moments, but eventually they'll dump you." *Sports Illustrated*'s Frank Deford portrayed the coach at the Jesuit program as pumping his team up before taking the floor like so: "All-right-let's-show-them-we're-the-No.-2-team-in-the-country-and-beat-the-bleep-out-of-them-Queen-of-Victory-pray-for-us."

By the mid-1970s, when he was on the speakers' circuit, McGuire could simply group his greatest one-sentence hits end to end, like a chain of boxcars in free verse: "Winning is only important in surgery and wars. Myself, I like seashells and balloons. Ribbons and medals. Bare feet and wet grass. Most of us rush for the stars as we crawl for our graves. You know, for years I was a nut. Now that we're winning, I'm an eccentric. The only difference between a nut and an eccentric is finer threads and a bigger car."

With the exception of references to "winning," nothing there gestures even obliquely toward basketball. And perhaps one or two sentences feel manufactured, the work of an aspiring truth teller expected to be profound on a deadline. Majerus said McGuire's "lines weren't as spontaneous as you think. He would go to the ends of the earth to get a phrase and read it." Enberg would one day be moved to write an entire play, *McGuire*, about his former broadcast partner. Not many coaches past or present have inspired thespian portrayals.

When McGuire worked the 1981 Final Four with NBC, he was concerned about proceeding as scheduled with the national title game between Indiana and North Carolina in the wake of the assassination attempt that day on President Reagan. "My style might insult some people. They'd say, 'What's this saloon guy doing with these one-liners?'" Then, referring to himself and to the higher-ups who'd decided to play the game, McGuire asked, "What does a court jester do when he finds his court is full of fools? He just goes on."

11.

Gavitt and Thompson

ohn Thompson was raised Catholic. While this fact presaged his entire high school and college playing and coaching careers, it was hardly an unalloyed good for an African American male in Washington, DC, in the 1940s and 1950s.

When he was a boy, Thompson was told by a parish priest that he could grow up to be a murderer. In spite of such experiences, Thompson's parents wanted their son to receive a Catholic education in the District. That education was interrupted by a secular detour when the nuns at Our Lady of Perpetual Help informed the Thompsons that their son should not return for the sixth grade. Three years later, he was tall enough and good enough at basketball that the Catholic schools were suddenly far more welcoming. He earned a scholarship from the archdiocese to play for Bob Dwyer at Archbishop Carroll High School in Northeast Washington. Carroll in the late 1950s was, in DC high school basketball terms, as dominant as Russell-era San Francisco and as pioneering as early-1960s Cincinnati or Loyola Chicago. With Thompson in the lineup alongside teammates like George Leftwich, Edward "Monk" Malloy, and Tom Hoover, the Lions won 55 straight games and would often be referred to in subsequent years as possibly the District's greatest team ever. Dwyer's starting lineup featured four Black players in Thompson's sophomore and senior years.

The Rev. Thomas Collins got in on the ground floor with Thompson's recruiting on behalf of Providence. Collins was a Dominican priest, a 1934 graduate of PC, a Washington, DC, resident, and a self-described "basketball nut." While Thompson also received feelers from Jack Ramsay at Saint Joseph's and from then assistant coach Lou Carnesecca at St. John's, he and his family ultimately decided to go with Providence. When he arrived on campus as a freshman in the fall of 1960, Thompson found a Friars program that was coming off easily the best season in its history. Led by Lenny Wilkens in his senior year, PC had reached the finals of the 1960 NIT before falling to Bradley. Then, with Thompson watching and waiting in an era when freshmen were still ineligible, Providence advanced through an all-Catholic final four—consisting additionally of Holy Cross, Dayton, and Saint Louis—at the 1961 NIT. The Friars won the title over the Billikens behind 18 points from center Jim Hadnot, a protégé of Bill Russell's who, like the Boston Celtics legend, was a product of McClymonds High School in Oakland, California.

Head coach Joe Mullaney had to like his chances going into the 1961–62 season. With Hadnot and Thompson both listed at 6 foot 10, Providence would have one of the tallest and most skilled front lines in the country. The pollsters agreed, and the Friars entered the season at No. 5 in the AP poll, by far the highest ranking in the program's history up to that time. The adulation, however, turned out to be premature. Providence started the season 4–4, fell out of the rankings, never to return, and lost to Temple in the first round of the 1962 NIT. Mullaney wouldn't have Hadnot anymore, but he did still have Thompson and Ray Flynn. A future mayor of Boston, Flynn was already being lauded as "one of Southie's favorite sons" by the *Boston Globe*. Thompson and Flynn both averaged exactly 18.9 points the year after Hadnot's departure, and Providence entered the 1963 NIT on a 12-game win streak. Flynn erupted for 38 points in the quarterfinals against Miami, and the Friars' 106–96 win was sealed in the last two minutes when Hurricanes sophomore Rick Barry received a technical foul for flinging the ball at the rim after his fifth foul.

A six-point victory over Marquette then put Providence in its third NIT final in four years, where the Friars faced Canisius. As counter-programming to the nationally syndicated telecast of the NCAA final between Loyola Chicago and Cincinnati that same Saturday, the Canisius-Providence game was broadcast coast to coast by NBC on a two-hour tape delay. Viewers grasped at a glance that Thompson had perhaps six inches on the Golden Griffins' tallest starter, and PC defeated Canisius 81–66. Sunday papers all over the country that weekend featured a wire photo showing Mullaney's bespectacled junior swatting away a shot at the rim.

That 1963 NIT title would endure as Providence's best postseason run for the next decade. As a senior, Thompson's scoring jumped to 26 per game and the Friars accepted their first-ever NCAA bid, but the defense took a step back and PC lost by 11 to Villanova at the Palestra in the first round of the 1964 tournament. After Thompson's graduation, Mullaney gave the keys to the offense to Jimmy Walker, an extraordinary scorer and first-team All-American who would amass over 2,000 points in a career that spanned just 81 games. Nevertheless, a Final Four berth eluded the Friars in the wake of Thompson's departure. In fact, in 1965, Mullaney suffered the worst defeat of his Providence career up to that point at the hands of Bill Bradley and Princeton, in a 109–69 NCAA East regional final.

By that time, John Thompson was playing professionally. In a 1964 NBA draft that included the likes of Walt Hazzard, Paul Silas, Willis Reed, and Jerry Sloan, Thompson had been selected by the Celtics with the 25th pick (the third round for what was then a nine-team league). "He's center insurance," Boston head coach Red Auerbach said of Thompson moments after the draft. "He'll make this club, mark my words." Per Auerbach's forecast, Thompson became Russell's backup at center, and the rookie was even referred to within the locker room as "the caddy" in relation to the Hall of Famer. Certainly, on the rare occasions when Russell took a breather, Thompson would customarily be the substitute coming into the game. The key word, however, is "rare." In the two years Thompson spent with the Celtics, Russell averaged between 43 and 45 minutes a game. Thompson's appearances were brief, but he did log more than three to five minutes per outing. In fact, Thompson spelled not only Russell but also Tom "Satch" Sanders and the frontcourt as a whole. That was more or less the problem for Thompson as an NBA player. As he told more than one reporter, he was not a "corner man," i.e., a forward. Big John was most at home in the paint, and Russell was still in his prime. Thompson's professional career was at a crossroads before it had truly begun.

In April 1966, Russell was named player-coach of the Celtics to replace Auerbach. The occasion afforded Thompson the opportunity, in one of his final interviews as an NBA player, to respond to a reporter's condescension by offering a glimpse of the essential qualities that would become so familiar in the decades to come:

> Q. Are you happy that one of your race has received such an outstanding honor?
> A. It's not only that he's one of my race. It's that he's qualified.

Two weeks after Russell was named coach, Thompson was selected by the newly created Chicago Bulls in the expansion draft, but he decided not to make the move to the Windy City. After a mere 74 appearances over two NBA seasons, John Thompson effectively retired. He was 24.

When Providence won the 1963 NIT title behind Thompson and Ray Flynn, there was a 25-year-old assistant coach named Dave Gavitt on the bench, who was in his first season with the Friars. The Dartmouth guard had arrived on Joe Mullaney's staff by way of an ill-fated stint at AT&T. "I didn't like it very much," Gavitt would recall, "and I wasn't very good at it." Fleeing corporate life, Gavitt enjoyed a more pleasurable if less remunerative two-year tour of duty as an assistant coach in basketball, baseball, and even, for a short time, cross-country and hockey at Worcester Academy. Gavitt learned a good deal from Mullaney, whom he would later refer to without hesitation as "a genius." After four seasons with the Friars, Gavitt returned to his alma mater. The plan was for him to serve a one-season apprenticeship as an assistant under the venerable Doggie Julian, who coached Mullaney, Bob Cousy, and George Kaftan to the 1947 NCAA title at Holy Cross. Dartmouth and Julian had told Gavitt that he would assume the duties of head coach as of 1967–68, but the apprenticeship was shorter than expected.

On December 29, 1966, Dartmouth was in Rochester, New York, to play in the Kodak Classic. The 65-year-old Julian had announced publicly that the season would be his last, and he was to receive a special service award at halftime at Rochester's War Memorial. He never showed. Julian had suffered a stroke that afternoon in his room at the Downtowner Inn and was taken to Strong Memorial Hospital. Assistant coach and former Boston Red Sox first baseman Tony Lupien coached the Big Green that evening in a loss to Georgetown. Six days after Julian was stricken, a small item appeared in the *Boston Globe*'s Sports Lines column:

> Freshman coach David R. Gavitt has taken over the varsity basketball assignment at Dartmouth...He will be filling in for veteran coach Alvin "Doggie" Julian, who suffered a stroke last Thursday.

Gavitt had played for Julian at Dartmouth in the late 1950s, and he was confident he could duplicate the 1959 Ivy title the two had won together. Yet Gavitt found being a head coach more difficult than he'd imagined. "Those were two very beneficial years for me," Gavitt would tell the *Globe*'s Bob Ryan in 1978. "It helped me as a coach because I learned humility very quickly." When Dartmouth finished fourth in the Ivy standings in 1968, Gavitt was named New England coach of the year. He'd won 35 percent of his games over two seasons as the full-time head coach in Hanover when, in the summer of 1969, Mullaney left Providence after 14 seasons to become head coach of the Los Angeles Lakers. Gavitt's name surfaced as Mullaney's likely replacement at Providence within 24 hours.

The Friars' new head coach inherited a team that returned leading scorer Jim Larrañaga, who was coming off an impressive debut as a sophomore. But PC was undersized, and the team recorded its third consecutive middling season. That first season for Gavitt would mark the last time the Friars would win less than 70 percent of their games for the next four years. Local product Ernie DiGregorio had grown up idolizing Jimmy Walker, and the scoring guard emerged as a star in his first season in 1970–71. Providence hosted Julius Erving and undefeated UMass in January, and, when the Friars prevailed 73–72, Gavitt credited his 6-foot-0 junior Don Lewis with holding Erving to a mere 19 points. In March, PC accepted its first NIT bid in four years and won a first-round game against Louisville before falling to Dean Smith and eventual champion North Carolina in the quarterfinals. Gavitt was named athletic director at Providence that June. He was 33.

Though the NIT loss marked the end of Larrañaga's playing career, it was DiGregorio, as a sophomore, who had led the team in scoring. Meanwhile, the head coach had already shown he was playing for keeps on the recruiting trail. Gavitt beat out Cincinnati and signed Providence Central High School product Marvin Barnes, who made his debut for the Friars in 1971–72. The 6-foot-8 sophomore's impact on New England basketball was immediate and profound on and off the floor.

In the second game of his college career, Barnes recorded a triple-double consisting of 18 points, 12 blocks, and 34 rebounds. With Barnes locking down the defensive rebounding, Providence crossed a significant programmatic threshold in January 1972, when it traveled to USC to play a nationally televised game against Paul Westphal and the No. 7–ranked Trojans. PC emerged victorious 70–66, and, by February, the Friars were ranked in the AP poll for the first time in Gavitt's tenure. Nevertheless, the season was bumpy off the court. Lewis, the player Gavitt had singled out for praise the year before when Providence defeated Erving and UMass, had refused to travel with the team to New York in December to play in the Holiday Festival tournament. A senior and team captain, Lewis had gone to Gavitt's house with five other Black players, according to the Associated Press, "to complain that several players hadn't been playing enough." The group was also unhappy that Gavitt had dismissed Gary Wilkins and Alan Baker from the team.

DePaul's George Mikan defends against Long Island University at "old" Madison Square Garden. Mikan led the Blue Demons to the 1943 Final Four and the 1945 NIT title. *(Credit: Collegiate Images via Getty)*

Bob Cousy was a freshman when Holy Cross won the 1947 national title. He was reputed to be the first college player ever to dribble behind his back during a game. *(Credit: Courtesy of Holy Cross Athletics)*

Seton Hall won the 1953 NIT with a lineup featuring Walter Dukes (No. 9) and Richie Regan (No. 18). *(Credit: Sporting News via Getty)*

Tom Gola powered La Salle to the 1952 NIT and 1954 NCAA titles. He is still the all-time leading rebounder in Division I history. *(Credit: Mark Kauffman via Getty)*

Bill Russell is carried off the court by fans at Kansas City's Municipal Auditorium after San Francisco defeated Tom Gola and La Salle to win the 1955 national championship. The Dons defended their title the following year and, at 29–0, became the first NCAA tournament champion to post a perfect record. *(Credit: Rich Clarkson/NCAA Photos via Getty)*

Elgin Baylor led Seattle University to the 1958 national title game, where SU fell to Kentucky. *(Credit: Bettmann via Getty)*

Despite never having played in a varsity game, Roger Brown was expelled from Dayton in the midst of college basketball's 1961 point-shaving scandal. He later starred for the Indiana Pacers in the early years of the ABA. *(Credit: Bettmann via Getty)*

Loyola Chicago's Jerry Harkness (left) shakes hands with Mississippi State's Joe Dan Gold (right) before their 1963 regional semifinal. MSU defied the state of Mississippi's "unwritten law" in taking the floor with Black opposing players. The Ramblers went on to win the 1963 national title, and their game against Mississippi State would later be called the Game of Change. *(Credit: Rich Clarkson/NCAA Photos via Getty)*

Marquette head coach Al McGuire surprised his university by holding a press conference in 1968 to confirm his interest in serving as coach and general manager of Milwaukee's new and as yet unnamed NBA franchise. The Jesuits held their coach to his contract, however, and McGuire stayed at MU. *(Credit: Bettmann via Getty)*

Ernie DiGregorio (left) and Marvin Barnes (right) cut down the net after Providence defeated Maryland to reach the 1973 Final Four. (*Credit: Eric Schweikardt/Sports Illustrated via Getty*)

Notre Dame's Adrian Dantley drives to the basket against UCLA's Bill Walton on January 19, 1974. The 71–70 victory by the Fighting Irish ended the Bruins' 88-game win streak. (*Credit: Rich Clarkson/NCAA Photos via Getty*)

Al McGuire and his assistant coaches, Hank Raymonds and Rick Majerus (left to right), watch the action during the 1977 national championship game against North Carolina. Marquette won 67–59, and McGuire joined John Wooden as the only coach up to that time to win a national title in the final game of his career. *(Credit: Collegiate Images via Getty)*

Patrick Ewing celebrates with his coach, John Thompson, after Georgetown defeated Houston to win the 1984 national championship. *(Credit: Rich Clarkson/NCAA Photos via Getty)*

Thompson shows his own version of St. John's head coach Lou Carnesecca's lucky sweater to a surprised Carnesecca before their two teams meet at Madison Square Garden on February 27, 1985. No. 2-ranked Georgetown defeated top-ranked St. John's 85–69. *(Credit: New York Daily News Archive via Getty)*

Villanova head coach Rollie Massimino cuts down the net after his team shocked George-town to win the 1985 national championship. The Wildcats shot 22-of-28 from the floor in what was called a perfect game. *(Credit: Rich Clarkson/Sports Illustrated via Getty)*

Loyola Marymount star Hank Gathers. *(Credit: Tim DeFrisco/ Stringer via Getty)*

During Loyola Marymount's run in the 1990 NCAA tournament, Bo Kimble shot his first free throw in each game left-handed to honor the passing of his teammate and friend, Hank Gathers. *(Credit: Andy Hayt/ Sports Illustrated via Getty)*

Dwyane Wade confers with head coach Tom Crean during Marquette's 83–69 win over top seed Kentucky in the 2003 Elite Eight. Wade recorded a 29-11-11 points-assists-rebounds triple-double against the Wildcats. *(Credit: Al Tielemans/ Sports Illustrated via Getty)*

From left: Jeremy Pargo, David Pendergraft, Adam Morrison, and Erroll Knight huddle during Gonzaga's 90–80 win over Indiana in the 2006 round of 32. *(Credit: Sporting News Archive via Getty)*

Off an assist from Ryan Arcidiacono, Kris Jenkins hit a buzzer-beater against North Carolina to give Villanova the 2016 national championship. *(Credit: Mitchell Layton via Getty)*

Mark Few does a handstand in the locker room after Gonzaga defeated Xavier 83–59 in the 2017 Elite Eight. The victory earned the Bulldogs their first Final Four berth in program history. *(Credit: Jed Jacobsohn/NCAA Photos via Getty)*

Loyola Chicago team chaplain Sister Jean Dolores Schmidt became a celebrity when her Ramblers won four consecutive games as underdogs to reach the 2018 Final Four. *(Credit: Kevin C. Cox/Getty Images Sport via Getty)*

Villanova head coach Jay Wright won his second NCAA tournament in three years as his Wildcats defeated Michigan 79–62 in th 2018 national championship game. *(Credit: Tom Pennington/Getty Images Sport via Getty*

Lewis returned to the team in a week's time, but, in March when PC accepted its first NCAA tournament invitation in six years, he voiced his displeasure on local television in Providence. "I'm not happy," Lewis said before his team's tournament game against Penn. "I'm distracted...I don't want to identify with basketball." Six days later, the Friars were outscored 45–33 in the second half of a 16-point first-round loss to head coach Chuck Daly and his Quakers. Barnes was limited to seven points, in what Gavitt termed "perhaps" his sophomore's "worst game of the year." Just the same, PC fans were hopeful for the future. Lewis was the lone senior in the rotation, and the team would be moving to the new $13 million Providence Civic Center for 1972–73.

When the new season arrived, it turned out both the rotation and the home court were in flux. In October, the college issued a cryptic news release:

> Larry Ketvirtis, a 6-10 senior on Providence College's basketball team, suffered a fractured cheekbone which will be operated on later in the week. The injury was incurred when Ketvirtis was struck by teammate Marvin Barnes in a post practice incident.

A week later, another release stated only that "Providence College's Disciplinary Council should rule this week on the status of basketball star Marvin Barnes."

Gradually, it emerged that, in practice on October 19, Ketvirtis accidentally elbowed Barnes while going for a loose ball. Later that evening, Barnes confronted his teammate outside the PC dining hall, and the episode ended with Ketvirtis in the hospital. Scouts from the ABA reportedly gathered in Providence in eager anticipation of the talented junior being ruled ineligible, but, to their chagrin, Barnes was cleared to play. Ketvirtis, on the other hand, was nowhere to be seen on the floor or even on the bench when the Friars opened their season.

The season in question commenced amid ongoing construction at the Providence Civic Center (rechristened decades later as the Dunkin'

Donuts Center). The arena had confidently booked acts for November, but the Lipizzaner Stallions, Bob Hope, and a roller derby all had to be rescheduled. Construction equipment still filled the hallways and there would be no ribbon cutting until 1973, yet the Friars opened their season at the Civic Center anyway, on December 11, 1972, with a win over Fairfield. *Sports Illustrated* ranked PC in its preseason top 10, and Providence looked the part, with future NBA talents in Barnes, DiGregorio, and Kevin Stacom, a newly arrived transfer from Holy Cross.

As for Ketvirtis, wire service updates were soon referring to him as "a former player on the Providence College basketball team," one who had just lodged a criminal assault complaint against Barnes. Ketvirtis alleged he'd been struck in the face with a tire iron, a charge Barnes denied. "There was no fight, and I didn't hit him with a tire iron," he said. "There is no assault at all and I don't know what he is talking about." Technically, Barnes was on probation at Providence, but he continued to play basketball and attend classes.

In January, the Friars embarked on the program's second annual nationally televised western swing, this time to face six-time defending national champion UCLA at Pauley Pavilion. The Bruins had won 58 straight games, dating back to 1971, and, with Coach Wooden's program approaching the NCAA record of 60 consecutive wins, set by San Francisco between 1954 and 1956, former Dons star K. C. Jones was on hand to watch Bill Walton and Larry Farmer host Providence. The result wasn't in doubt for long, as UCLA won 101–77. DiGregorio nevertheless impressed Wooden with a 22–13 points-assists double-double.

Within a few weeks, DiGregorio would dismiss the loss as a fluke, saying "Barnes and I had the flu that week," and claiming that in "Pauley Pavilion the referees blow that whistle like it's a Hollywood script." Soon after the team returned to Providence, Barnes was arraigned on one count of assault with a deadly weapon. The junior was in court on the last Tuesday in January and released on a $5,000 bond. The next night, Barnes recorded a double-double in a win at Boston College. With their two local stars in the lineup, the Friars finished the regular season 23–2.

The 1973 NCAA tournament dealt a blow to that year's NIT by locking up all eight independent programs ranked in the AP top 20, including No. 6 Providence. The Friars opened the tournament with a 13-point victory over Saint Joseph's on the campus of William & Mary. Advancing to the East regional in Charlotte, PC then avenged its loss in the previous year's tournament with an easy victory over Penn. Gavitt's team was averaging 52 points after halftime in its NCAA tournament wins, a fact that did not appear to cause the Friars' next opponent undue concern. Maryland had brushed aside Syracuse, and now the Terrapins, including John Lucas, Tom McMillen, and Len Elmore, awaited the Friars.

Gavitt and his staff were known and often lauded for a low-key manner that was unusual in the coaching profession. Nevertheless, the press in Charlotte didn't have to work hard to gather bulletin board material from either program in advance of the regional final. Terrapins head coach Lefty Driesell claimed that he could not pronounce DiGregorio, and instead referred to the senior as No. 15. As for Stacom, he was, in Driesell's rendering, "the other one." Gavitt responded in kind. When asked about the Terps styling themselves as "the UCLA of the East," he replied with uncharacteristic combativeness: "It's all in their heads." Friars assistant coach Nick Macarchuk was more direct. "There's one area we won't have to worry about," he said gesturing toward Driesell. "We know we won't be outcoached."

Whether it was coaching, talent on the floor, or both, Providence won 103–89. "We got here by playing good defense," Driesell said after the game, "and we got beat by playing bad defense." DiGregorio, who led all scorers with 30 points, couldn't resist twisting the knife. "Do you think that Driesell knows how to pronounce my name now?"

UCLA was an overwhelming favorite to win its seventh consecutive national title at the 1973 Final Four in Saint Louis. The Bruins faced Indiana and 32-year-old head coach Bob Knight in one semifinal, while PC was paired with Memphis State in the other. Gavitt's team had built an early eight-point lead on the Tigers when, with a little more than 12 minutes left in the first half, Barnes injured his knee as he landed awkwardly on Memphis State's Ronnie Robinson. Barnes was treated on the bench and sent back into the game, but he was unable to put weight on the injured leg. Providence still led by nine at the half, Barnes returned late in the game with his knee heavily taped, and his lay-in with 4:04 left in regulation cut the Tiger lead to one. That basket was, and would remain for the next several decades, the Friars' closest brush with a national championship game. Memphis State closed the contest on a 13–1 run. PC ended arguably its best season in program history with a 98–85 loss.

In the years that followed, the injury suffered by Barnes took on mythic proportions in New England as the stroke of bad luck that sealed the Friars' demise. The injury was, indeed, all the more devastating due to Gavitt's thin rotation in the frontcourt. What if Larry Ketvirtis were still on the roster for the 1973 NCAA tournament? He wasn't an NBA-track talent like Barnes, but he was at least a 6-foot-10 senior who'd averaged 16 minutes as a junior and recorded a 22–11 double-double against No. 11–ranked Villanova. The Friars could have used a player with a profile like that in the second half against the Tigers.

Barnes led the nation in rebounding as a senior, and was selected with the second overall pick in the NBA draft after Bill Walton. Spurning the Philadelphia 76ers, Barnes signed with the Spirits of St. Louis in the ABA, where he was, to use *Sports Illustrated*'s term, "brilliant," averaging a 24–16 double-double as a rookie. By the time he entered a guilty plea in the Ketvirtis case, Marvin "Bad News" Barnes had a $2.5 million contract with the Spirits. He was given three years' probation, which he violated when an unloaded pistol was found in his luggage at the Detroit Metropolitan Airport. After serving five months at the Adult Correctional Institute in Cranston, Rhode Island, Barnes was flown to Buffalo the day he was released in October 1977 for a preseason game between his current team, the Detroit Pistons, and the Buffalo Braves. He cycled through stints with Buffalo, the San Diego Clippers, and even with the Dave Cowens–era Celtics, but never delivered on the promise he'd displayed in the ABA. Barnes later said he regretted his use of cocaine during these years.

Stories written about Barnes when he was still in college occasionally marveled that an African American from South Providence was teaming so effectively with DiGregorio, an Italian American from North

Providence. Barnes later described how friends from his neighbor-hood looked askance at DiGregorio. "When I was at PC," he recalled, "everyone would be calling Ernie a punk...I always defended him. They kept saying to me to bring Ernie down to [the South Providence Rec Center] and they'd kick his butt. So one day I did...He kicked all their butts." Gavitt was just as impressed as Barnes's friends. The coach made a significant shift on offense for the Final Four season and placed a much greater emphasis on DiGregorio. It worked: Ernie D averaged 25 points and nine assists per game as a senior.

DiGregorio's coach was at the top of the profession by 1973, a leading light in a new generation that included celebrated young con-temporaries like Bob Knight and Digger Phelps. Less volatile than the former and not as voluble as the latter, Dave Gavitt was also observant, meticulous, and continuously experimenting. Already in his time at Providence, the 35-year-old head coach had displayed an unusual degree of flexibility in matters of style and scheme. Gavitt adapted his X's and O's to the talent on hand, and when DiGregorio went to the NBA after his senior season, the Friars seamlessly shifted to an offense predicated on getting the ball to Barnes in the paint.

Most of all, Gavitt arrived at three foundational conclusions on how to succeed in eastern college basketball. First, lock down the east-ern talent. Second, get your team on national television. The games Providence played at USC and at UCLA in successive Januarys in 1972 and 1973 elevated the program's profile in a way that had never been achieved by beating Boston College and Holy Cross. Still, the Friars had been forced to play road games in order to make that leap. This led to Gavitt's final conclusion. Build an arena large enough that quality opponents will come to play on your home floor. Soon, Gavitt would apply all three lessons in creating an entirely new "power" conference. In the process, he would transform East Coast basketball.

While Dave Gavitt was scaling the coaching ranks at Dartmouth and Providence, John Thompson was doing the same thing in very much his own manner in Washington, DC. The onetime PC star who had broken off negotiations with the expansion Chicago Bulls in 1966 later characterized the move as the decision of someone who "was too young and dumb to be frightened." No longer on salary with the NBA but blessed with a wife and infant son, Thompson accepted an offer with the United Planning Organization, the community action agency for the District of Columbia. He also ran a locally tailored 4-H program affiliated with the US Department of Agriculture, telling the *Washington Post* in an early Thompsonian flash, "Our kids don't need to know how to make Indian headbands, they need to know how to survive in the city."

His old high school coach, Bob Dwyer, approached Thompson soon after he returned to the District about possibly taking the head coaching position at St. Anthony in Northeast Washington. The St. Anthony basketball program was nowhere near what Thompson had been an instrumental part of at Archbishop Carroll just a few years before. The Tonies represented a school with an enrollment of just 300, of whom perhaps 200 could fit into the gymnasium to watch the team play. Nevertheless, Thompson was intrigued by the opportunity to coach part-time while keeping his day job. He accepted the position, and after his first season he spotted Donald Washington in a pickup game against one of the coach's own freshmen. Washington was a 6-foot-4 eighth grader, and he was soon taking and passing the St. Anthony entrance examination. When one of Washington's parents passed away and the other was hospitalized, the Thompsons took the high school student into their home and became his legal guardians. Washington grew to 6 foot 8 and became one of the most heavily recruited players in the metro area. Dean Smith won that battle for North Carolina with Thompson's endorsement, a notable vote of confidence for Big John to bestow upon a white coach from the ACC. Thompson and Smith would long remain close.

By the late 1960s, with Thompson on the sidelines and Washington in the paint, St. Anthony was rivaling Morgan Wootten's legendary DeMatha teams as a local power. Yet the two coaches never faced each other while Thompson was at St. Anthony. Thompson felt Wootten was ducking his team, a charge the DeMatha coach would deny repeatedly. According to Wootten, it was just that the two coaches could not agree on scheduling. Wootten proposed that the teams play on the campus of either Maryland or Georgetown. Thompson named Howard University as his preferred site. When the two programs at last faced off against each other, after a fashion, in a 1970 summer league game sponsored by the Jelleff Boys Club, Thompson didn't even attend. Instead, he left instructions for assistant coach Bob Grier to bench the starters and play St. Anthony students who weren't even on the team.

DeMatha won the "game" 108–26, and Thompson explained his rationale for not letting his starters play. He said he wanted DeMatha to be as disappointed as his seniors had been that spring when St. Anthony was left out of an annual doubleheader for elite high school teams sponsored by the University of Maryland. Once Thompson took over Georgetown's recruiting as head coach, in 1972, the Hoyas did not sign DeMatha graduates. Famously, no player from the celebrated high school just a few miles from campus would don a Georgetown uniform until, finally, Austin Freeman played for Thompson's son, John Thompson III, in 2007. Asked a few years after the fact about the rivalry with Wootten, Big John would say simply, "People can live on the earth away from one another." The two did eventually get together on a radio show that Thompson hosted after his coaching days. On the air, the rivals expressed mutual admiration, insisting there had never been any truly ill will. It had not appeared that way to observers in real time.

Even as Thompson was lifting St. Anthony to unprecedented heights, the basketball program at Georgetown University was struggling. Jack Magee's best year as head coach was 1969–70, when he led the Hoyas to an 18–8 record and an NIT appearance. However, the onetime Boston College assistant under Bob Cousy won just 43 percent of his games in six seasons at Georgetown, bottoming out at 3–23 in 1971–72. In an unusually sweeping acknowledgment that the status quo was unacceptable, the Jesuits on the Potomac fired both Magee and athletic director Bob Sigholtz in the spring of 1972.

Thompson was on Georgetown's radar from the beginning, but his was far from the only name being discussed. Wootten had been considered for the same position back in 1966 before Magee was hired, and the DeMatha coach was again viewed as a potential successor. Another serious candidate was George Raveling, a District native who'd played at Villanova and was then serving as an assistant under Lefty Driesell at Maryland.

Thompson called trusted colleagues for advice, and, for a 30-year-old high school coach, he had an amazing professional network, up to and including Dean Smith, Dave Gavitt, and Red Auerbach. When search committee chair Charles Deacon initially reached out to him, Thompson asked why he should believe the school was ready for a Black coach in 1972, when he knew from personal experience it had not been ready for a Black player in 1960. At length, the Jesuits expressed a desire to turn over a new leaf, entering into detailed discussions with Thompson on increasing diversity on the campus and providing academic support for the basketball program. Georgetown's president, the Rev. R. J. Henle, introduced Thompson as the next coach on March 13, 1972. Thompson's boss would be newly hired athletic director Frank Rienzo, formerly the coach of the Hoyas' track team. "We don't expect John Thompson to work a miracle," Rienzo said that first year, "but we'll be happy if he does." Rienzo and Thompson would work in partnership together for the next 27 years.

Freshmen were once again eligible for varsity basketball as of the 1972–73 season, and Thompson brought a nucleus of St. Anthony talent with him to play at Georgetown. It was, however, young talent, and the Hoyas were 25–27 under their new coach in his first two seasons. In Thompson's third year, as Georgetown struggled with injuries, shouts of "Bring back Magee" were occasionally heard in McDonough Gymnasium. That taunt turned out to be mild in the extreme. At a home game against Dickinson College that season, unknown persons unfurled a banner as the national anthem began to play. It read: THOMPSON THE [N-WORD] FLOP MUST GO. The banner was visible only for a few seconds before it was pulled down by fans, and at the time it wasn't clear if Thompson or anyone else on the floor had seen it. Regardless, the coach was informed of it immediately. After the game, he told a *Washington Post* reporter, "Things like that bother me. I still can't get used to them."

Henle condemned the perpetrators as "bigots," and praised the coach as "my man, and I'm happy to have him with us as the coach and as a human being." Thompson's players drafted a lengthy statement, one that was read at a press conference by St. Anthony graduate and current Georgetown freshman Felix Yeoman. The players sought to negate the hateful epithet through its repetition, citing numerous personal examples demonstrating why their coach was in fact an outstanding success. "All of us on the team," Yeoman concluded, "know of personal instances when Mr. Thompson has protected us from public criticism and shouldered the blame himself. That's why we've decided that it's time that we speak up."

While Georgetown's players were speaking out on behalf of their coach, they were also rallying to finish 18–10 that same season, earning the program its first NCAA bid in 32 years. The team promptly repeated that feat in 1976, though both tournament appearances were brief. A controversial finish had left the Hoyas on the wrong side of a 77–75 final score against Central Michigan in the opening round of the 1975 NCAA tournament. The following year, a combined 42 points from Derrick Jackson and Jon Smith couldn't prevent another first-game exit, this time at the hands of Arizona. A career 0–2 mark in the NCAA tournament for Thompson, however, merely served to highlight indirectly the success the program was achieving. Georgetown had never before appeared in two consecutive NCAA tournaments. Dean Smith selected Thompson as his assistant coach for the 1976 Olympic team at a time when the Hoyas' recruiting was already on the upswing. Georgetown's wins on the recruiting trail included local standouts Craig Shelton and John Duren from Dunbar High School and, in the spring of 1978, Eric "Sleepy" Floyd from Gastonia, North Carolina.

In addition to raising an entire basketball program from the ashes, Thompson was already displaying a number of qualities that would become familiar, if not iconic, later in his career. To be sure, the two facets of the program that would change dramatically were perhaps its degrees of success and (media) access. Otherwise, Thompson might fairly be said to have been Thompson long before Patrick Ewing or the Big East were a gleam in his eye. In the 1970s, he was already insisting— vocally and repeatedly—that in his program, education would come first. He was already waving aside follow-up questions about the extent to which this could truly be the case within an elite basketball program located within an elite university. He was already displaying a genius for choreographing basketball gestures as expressions of principle: Thompson's premeditated no-show against Wootten and DeMatha in 1970 presaged the walkout he would stage almost two decades later in opposition to an NCAA eligibility rule known as Proposition 42. He was already a highly effective spokesman for his program or for any cause he supported, one who possessed what Georgetown's president would one day term "a devastating gift for one-liners." And he was already winning with ferocious defense, fast breaks, and an emphasis on post scoring. The more his team won, the larger Thompson's qualities loomed.

Georgetown was nominally an independent program in the mid-1970s, yet the Hoyas were playing their way into NCAA brackets by winning the four-team Southern division tournament as part of a collective known as the Eastern College Athletic Conference. Strictly speaking, an ECAC entrant wasn't a "conference champion" in the eyes of the NCAA tournament. Rather, Georgetown was said to be a "regional representative." An entity that had "Conference" in its very title yet wasn't quite what most people thought of as a conference caused no end of confusion outside the East. "There'd always be questions from people in the South or Midwest," Gavitt would attest in retrospect in 1982. "'What conference are you in? Tell us about your league.' I tried to explain it and talk about basketball in the East and mention the ECAC. But the people would look puzzled."

The establishment of four different ECAC tournaments in 1975 with an NCAA bid as the reward for each winner spoke to a moment of great ferment in the process by which the national championship was determined. The changes were felt nationally, but the impacts would prove particularly dramatic on the East Coast. Most fundamentally, the NCAA abandoned the model whereby its tournament, while granting a few at-large bids for independents, functioned as a "playoff" for conferences that received automatic bids. The limit of one NCAA tournament bid per conference had long resulted in foreseeable injustice. Whether a would-be reformer's preferred example was USC in 1971 or Maryland in 1974, it was clear that some of the nation's best teams were being excluded from playing for a national title while many far weaker programs were afforded the opportunity to do so.

For a fleeting moment, it appeared the NCAA's response to this state of affairs would be simply to compete with, and possibly eliminate, the NIT by starting a new tournament for second-place finishers. An eight-team Collegiate Commissioners Association Tournament was won by Indiana in 1974, and Drake emerged victorious at a renamed National Commissioners Invitational Tournament in 1975. Better thinking prevailed, however, and the second-place tournament, under any name, ceased to exist. Instead, allowance was made for conferences to receive multiple bids starting with the 1975 NCAA tournament.

Changes to the NCAA tournament were initially of little consequence for the venerable Catholic independents of the Midwest. In addition to Marquette's 1977 national title, Phelps and Notre Dame advanced to the Final Four the following year, with no fewer than eight players who would one day earn at least a cup of coffee in the NBA. Freshman Kelly Tripucka was a year away from consensus second-team All-American honors, and he was teaming with future pros like Orlando Woolridge, Bill Hanzlik, and Bill Laimbeer. To reach the national semifinals, Tripucka and the Fighting Irish had trounced DePaul by 20 at Allen Fieldhouse in Lawrence, Kansas. Coach Ray Meyer could be forgiven if he didn't sulk. The Blue Demons would bring in arguably the most celebrated recruit in the program's history the next season: Mark Aguirre, out of Chicago Westinghouse. Aguirre averaged 24 points on 52 percent shooting as a freshman and led DePaul to the 1979 Final Four. That season marked the first time the Blue Demons had played in a national semifinal since George Mikan had come up short against Georgetown at old Madison Square Garden in 1943. This time, Meyer's team lost a two-point heartbreaker in Salt Lake City to Larry Bird and undefeated Indiana State.

Between 1974 and 1980, the tournament field expanded from 25 to 48 teams, regions became much less geographically literal (Georgetown was assigned to the West region in the 1976 NCAA tournament), and seeding was introduced. The upshot of these innovations was that independents in the East, with greater or lesser degrees of alarm depending on the school, saw their traditional paths into the NCAA tournament being imperiled. Under the new way of doing things, it was feared that powerful conference teams from the rest of the country would take away East region at-large bids—small in number yet previously shielded by geography—that had long been awarded to independents along the Boston-to-Washington, DC, axis. As if to reinforce this fear, the NCAA eliminated one of the ECAC's four bids in 1977. With just three spots available, the ECAC folded two of its regions, from the "Southern" and "Upstate" divisions of the confederation, into a single postseason tournament. The net effect in March 1977 had been to throw the 35-year-old Thompson into the same four-team bracket annually with the 32-year-old coach who was completing his first season at Syracuse, Jim Boeheim.

Each March in the ECAC semifinals, Georgetown faced a geographically appropriate opponent, like Virginia Commonwealth or Old Dominion. On the other, Upstate, half of the bracket, Syracuse would usually play St. Bonaventure. Finally, on March 3, 1979, Thompson and Boeheim met in the ECAC Upstate/Southern finals at the University of Maryland's Cole Field House, with a guaranteed NCAA tournament bid on the line. The Hoyas won 66–58, against a Syracuse team led by 6-foot-11 center Roosevelt Bouie, one that entered the game 25–2 and ranked No. 6 nationally. After the loss, Boeheim said that "unless the ECAC can get a neutral site, the playoffs are not a fair situation for either team." However, both teams proceeded into the 40-team NCAA field. Syracuse defeated Connecticut by eight in a game played at the Providence Civic Center before bowing out by the same margin in Greensboro, North Carolina, against eventual Final Four participant Penn. Georgetown, also in Providence, lost by six to Rutgers.

The Hoyas' defeat at the hands of the Scarlet Knights marked the last time John Thompson would coach in an NCAA tournament as anything other than a representative of the Big East conference.

12.

The Rise of the Big East

While the NCAA tournament was undergoing its gradual but unmistakable metamorphosis in the late 1970s, Providence head coach Dave Gavitt was at a professional crossroads. His teams after the Marvin Barnes era continued to make appearances in the top 15 of the AP poll even as the Friars suffered first-round exits in the 1977 and 1978 NCAA tournaments to Kansas State and Michigan State, respectively. Additionally, Gavitt had long been mentioned for openings not only collegiately but also in the NBA.

By the fall of 1978, Gavitt felt the moment had arrived for a change. That July, he'd been named Team USA's coach for the Moscow Olympics in 1980. (Dean Smith, based on his experience in Montreal in 1976, had advised Gavitt to turn it down, but the PC coach believed doing so would be "unthinkable.") Closer to home, Providence had lost its top four scorers from the previous season, and Gavitt expected his next team to struggle. All of the above may have figured into his announcement that he would step down as head coach at the end of the 1978–79 season. As both the US Olympic coach and, no less, the athletic director at Providence College, he could ride out, and take the hit for, the "down" year worry-free before turning over the reins to a successor. Anyway, Gavitt had never envisioned coaching as his terminal destination professionally. "You make a lot of foolish statements when you're young," he explained, "but I remember telling my wife I was not going to be a coach when I'm 40. Now I'm 41. It's time."

The coach was correct about 1978–79 being a down year. Providence posted a 10–16 record and failed to advance to either the National Invitation or NCAA tournament for the first time since 1970. Among the names mentioned as likely candidates to replace Gavitt as the next head coach of the Friars was the 31-year-old head coach at Army, Mike Krzyzewski. As for Gavitt, by the time he coached his last game in February 1979 he'd already been hard at work for months on his next project, one he'd been musing about as far back as 1975.

When the Eastern College Athletic Conference instituted its play-in system for NCAA tournament bids that year, it did no favors to a regional hegemon like the Friars. Instead of simply building its body of work over an entire season in competition for one of the East region's at-large NCAA bids, PC had to face Connecticut or Holy Cross or Fairfield in a four-team ECAC New England division bracket. "Teams that had gotten a lot of attention nationally were being brought down," Gavitt would say later of those ECAC tournaments, "while teams that played a Yankee Conference schedule were being brought up. It seemed like we had worked hard for 30 years [at PC], and the work was for naught."

In 1978, the NCAA was considering legislation that, by 1981, would require conferences receiving automatic tournament bids to play round-robin schedules. For Providence, the strongest member of the ECAC's New England division, this was too much to swallow. "We could not comply with this round-robin thing," Gavitt would later say. "It just would have been a disaster." By the late 1970s, the idea of forming an eastern superconference of sorts with only the region's best basketball programs had, in the estimation of St. John's coach Lou Carnesecca, been discussed for 20 or 25 years. "But this time," Carnesecca added, "you had people who were serious."

Gavitt was serious. He lobbied the resistant Carnesecca over wine at a Milan restaurant during an eight-hour flight delay following a series of basketball clinics in Italy, and for a few hours more once they were on board the plane. A meeting was held in May 1978 at St. John's, with representation from the host school, Providence, and Georgetown. In September of that year, Syracuse joined the discussions. The four athletic directors at the table were now Gavitt, Frank Rienzo from Georgetown, Jack Kaiser from St. John's, and Jake Crouthamel from Syracuse. Gavitt and Crouthamel had been fraternity brothers at Dartmouth in the 1950s.

Over the next few months, the four schools stayed committed to the vision of a smaller and stronger league, gathering a number of times in a conference room at LaGuardia Airport to hash out details. When the 1978–79 basketball season ended, it became clear that other eastern programs were queueing to climb aboard. One foundational idea behind the new conference was to assemble its membership from the East Coast's largest media markets. That sounded advisable, certainly, yet the devil was going to be in those details. Would Holy Cross or Boston College be the stronger draw in the Boston market? Besides St. John's, which programs should be included from greater New York City? If the Friars and UConn were included, why not Rhode Island or UMass? Or both? What about Philadelphia?

In short, what would be represented after the fact, correctly, as a spectacular success could have been a success with any number of different beneficiaries. The reporting on the new conference's formation in May 1979 captured this aspect of the discussions quite well, and the stakes were high. On May 10, Holy Cross athletic director Ron Perry and his counterpart at Boston College, Bill Flynn, both arrived in Providence to meet with Gavitt. A few years later, the host of that meeting would say forthrightly that he and his colleagues really had wanted the Crusaders in their new conference. "When the league was being formed," Gavitt would state in 1985, "we were very interested in BC and HC...But Holy Cross turned out to be Doubting Thomases. They seemed to have reservations and never did stand up and say, 'We want in.'"

The reservations were harbored by the president of Holy Cross, the Rev. John E. Brooks, who resisted making accommodations in admissions for athletes. Brooks felt strongly enough on this point to later veto membership in the Atlantic 10, as well. By the mid-1980s, those decisions looked disastrous from an athletic director's perspective, but Brooks was defended by the holiest Holy Cross basketball legend of all, Bob Cousy. "Father [Brooks] is a sports fan who loves nothing better than to have competitive programs," Cousy said, "but he has equal enthusiasm for why the damn school is there in the first place."

With Holy Cross, in effect, withdrawing from negotiations, the new conference was set except for its official name. Sportswriting naturally abhors a vacuum, and default names continued to be floated in the press, including the Eastern Super Seven, for the seven members: Boston College, Connecticut, Georgetown, Providence, Seton Hall, St. John's, and Syracuse. But the membership had made it clear from the first week of its existence that there would be room in the second season for the addition of a program from Philadelphia, possibly Villanova or Temple. Initial reports, however, suggested the Wildcats were not yet sold on the idea.

If Villanova was hesitant, officials at a few schools that had been left out were irate. Things became a bit awkward on May 30, when a large testimonial dinner to honor the end of Gavitt's tenure as Providence head coach coincided almost to the day with the creation of what would eventually be called the Big East. Rhode Island athletic director Maurice Zarchen was attending the dinner, and when a reporter noted that the AD had been difficult to contact in recent days, Zarchen replied tartly, "I've been in Philadelphia, looking for a place to move my campus."

The creation of a seven-team eastern league with five Catholic members represented a watershed moment, one that both exemplified and accelerated an eastern Catholic migration toward conference memberships. By the late 1980s, the ranks of remaining independent programs would be down to Notre Dame, DePaul, and just a few others. Above all, the formation in 1979 of what would become the Big East conference reflected an acknowledgment that the NCAA tournament was now the only game in town. Where once Catholic independents had tailored their schedules to their own preferences and alternated contentedly between the National Invitation and NCAA tournaments, those same programs now formed leagues in the collective pursuit of NCAA bids.

Now that the Big East had come into existence, it needed a television package for its first season. The conference front office that first summer in downtown Providence was piloted by Gavitt in partnership with his onetime sports information director at PC, Mike Tranghese. "We made a decision," Gavitt would explain in 1982, "that the single most important thing to do with television was a prime-time package." When he and Tranghese drafted a six-page request for proposals and sent copies out to TV networks, one of the recipients answered, "When you guys grow up, call us back." Tranghese then traveled to Bristol, Connecticut, and spoke with officials at ESPN, which was scheduled to launch in September of 1979. Eventually, the Big East negotiated a nine-game deal for its inaugural season with the William B. Tanner Syndicate in Memphis. While the deal looks modest in retrospect, those nine games were syndicated at a time when weeknights were virtually a blank slate in terms of sports. The national networks carried college basketball on the weekends, but, as Tranghese would later say, the games were just as good during the week.

The first Big East season proved to be a time of both optimism and disappointment for Gavitt professionally. The conference was making its debut at a moment when more weighty developments were being tracked in the news pages. In February 1980, the Carter administration confirmed that the United States would join more than 60 countries in boycotting the Moscow Olympics in response to the Soviet Union's invasion of Afghanistan. Gavitt would not have the opportunity to coach Isiah Thomas, Mark Aguirre, Sam Bowie, Rolando Blackman, and Michael Brooks, among others, at the Olympics after all. His work creating and establishing a new major conference would have to suffice.

Big East teams played just six conference games apiece that first season, as programs were allowed to honor scheduling commitments they had already made before the formation of the new league. This meant that, in total, there were a mere 21 Big East conference games played in

1979–80. One was a classic. In February 1980, Syracuse had won 57 straight games, dating back to 1976, on its home court in Manley Field House. Jim Boeheim's team would move to a domed venue the next season, and the last game ever played at Manley was scheduled for February 12 against Georgetown. Syracuse entered the contest 21–1 and ranked No. 2 in the nation behind undefeated DePaul. The 17–5 Hoyas were unranked but figured to be on solid ground in terms of an NCAA tournament berth. Boeheim had never lost at Manley.

John Thompson's team was held to 16 points in the first half, and Syracuse was up 38–23 with 13:58 remaining when fans began singing "Auld Lang Syne" as a farewell to Manley. But despite the home team's attempts to run out the clock with a four-corners offense of sorts, the Hoyas rallied and, according to one reporter, "the crowd tensed up and grew strangely quiet." Boeheim's team committed four turnovers in the last 5:20, allowing Georgetown to tie the score at 50. All season long in practice, Thompson had told Sleepy Floyd that shooting free throws was as "easy as ice cream." Now, as Floyd stepped to the line with five seconds remaining, he glanced over at his coach and saw him mouth the words "ice cream." Floyd hit both free throws, Louis Orr missed a desperation 30-footer at the buzzer for Syracuse, and Georgetown emerged with a 52–50 victory.

After the game, Boeheim stayed behind closed doors with his team for eight minutes, affording Thompson the opportunity to greet the waiting media with six words destined for legendary status: "Manley Field House is officially closed." Whether he realized it or not, Thompson had coined one of the most famous postgame quotes in college basketball history. To this day, typing "Manley Field House" into a search window elicits one suggested algorithmic completion in particular: "is officially closed."

The win at Manley was no fluke. Thompson had far and away his best team to that point at Georgetown, a team that won the first-ever Big East tournament (played at the Providence Civic Center) and reached the Elite Eight at the 1980 NCAA tournament before falling 81–80 to Iowa at the Spectrum in Philadelphia. Thompson was in high demand by then, both professionally and as a speaker and interview subject. In a widely reprinted feature that March, the *New York Times* remarked that Thompson "has been called a social worker, a father figure to his team of inner-city players, a black version of the White Shadow." Oklahoma, in particular, made a determined effort to hire Thompson. He was flown to Norman and given a tour of the campus and the area by OU football coach Barry Switzer. Reports suggested Thompson was being offered as much as $120,000 a year to become the next coach of the Sooners. "It would be foolish with the kind of money they're talking about not to evaluate it," Thompson said, and he spent 48 hours doing so before deciding to stay where he was.

Thompson's Hoyas had survived far longer in the 1980 NCAA tournament than No. 1–ranked DePaul. The Blue Demons had added freshman Terry Cummings to a rotation that, for a second year, featured Aguirre. DePaul entered the tournament 26–1, but Ray Meyer's team was defeated in its first game 77–71 by UCLA. An emotional Aguirre nodded in agreement when Meyer said at the postgame press conference that his team was committed to coming back from this loss and that the Blue Demons had made a pact to win the 1981 NCAA tournament. The nod set off speculation that Aguirre would return for his junior season rather than enter the NBA. And he did indeed return, along with virtually the entire roster. Again, DePaul entered the tournament with just one loss on the season. Again, the Blue Demons went down to defeat in the first game, this time by one point to Saint Joseph's, courtesy of a game-winning shot by John Smith. (The Hawks engaged in Catholic fratricide in the 1981 bracket, winning one-possession games against DePaul, Creighton, and Boston College before falling to eventual champion Indiana.) By the time 1982 rolled around, Meyer was sounding a much different note. "Hope you make it to New Orleans," a coach told him, referring to the Final Four site. Meyer responded, "I'll be there, but I'm sure my team won't."

While DePaul would continue to maintain its status as an independent program all the way to the early 1990s, the Big East was already expanding as of its second season. Whatever Villanova's initial reservations may have been, athletic director Ted Aceto contacted Gavitt in December 1979, and the Wildcats signed on the dotted line in March 1980. Everyone was all smiles at the press conference, yet there was intrigue in the air. Even as Villanova was joining a new conference, head coach Rollie Massimino was considering a new job at the University of Pittsburgh. The coach of the Wildcats was reportedly being offered up to $45,000 a year by the Panthers, a significant upgrade for an existing salary pegged at $27,000 in the press. In the end, Massimino elected to stay put and lead his team into its new conference, one where he and his school's administration would be pressured to find a new home court.

A sticking point in the negotiations between Villanova and the Big East had been the school's field house, constructed in 1932 and offering a capacity of just 1,500. When asked about potentially having to play road games at such a venue every year, Boeheim replied pointedly, "When we formed the league, we decided schools would play their games in the biggest arena they could find, use, and fill. Hopefully, all teams will stick to that." As if to demonstrate the possibilities inherent in a somewhat larger venue to new member Villanova, the Big East held its 1981 conference tournament at the brand-new 34,000-seat Carrier Dome in Syracuse.

Gavitt was preparing to watch a first-round game between Georgetown and Seton Hall when the phone in front of him at mid-court rang. "I thought something was wrong with my family," Gavitt would say. Instead, he picked up the call and heard the voice of Bill Raftery, the head coach of the Pirates. "It was Billy," Gavitt recalled later, "who knew he was overmatched against Georgetown. 'Whose idea was this damn league, anyway?' Billy yelled into the phone. I looked across the floor, and there he was with that ridiculous grin." The Seton Hall coach was 40 minutes away from hanging up his clipboard for good and going into announcing. He would start in 1981–82 as analyst on *Big East Game of the Week* telecasts with Len Berman.

Change was afoot outside the Big East, as well. In 1981, the NCAA used its new rating percentage index (RPI) for the first time in the selection and seeding process. "The computer ranking system is unique," the Associated Press reported that March, "in that teams will be penalized for scheduling non–Division I opponents, whether they win or not." The NCAA would henceforth put together its brackets, in the words of committee chair Wayne Duke, "utilizing material not available to the average person or to a writer voting in the AP poll or a coach voting in the UPI poll."

The winner of the 1981 Big East tournament was not pleased with how the NCAA utilized its material. Syracuse had captured the conference tournament crown, but, with the Big East still lacking an automatic bid, Boeheim's men were nowhere to be found in the NCAA bracket. "No question in my mind we won a bid on the court," Boeheim announced in a prepared statement. This was the last year when there was no televised selection show. Schools, instead, waited by their phones on Sunday, March 8. The phone at Syracuse never rang, while those at Georgetown, Villanova, and Boston College did. However, the Hoyas had taken a measurable step back, particularly on offense, after Craig Shelton and John Duren completed their senior years in 1980. Thompson's team lost by six in the opening round to James Madison.

While no Big East teams reached the Elite Eight, this was the last time that would happen until 1986. Some remarkable four-year careers were about to begin within the conference. In the fall of 1981, Ed Pinckney arrived at Villanova, Chris Mullin began playing at St. John's, and the Patrick Ewing era dawned at Georgetown.

The recruiting process for Ewing followed a highly structured sequence set forth by his parents and by Mike Jarvis, the coach at Rindge and Latin School in Cambridge, Massachusetts. Some 200 schools were initially contacted, and from this list, 15 coaching staffs were invited to come to Cambridge and speak to the Ewings and to Jarvis at the high school. The coaches arrived over a period of two weeks in September 1980 in alphabetical order according to their school name. John Thompson was preceded by Ed Badger and Cincinnati, and he was followed by Hank Raymonds and Marquette.

Ewing's mother, Dorothy, had come to the United States from Jamaica in 1971 and taken a job at Massachusetts General Hospital. By 1975, she and her husband, Carl, had a five-room apartment for themselves and their seven children in Cambridge. Five years later, when Thompson was making his pitch for why Dorothy Ewing's son should play basketball at Georgetown, the coach surmised that she was in fact the key player in this room. "This lady was watching me the whole time and I swear I don't think she ever blinked, not once," he would later recall. When Thompson finished his prepared remarks, Dorothy Ewing asked him what social opportunities her son might be afforded if he enrolled at Georgetown.

"I said, 'Mrs. Ewing, it is not a responsibility of mine to get involved with your son's social opportunities,'" Thompson recounted. "'But the city of Washington is 70 percent black, if that interests you. And if there are no social opportunities that Patrick can find there as a young black man, he has a problem, ma'am, that I frankly can't solve.' And she looked at me for a while, like maybe she sort of liked that. But she never smiled, never broke into a laugh to let me be sure. She just looked at me and said, 'Ha, funny man, funny man.'"

Assistant coach Bill Stein was also present for the interview, and he feared that the funny man may have just talked Georgetown out of the running with Dorothy Ewing. Stein was therefore relieved when Patrick Ewing announced his six finalists: Thompson and Georgetown, Tom Davis and Boston College, Rollie Massimino and Villanova, Rick Pitino and Boston University, Dean Smith and North Carolina, and Larry Brown and UCLA. Ewing visited the six campuses between October and December 1980, and a press conference was scheduled at Satch Sanders's restaurant in Boston for February 2, 1981. The restaurant was packed with members of the press, but a tiny number of Georgetown fans had managed to wriggle their way into the back of the room, and they burst into cheers when Ewing announced he would play for the Hoyas.

Ewing's announcement tipped off a momentous year not only for Georgetown but also for the Big East. Upon learning that Ewing would be joining the league, Gavitt picked up the phone and began

negotiations to book Madison Square Garden for the Big East tournament starting in 1983. "The Garden is basketball," he explained. Even
with Ewing in the fold, however, the new league was already facing the
first challenge to its existence. As would be the case throughout the
Big East's history, the threat was football. Boston College and Syracuse
nourished ambitions in that direction that were not shared by the rest
of the conference.

By 1981, Penn State's Joe Paterno was pitching what was termed, in
a bit of a swipe at the basketball-focused Big East, a "total conference."
Paterno envisioned prying BC and Syracuse away from the Big East
and adding them to a league with Pitt, Rutgers, Temple, West Virginia,
and, of course, the Nittany Lions. Concurrently, Boston College and
Syracuse were lobbying within the Big East for the football-driven
additions of Pitt and Penn State. Gavitt noted at the time that the
idea was being resisted by some "of our members [who] felt that our
basketball strength would be diluted by the additions."

In the end, both sides in the dispute within the conference were
given half a loaf. Gavitt negotiated a deal for Pitt to join the Big
East in basketball and six other sports as of 1982–83 while remaining
independent in football. The league would add one new member with
an eye toward football, but not two.

As of September 1, 1981, the indefatigable Gavitt also served as the
NCAA's committee chair for men's basketball, an influential position
from which he opposed proposals then under discussion to expand the
field to 64 teams. "I am personally very much against expansion," he
said in an interview shortly before assuming his duties as chair. "I'm
prepared to speak against it. I'm prepared to vote against it. Whether I
have the prevailing opinion, I don't know."

The issue first arose indirectly in January 1982, when, in a rare
development, the national membership voted in convention to over-
ride a basketball committee recommendation already approved by the
NCAA's executive council. Armed with printouts furnished by the
new RPI, the basketball committee had proposed replacing four automatic bids with a like number of at-large invites in 1983. When the

membership vetoed the measure, Gavitt predicted correctly that pressure to move to a 64-team field would increase further still. "I'm not anti-64," he told a reporter. "But I am greatly concerned about what it will do to the quality of in-season play. It scares the hell out of me."

Nevertheless, expanding to 64 teams had two powerful forces operating in its favor. The idea was strongly supported by the National Association of Basketball Coaches, and, by late 1983, it had emerged as the middle position between the status quo and creating a single-elimination bracket for all of Division I. On December 3, 1983, when the basketball committee voted 8–1 in favor of expanding the 1985 NCAA tournament to 64 teams, Gavitt's was the lone vote in opposition. However, the Big East commissioner was also an early and vocal supporter of a shot clock, and he helped pave the way for its adoption throughout Division I soon after his term ended on the men's basketball committee.

During the time that Gavitt was holding down responsibilities with both the Big East and the NCAA, Thompson was taking his basketball program to places it had never been before. Literally. Georgetown would for the first time play several home games at the Capital Centre in 1981–82. The Hoyas would appear 12 times at the larger venue in Landover, Maryland, in Ewing's freshman season and five times at McDonough Gymnasium. Georgetown sold 6,000 season tickets at its new venue, 2,000 more than the Washington Bullets sold that season while playing in the same arena. Ewing was the team's second-leading scorer behind Floyd, and the freshman led a defense that allowed 10 fewer points per game than it had the previous season.

Still, a three-game losing streak in January effectively opened the door for Villanova in the Big East title race. Pinckney was making a highly impressive freshman debut of his own alongside featured scorer John Pinone, and the Wildcats captured the regular-season title at 11–3, despite losing twice to Georgetown. Villanova was destined to record yet another loss to the Hoyas, this time in the Big East tournament title game at the Hartford Civic Center. The closing seconds of Georgetown's 18-point win marked the last time Big East tournament basketball was played anywhere besides Madison Square Garden.

Thompson's team was given the top seed in the West region of the 1982 NCAA tournament, and the Hoyas defeated Wyoming, Fresno State, and No. 2 seed Oregon State by an average margin of almost 17 points, in games played in Logan, Utah, and in Provo. The national semifinal against Rodney McCray and Louisville at the Superdome in New Orleans, on the other hand, was a much closer contest. Denny Crum's team denied Ewing the ball and held him to just eight points, but Georgetown's zone defense was tough enough in its own right to deliver a 50–46 victory. Now, at last, the Hoyas were back where they'd been 39 years before, in the NCAA title game. This time, the opponent would be North Carolina. Writers in New Orleans were so persistent in asking Dean Smith about his close friendship with Thompson that the UNC head coach finally responded, "It's not going to be Dean Smith vs. John Thompson. It's players against players. If we were playing, he'd take me inside and kill me." Smith had great players, including James Worthy, Sam Perkins, Jimmy Black, Matt Doherty, and a freshman who was still, on occasion, referred to in print as "Mike" Jordan.

The 1982 national championship game began with North Carolina scoring its first eight points on four goaltending calls against Ewing. Three of the four swats were obvious violations at the rim, the product of Thompson's standing order for Ewing to open each game by simply going after any shot he could reach. ("When Patrick makes an impression early," the coach would explain the following season, "that impression tends to last.") Ewing played easily his best game of the tournament, recording a 23–11 double-double, on a night when his teammates were also rising to the occasion. Floyd's floater in the lane with 32 seconds left in the game gave Georgetown a 62–61 lead. Dean Smith called time-out and told his players to take the first open shot, knowing that plenty of basketball remained to be played even in the event of a miss. That open shot was taken by Jordan, who nailed a 15-footer from the left side with 15 seconds on the clock. Thompson elected not to call time-out, and Hoya guard Fred Brown brought the ball across midcourt, with Eric Smith calling for a pass on his right.

Worthy flashed out well beyond the top of the key to deny the pass, and

Smith reacted by cutting to the foul line. It could have been a five-on-four advantage for Georgetown as, strangely, Worthy continued to linger out top, alone in space and guarding no one. Instead, Brown's peripheral vision registered the presence of a player in the spot where Smith would normally be found. Brown threw that player the ball, but it turned out to be James Worthy. "I was surprised," Worthy said after the game. "He threw it right at my chest." Worthy was fouled with two seconds left, and, while he missed both free throws, Georgetown was unable to get a good shot off at the buzzer. North Carolina had won 63–62, giving Dean Smith his first national title in his seventh Final Four appearance.

As the Tar Heels celebrated, a national audience watched Thompson hug Brown and speak reassuringly to him on the sideline. In a matter of weeks, recruits David Wingate and Horace Broadnax would sign with Georgetown, and both players would specifically cite Thompson's embrace of Brown as a major factor in their decisions. "David told me he just had to be associated with a coach who cares so much about his players," Wingate's high school coach would tell the *Washington Post*.

There were hugs all around in New Orleans that evening. Dean Smith came over and gave Thompson a consoling embrace, and Georgetown's coach long kept a photo of that moment. "I hope I would have been classy enough to do that," he would say in 2007, "because I would probably have been doing what [Jim] Valvano did, running around and hollering."

The 1982 Final Four had not been without drama. This was the first tournament where Thompson made news by sequestering his team far away from the tournament site. While the North Carolina team stayed at a hotel in the heart of the French Quarter, Georgetown was billeted in Biloxi, Mississippi, nearly 100 miles away from the Superdome. Such decisions would come to be known in the press as "Hoya paranoia," though in this instance what appeared to be paranoia may have been prudence. Thompson would reveal that weekend that a threat had been made on Ewing's life three weeks earlier. The coach was moved to share the information by something he saw on his Mississippi hotel's TV that Saturday night after the semifinals had concluded. "I turned on ESPN," he said, "and there's this guy just ripping us."

ESPN had aired a segment of editorial comment that evening by free-lancer Bill Currie in which Ewing's presence at Georgetown University was held up as proof that the Jesuits had sacrificed academic integrity on the altar of basketball glory. Officials at Georgetown, including Rienzo, were reportedly furious, and ESPN president Chet Simmons apologized in two separate appearances on the air the following night. "I personally... do not subscribe to [Currie's] viewpoint of Georgetown and Patrick Ewing," Simmons stated. But Thompson was not placated. "It's too late for that," he said of Simmons's apology. "The damage was done."

When the *Washington Post* asked Georgetown's president, the Rev. Timothy Healy, to comment on the ESPN segment, he dismissed what had been broadcast as "the same old *Boston Globe* story." He was referring to a feature that had run in February 1981, after the *Globe* obtained a copy of the letter high school coach Mike Jarvis had sent out to every school interested in recruiting Ewing. In the letter, Jarvis had spelled out the level of academic support that Ewing would be seeking, including the use of a tape recorder in lectures and permission to take examinations in untimed sittings. The *Globe* called the conditions "extraordinary," and the space and placement given the story, which occupied the entire front page of the sports section, above the fold, con-veyed a sense that this was scandalous or, at a minimum, salacious.

To be sure, there were indeed a number of stories garnering coverage in the early 1980s that seemed to underscore troubled times in college athletics. A few of the stories took place on Catholic campuses.

In the summer of 1982, the University of San Francisco dropped men's basketball as a varsity sport after former player Quintin Dailey was charged with five counts of felony assault. Dailey was drafted into the NBA with the seventh overall pick four days after he entered a guilty plea on one count of the charges, which stemmed from a sexual attack on a female student in December 1981. The Dons had already been placed on probation for recruiting violations and impermissible benefits in two separate rulings handed down by the NCAA, covering both 1979–80 and 1980–81. By the time charges were filed against Dailey, USF's president, the Rev. John Lo Schiavo, had seen enough. "There is no way of measuring the damage that has been done to the university's most priceless assets, its integrity and its reputation," he announced. (San Francisco would relaunch its men's basketball program in 1985.)

Making news at the same time as San Francisco's suspension of all men's basketball activities was the lamentable tale of Kevin Ross. If Dailey was shielded by an overemphasis on basketball, Ross was portrayed as the academic victim of that same myopia. He made national headlines in 1982 when he finished his athletic eligibility in the Creighton basketball program and promptly enrolled at age 23 in a Chicago elementary school, Westside Preparatory, in order to learn to read. His transcript from Creighton included courses in ceramics and first aid. Ross appeared in *People* magazine and on the *Donahue* show before making further news by throwing every piece of furniture in his Chicago hotel room off its eighth-floor balcony. He explained afterward that he had imagined the furniture to be Creighton's administrators, and he sued the school for negligence and breach of contract. The coverage given to Ross surfaced at the same moment when questions were being raised regarding the quality of education afforded to prominent athletes, including football player Dexter Manley at Oklahoma State and basketball player Chris Washburn at North Carolina State. It was in this context that the call went out for rigorous academic standards. NCAA minimum standards, codified as Proposition 48, were adopted in 1983, requiring freshman college athletes to record a 2.0 grade point average in core courses in high school and to post at least a 700 on the SAT or a 15 on the ACT.

It was after Proposition 42 was drafted later in the decade that Thompson staged his famous protest, in the form of a walkout at a home game in 1989 against Boston College. The new rule would deny not just eligibility to nonqualifiers but also athletic scholarships. To Thompson and allies like Temple's John Chaney, these nominal reforms were racist in their impact if not in their intent.

NCAA executive director Walter Byers disagreed, and he would devote a portion of his memoirs to an effort to marshal data in support of his position. Athletic scholarships wouldn't solely or even primarily be transferred from African Americans to whites under these measures, Byers claimed. The scholarships would instead in some instances be conferred to another population of Black students that had earned better academic credentials. Better credentials as defined by whites, critics were quick to add. Whatever the merits or weaknesses of Byers's position may have been, however, they were doomed to obscurity by his own hand. Ironically, the most deeply felt passages in his cri de coeur would be overlooked completely. His book would instead be used as a polemical drive-thru window for decades due to a brief aside in which he revealed that the term "student-athlete" had been coined within the NCAA as a defense against litigation.

This debate over academic standards formed the maelstrom into which Ewing stepped with a singular prominence that to later eyes is baffling. In the long, and on occasion educationally problematic, annals of college sports, one is hard pressed to find anything especially aberrant academically about the Ewing-era Hoyas. Actually, in 1980, Thompson was being praised to the skies by the national press as the no-nonsense authority figure who kept a deflated basketball on his office shelf to illustrate the importance of life after college sports. He was lionized as a coach who made his players go to class, do their homework, and wear coats and ties on road trips.

Yet something about Ewing in particular attending Georgetown in particular clearly wound up a particular segment of the 1980s public at large. That segment was very much in evidence in the racist signs displayed by fans of other Catholic Big East schools. At the 1982 Big East tournament title game at the Hartford Civic Center, Villanova fans caught the eye of *Boston Globe* columnist Leigh Montville. "The ugly sweethearts in the stands who held a sign saying that an 18-year-old college freshman was the missing link in Darwin's theory," he wrote, "can take their long and sad ride home to Philadelphia." Such banners continued to appear in Ewing's sophomore year. When he stepped to the line late in the first half at Providence, a fan under the basket revealed a sign stating EWING CAN'T READ. Thompson was livid, and he pulled his team off the floor briefly "as an alumnus, not as a coach," he explained afterward. "I saw [the sign] as a reflection on the Dominican education I received."

Nine days later at the Palestra, a Villanova fan threw a banana peel on the court when Ewing's name was called during pregame introductions. Signs in Philadelphia that day included EWING IS AN APE and EWING CAN'T SPELL HIS NAME. A T-shirt said EWING KANT READ DIS. Decades later, Nova's Ed Pinckney would recall that game, saying, "It's surreal, because you're being supported by fans who encourage that." Gavitt had stepped down as Providence athletic director in the summer of 1982 to become the full-time commissioner of the Big East. In February 1983, he sent a two-page letter to every athletic director and coach in the league, spelling out preventive and, if need be, enforcement steps to be taken by security staff. "I think it's despicable that any player or coach has to be subjected to those kinds of signs," he said.

The 1982–83 season marked by such venom in the stands was simultaneously characterized by a bit of a letdown for Georgetown on the court. Sleepy Floyd and Eric Smith had graduated, and Fred Brown's absence for a little more than half the season due to injury coincided with a measurable drop in the effectiveness of Thompson's defense. The year had nevertheless opened with a No. 2 ranking in the preseason and high expectations. In December, Ewing faced off against 7-foot-4 center Ralph Sampson and Virginia in an eagerly awaited showdown that by itself set off a bidding war among television networks. In the end the Cavaliers' five-point win at the Capital Centre was carried by Ted Turner's emerging TBS network in Atlanta. The Hoyas eventually lost to Syracuse by seven in the opening round of the Big East tournament at Madison Square Garden, and entered the 1983 NCAA tournament as a No. 5 seed. Georgetown defeated Alcorn State by five before bowing out 66–57 against Keith Lee and Memphis State at Freedom Hall in Louisville. It went in the books as a 22–10 season for Thompson's young team.

The coach returned virtually the entire roster for 1983–84, Brown was once again healthy, and Reggie Williams and Michael Graham joined the rotation as freshmen. Georgetown dropped a two-point decision at DePaul in December and also came up short in two overtimes at home against Villanova in January. As a result, the Hoyas were 23–2 in late February when they hosted 15–8 St. John's, a team they'd defeated by 22 at the Garden in January. Nevertheless, the Johnnies' Chris Mullin scored a career-high 33 points and recorded a key steal against Horace Broadnax in the final minute to give Lou Carnesecca's men a four-point victory.

Four nights later, Ewing was ejected in the waning moments of the Hoyas' easy win against Boston College in Springfield, Massachusetts, when he charged at Michael Adams after having grabbed him and flung him to the ground. Adams was listed at 5 foot 9 and 162 pounds. "I guess he wanted a heavyweight against a lightweight," Adams said afterward. "He threw me back a couple of yards and then came at me, but I was ready to use my speed at that time." Thompson voiced what by Georgetown's lights was a tacit acknowledgment that Ewing had erred: "Nobody condones this, but it was kids making a mistake." Dick Paparo was the referee at the center of the scrum that emptied both benches. Though no one at the game in Springfield could have known it, Paparo's lasting moment in Hoya and, especially, Syracuse lore was yet to come.

Georgetown faced Boeheim's team in the title game of the 1984 Big East tournament, a clash that on paper figured to be no great obstacle for the Hoyas. Thompson's group had won the two previous meetings against Syracuse by an average of 14 points, but this evening was to be different. Dwayne "Pearl" Washington, Boeheim's sensational freshman, torched and humbled the proud Georgetown defense to the tune of 27 points. "We had our best defender, Gene Smith, guarding him," Ewing would say in enduring disbelief 30 years later. "And [Washington] was taking it to the house." On the strength of Washington's heroics, Syracuse had built a three-point lead entering the last four minutes of regulation. Then, with 3:52 on the clock, Syracuse's Andre Hawkins pulled down a rebound and got into a tie-up with Graham.

Attempting to wrest the ball away, Graham appeared to escalate from a possibly inadvertent right swinging elbow to what looked to many observers to be a more purposeful attempt to throw a punch with the left hand. Paparo rushed between the two players, signaling repeatedly, with the extended thumb on a right hand that was flailing high in the air, that Graham was being ejected. But Graham was not ejected. After Paparo huddled with colleague Jody Sylvester, Graham was allowed to stay in the game.

Georgetown eventually won by 11 in overtime, and Boeheim staged one of the greatest tantrums the interview room at Madison Square Garden has ever seen. It ended with him literally throwing a chair.

"The referees pure and simple took the game away from us ... Michael Graham in front of 19,000 people punched my player," Boeheim said. "They didn't have the guts to call it, and then they had the nerve to call about four other things to take the game away from my players. It's pure and simple. Georgetown's got a great basketball team, but today the best team did not win. Thank you."

When the NCAA sent Georgetown to Pullman, Washington, as the No. 1 seed in the West region that year, Thompson elected to head-quarter his team some 75 miles away, in Spokane. The Hoyas were very nearly sent all the way back to Washington, DC, after their first game. The 1984 NCAA tournament was the second-to-last one where teams were still permitted by rule to hold the ball, which is what Southern Methodist did against Georgetown. The Mustangs also capitalized on the lack of a three-point line by playing a 2–3 zone huddled close to the basket. SMU coach Dave Bliss had studied tape of Villanova's win over Georgetown at the Capital Centre that season, and he patterned his zone after what Massimino and the Wildcats had done. It all worked beautifully. The Mustangs shocked scoreboard watchers across the nation by taking a 24–16 lead at the half. Georgetown rallied, and the score was tied at 34 with 51 seconds remaining when Gene Smith went to the line for the Hoyas. Thompson never used Ewing on a task as unrewarding as pursuing offensive rebounds on free throws, preferring instead to have him take his position at the back of the full-court press. This time Ewing asked Thompson if he could fill one of the spots on the lane, and the coach said yes. When Smith's shot bounced off the front of the rim, Ewing spun around SMU's Larry Davis and tapped the ball in, giving Georgetown a two-point lead. The Hoyas escaped, 37–36.

By comparison, the rest of Georgetown's tournament run was a piece of cake, at least on the court. At Pauley Pavilion, the Hoyas defeated UNLV by 14 and then beat surprising No. 10 seed Dayton by 12 to reach the Final Four at the Kingdome in Seattle.

Off the court, the college basketball world's discussion of and interest in Hoya paranoia reached a crescendo. "We're not secretive, we're private," athletic director Frank Rienzo said. "Who cares where he stays on the road? I don't. He's staying where he thinks it's most appropriate." John Thompson showed up smiling in Seattle and wearing one of the buttons being sold by vendors at the Final Four: GEORGE-TOWN WHERE ARE YOU? Georgetown undergraduates wearing HOYA PARANOIA . . . CATCH IT T-shirts had taken advantage of a special Final Four package offering a $320 airfare and Jesuit-furnished accommodations, such as they were, on the floor of Seattle University's gym.

Healy, Georgetown's president, marked his school's run to the Final Four by penning a *Washington Post* opinion piece that ran that Friday under a headline that put "Hoya Paranoia" in quotation marks. "Pundits on TV and on sports pages, like a sportily clad college of cardinals, cluck and mutter darkly," Healy wrote. He then seemed to reference incidents involving Graham, not only the one in the game against Syracuse but also one in the regional final against Dayton: "Freshman players can lose their heads in the heat of a game." Healy also mentioned, in passing, the public at large, noting that a "totally successful black man who succeeds in his own way and on his own terms in this competitive world is hard for many white Americans to swallow."

"Hoya paranoia" was coined as a description of the mindset that Thompson was said to have instilled within his program, but the term functioned equally well in encapsulating the all-consuming trepidation exhibited by opposing offenses. While the percentage of opponent shot attempts that Ewing blocked during his minutes was of course quite high, it wasn't quite proportional to what one expects from one of the greatest defensive players in the game's history and a future 11-time NBA All-Star. This slight deflation in Ewing's individual statistics was in fact the foundation of a patently outstanding Georgetown defense. Opponents were so preternaturally afraid to attempt shots anywhere near Ewing's vicinity that they instead launched long jumpers that, at that time, could net them a maximum of two points. Aversion on the part of opponents fueled the Hoyas' defensive hegemony.

The lack of correlation between Ewing blocks and opponent misery was demonstrated vividly in the second half of the Hoyas' national semifinal against Kentucky. In a game where Georgetown's star was credited with zero blocks, UK's Mel Turpin, Kenny "Sky" Walker, Sam Bowie, and their teammates made three of their 33 shot attempts after the intermission. The Hoyas won by 13, the same number of points that the Wildcats scored in the second half, and Thompson's team proceeded to the national final against Houston.

UH head coach Guy Lewis had long been beset with claims that, in the parlance of coaching, he "just rolls the ball out." In Seattle, he told the press with a straight face, "I've become a lot better, I try to roll them out now with both the left and the right hands. I've really improved." A roster featuring Hakeem Olajuwon and Michael Young was one of the few nationally that could hold its own on paper with Georgetown's, and the Hoyas were given further cause for concern when Smith injured his foot against Kentucky and was rendered unavailable for the title game. Nevertheless, Thompson's team found a way. Olajuwon played the last 19 minutes of the game with four fouls, and George-town's seemingly bottomless pool of talent was on display once again. Freshman Reggie Williams came off the bench and rang up 19 points to go along with 16 from David Wingate in an 84–75 victory.

Even as the game was still winding down in the final seconds, Thompson sought out the former assistant coach he had played for at Providence 20 years earlier. Shaking hands with Dave Gavitt,

Thompson asked, "How about that Big East now?" By this time, Bill Russell was coming down out of the stands to embrace his onetime teammate. "I'm more proud of him than if I did it myself," Russell said. "John and I have a special relationship and are philosophical allies." Thompson admitted he had been "obsessed" with winning a title. "Now I have one," he told reporters. "I don't want 10 like John Wooden, I just wanted to get one."

In any Catholic map of college basketball's history, Ewing-era Georgetown forms the Continental Divide. San Francisco with Russell was just as dominant, if not more so, but the Hoyas acquired a cultural prominence nationally, not all of it admiring, that simply was not possible for a college basketball team in the 1950s. Villanova would win one more national title between 2016 and 2018 than Georgetown did between 1982 and 1985, but the university president in Jay Wright's era would never feel it necessary to write an op-ed championing or explaining or defending his coach. In many ways, Georgetown in the early 1980s stands apart.

Thompson bristled every time a white sportswriter asked him in 1982 about being the first Black head coach to reach the Final Four or, as of 1984, about being the first to win a national title. He would say his predecessors, like Clarence "Big House" Gaines and John McLendon, had forgotten more about basketball than he would ever know, and that singling him out as "the first" implied that no one before him had displayed enough ability. It was, as was often the case with Thompson, undeniable truth packaged in a more or less combative form likely to intimidate.

Before Thompson's hiring in 1972, Georgetown as a program arguably was weaker across its history than was Holy Cross. After Thompson, it was the Georgetown we know today. He brought this about in a manner consonant with what the Jesuits running the university said they wanted, and they backed their coach to the hilt at every opportunity. On the court, of course, intimidation had measurable basketball benefits. It was and always has been a fine line between tough and too far. When the makers of ESPN's *30 for 30* documentary on the Big East came calling to talk to the principals three decades after the fact, this debate was still alive and well. Pearl Washington is shown in the 2014 film saying Georgetown was "dirty." Ewing, in his own interview, phrases his team's style instead as "physical."

When intimidation came to actual blows, it was ritually deplored from all sides, even as some observers asked if Thompson was encouraging the actions or, at least, creating "an environment." Which, of course, was a perfectly fair question to pose. There were plenty of opportunities to do so with other teams and with other conferences. If anything, matters grew worse in the late 1980s and into the 1990s. In 1988, a fight between St. John's and Providence escalated to the point where one of the Red Storm's players threw a folding chair at a spectator. In 1990, extra security was hired when Utah State hosted UNLV because of a brawl that had erupted earlier in the season when the two teams played in Las Vegas. One can well imagine the headlines if such events had occurred with Ewing-era Georgetown.

John Thompson tended to find himself at the center of these and other controversies in a way that no other coach save Bob Knight ever has. The Georgetown coach clearly relished it, but it's still interesting to note how in the 1980s the ground was contoured to roll these discussions his direction in a way that would be simply unthinkable with a Lou Carnesecca or a Jim Boeheim. Thompson used his prominence to push relentlessly, sometimes bluntly, and, quite often, eloquently for change.

When the coach passed away in 2020, Black adults who had grown up watching Patrick Ewing and the Hoyas on occasion remarked that as children they had assumed Georgetown was an HBCU. This may well have drawn a smile from Thompson, who by his own account had viewed the same institution as "a white school up on the hill" when he was growing up in DC. Thompson almost certainly changed more perceptions and more practices across more categories than any other college basketball coach. His is an example worth remembering and following.

13.

The "Perfect Game"

I f Rollie Massimino had not been named as Jack Kraft's replacement at Villanova on March 23, 1973, he'd had another opportunity in the works that appeared to be almost as enticing. The 37-year-old assistant on Chuck Daly's staff at Penn had literally had his bags packed for an interview to be the next head coach of Bologna in the Italian league. Massimino's job with the Quakers, however, turned out to be precisely what the doctor ordered for the Wildcats. Art Mahan, longtime Villanova athletic director and assistant to the president, had stated from the outset that his school was seeking someone who knows "what the challenge is in the Big 5. A man from Iowa or the West Coast wouldn't know that challenge. I don't think we'd like to get away from that local flavor." Ironically, Massimino would one day be vilified, fairly or not, as nearly killing the Big 5, but the irony was still many years and one national championship in the future.

Before the assistant job at Penn and the head coaching stop at Stony Brook that had preceded his arrival in Philadelphia, Massimino had earned for himself the curious form of underground fame that once flourished among pre-internet high school coaches. His work at Hillside High School in New Jersey was widely admired, particularly on defense. In 1963, Doggie Julian asked Massimino, then 28, to come and talk about defense to his Dartmouth team. Julian recommended Massimino for the job at the high school in Lexington, Massachusetts, and, in later years, those connected with that program would recall Bob Knight, then at Army, chatting about X's and O's at Massimino's house. In future years, Massimino's Villanova teams would practice at the Lexington High gym whenever the Wildcats played at Boston College.

The esteem in which he was held within the profession did not prevent Massimino from experiencing lean years in the mid-1970s. Villanova compiled a 16–37 record in the coach's first two seasons before the picture improved considerably. The Wildcats reached the semifinals of the 1977 NIT and then advanced all the way to the 1978 NCAA Elite Eight, respectable showings that had been powered in both years by Keith Herron and Rory Sparrow. By this time, the basketball program had shed its eastern Catholic tradition of independence and joined what was known as the Eastern Eight. In three years of rivalry with Rutgers, Pittsburgh, West Virginia, and Duquesne, among others, the Wildcats won or shared three regular-season titles before jumping to the one-year-old Big East. Notwithstanding Massimino's discussions with Pittsburgh about the head coaching job there in March 1980, Villanova's move to the Big East heralded a return to the kind of consistent multiyear success the program had not seen since the late 1960s and early 1970s. A native of northern New Jersey, Massimino recruited greater New York City intensively and signed John Pinone, Stewart Granger, and, in 1981, Ed Pinckney.

While he was at it, Massimino also snatched Dwayne McClain away from Holy Cross, the young man's hometown school in Worcester, Massachusetts. The Crusaders had just turned down membership in the Big East, but in an effort to sign McClain they sought assistance from Holy Cross legend and local resident Bob Cousy. "I was praying his parents didn't turn to me and ask, 'Where do you think our son should go?'" Cousy would later say of the visit. "The question was never asked, but if it had been, I couldn't have said Holy Cross. A player with his ability should not have gone to a small Jesuit school with no TV." McClain instead signed with a small Augustinian school with an abundance of TV.

Pinone and Granger were two years ahead of Pinckney and McClain, and the foursome carried Villanova to back-to-back regional finals in the early 1980s. If Massimino had a coaching weakness in this era, it was his terrible luck in bracketing. In the 1982 NCAA tournament, his team was put in the same region as eventual champion North Carolina. The next year, the NCAA placed the Wildcats in a bracket with Hakeem Olajuwon, Clyde Drexler, and eventual national runner-up Houston. Though Villanova bade farewell to Pinone and Granger in 1983 and then lost to Illinois in the round of 32 in 1984, the future looked promising. Harold Pressley, yet another New York product, had emerged that season as a trustworthy third scorer. Gary McLain was a solid point guard who'd entered the program along with Pinckney and McClain. The three classmates called themselves the Expansion Crew, and now they were seniors. Massimino had been at Villanova for over a decade. The pieces appeared to be in place.

Instead, the Wildcats took a step back. A team that had been 12–4 in the rugged Big East in 1984 with just one senior in the rotation (Frank Dobbs) somehow posted a 9–7 record in conference play in 1985. The low point came on the last day of the regular season, when Villanova suffered the worst defeat it had yet seen in its Big East history. At half-time of what was fated to be a 23-point loss at Pittsburgh, a disgusted Massimino told his starters they had exactly three more minutes to prove they deserved to keep playing. When the coach was not satisfied that his conditions had been met, he benched his entire starting five with 17 minutes left in the game. The starters remained seated for the rest of the contest. "I warned them," Massimino explained. The coach was unsure if his program would be selected for even a newly expanded 64-team NCAA tournament that year.

Everything that was surprising and disappointing about Villanova that regular season was predictable and impressive about St. John's. For three years, Lou Carnesecca had been working to get a trio of complementary players from the New York City metro area on the court together as his rotation's three leading scorers. It finally came together in 1984–85. The third-leading scorer and least celebrated figure of the three was Bill Wennington, a 7-foot-0 senior who had arrived at St. John's after playing for Bob McKillop at Long Island Lutheran in Brookville. Wennington's 12 points a game and low-key demeanor belied the fact that he was on the cusp of over a decade of steady work as an NBA reserve. In a league that included the likes of Ed Pinckney and Patrick Ewing, it was good to have a 7-foot senior in the paint.

Chris Mullin was Wennington's classmate and the team's featured scorer. His connection to the St. John's program had long predated his enrollment at the school. Carnesecca had seen Mullin for years at the camps the coach ran, and, on the same day that the high school senior led Brooklyn's Xaverian High School to the 1981 state title, he committed to St. John's. Both Mullin and Wennington had been pursued by new Duke head coach Mike Krzyzewski, and Coach K had placed particular emphasis on recruiting Mullin. When St. John's won that battle, Mullin emerged as a Big East–level scorer right away as a freshman. Over his first three seasons, the 6-foot-6 scoring guard increased both his production and his efficiency. By his junior season, Mullin was averaging 23 points while shooting a remarkable 57 percent from the floor. That season, he earned second-team All-American honors, no small feat in a year where the competition included Michael Jordan, Patrick Ewing, Hakeem Olajuwon, Sam Perkins, and Oklahoma's Wayman Tisdale, among others.

Mullin's co-featured scorer his senior season was Walter Berry, finally wearing a St. John's uniform for the first time after what had been a long struggle. Much like Mullin, Berry had checked every traditional box for greatness in New York City basketball. Like Mullin, he had starred for the renowned Hawks team at Riverside Church, where Berry played alongside future NBA mainstays like Kenny "The Jet" Smith and future St. John's teammate Mark Jackson. When the Hawks pummeled the visiting Soviet Junior National team in May 1983 and Smith was praised for his passing, he told the *Daily News*, "When you have players like

Walter [Berry]...they get open easily and it's easy to find them." Berry had already played well enough at Benjamin Franklin High School to be considered one of the top recruits in the class of 1982 nationally, along with Tisdale and future Louisville star Billy Thompson. The obstacle Berry encountered, however, was that he was not really in the class of 1982. He didn't earn enough credits to graduate. Berry thought he was studying his way onto the 1983–84 St. John's team when he earned his New York State high school equivalency diploma on the university's campus in Queens that summer, but the NCAA ruled that the diploma met a state but not a national equivalency standard.

St. John's went to court, seeking an injunction that would allow Berry to play that season, only to lose its appeal in September 1983. Instead, Carnesecca's staff arranged for Berry to enroll at reigning National Junior College Athletic Association champion San Jacinto in Texas. The Ravens had previously enrolled another one of Carnesecca's players, Billy Goodwin. After Berry averaged 26 points and 14 rebounds in his one year of junior college, San Jacinto coach Ronnie Arrow proclaimed, "There is no difference in talent between Walter and Hakeem Olajuwon or Michael Jordan or Wayman Tisdale. The only difference is intensity." Other Division I coaches besides Carnesecca drew similar conclusions, and Berry was recruited anew from San Jacinto by the likes of Maryland, UNLV, and Georgia. In the end, he stuck by Carnesecca and assistant coach Ron Rutledge.

With its three building blocks in place at last, St. John's was ranked a respectable No. 7 in the AP preseason poll for 1984–85. It was the lowest ranking Carnesecca's program would carry all season. In Mullin and Berry, St. John's had the players who would win the Wooden Award in 1985 and 1986, respectively.

Mullin's Wooden recognition at the expense of Ewing would raise some eyebrows. Indeed, the team that had held the top ranking every week without fail from the 1984–85 preseason into January was defending national champion Georgetown. If possible, the Hoyas looked even better than they had the previous season. On a roster loaded with veterans, Georgetown was less reliant on Ewing for scoring than the program had been since its star's freshman year. David Wingate, Reggie Williams, Bill Martin, and Michael Jackson were all a year older and more refined, offsetting the loss of two players from the national championship team, including defensive specialist Gene Smith. The program had also parted ways after just one season with Michael Graham, whose recurring altercations and image as an enforcer had attracted comment and criticism. Thompson dropped Graham from the roster in the off-season due to poor academic performance even as Georgetown kept him on scholarship as an inducement for a possible return. It never happened. In December 1984, Graham sought and was granted a release so he could transfer to the University of the District of Columbia. Still, even without two rotation players from the title year, the Hoyas appeared unstoppable in the early stages of the season.

By the time Georgetown hosted St. John's at the Capital Centre in late January 1985, the 18–0 Hoyas had won 29 straight games, dating back to the previous season. It was a win streak that had begun after a home loss to St. John's, and it ended with another loss on the same court to the same opponent. Carnesecca's team jumped on Georgetown from the start, held Ewing to three field goals and nine points, built an 18-point lead in the first 28 minutes, and then held on for a 66–65 victory. Mullin again excelled against the Hoyas, leading all scorers with 20 points and earning praise from the enraptured *Daily News* as "a little Larry Bird." When the next AP poll was released, St. John's was ranked No. 1 in the nation for the first time since Zeke Zawoluk and Ron MacGilvray were starring for Frank McGuire in December 1951. Writers filing game recaps from Landover, Maryland, also noted in passing that Carnesecca, for some reason, had now worn the same sweater for four consecutive games, all of which were St. John's wins. From such humble beginnings, the legend of "the sweater" was born.

The coach would invariably tell the tale as follows: Carnesecca had been under the weather when his team traveled to Pittsburgh in the middle of January. Looking to fight off chills during the game against the Panthers, he wore a sweater he'd been given as a gift by a friend. That night, St. John's shot 65 percent from the floor and won 87–56 on the road against a team that included future NBA regular Charles Smith and that would go on to that year's NCAA tournament. A happy Carnesecca said after the game, "I thought this was our best performance." St. John's had already won six games in a row before defeating Pittsburgh, so it was the magnitude and quality of the victory more than the win itself that launched the superstition of the sweater. The legend gathered force as St. John's continued to win, and the sweater truly became an object of intense media interest once it was displayed in all its glory by Carnesecca during the pivotal victory at Georgetown.

While the Hoyas stumbled again after losing to St. John's and came up short by two points at Syracuse, Carnesecca's win streak continued. And New York's tabloids loved the sweater. WINNING IS A STITCH, they declared while printing the actual instructions for how to "Knit a Lou Carnesecca sweater." By the time St. John's and Georgetown prepared for their rematch, the sweater was 13–0. Of course, St. John's itself was 24–1, and the team didn't appear to require much assistance from superstition. When Mullin's scoring average dipped slightly his senior season, for example, it was actually a good sign. It indicated that he now had help: Mullin, Berry, and Wennington all got excellent looks at the basket that season, and St. John's came within a hair of leading the nation in accuracy from the field, at 54 percent. It was an extraordinary performance for a team that had to play 16 games against Big East defenses.

It's possible that the sweater captivated the public due to the fact that it was, in the words of the person who kept wearing it, "the ugliest thing you ever saw." By contrast, no one particularly noticed or cared about the sweater, from a drawer full of identical sweaters, that Bob Knight wore so faithfully at Indiana. It was just a red sweater. But Carnesecca's pullover was red, blue, and, of all possible choices, brown. During a sideline interview, the dapper yet unfailingly blunt Al McGuire told Carnesecca, "That sweater looks like a pizza that was dropped in the street."

No. 1 St. John's hosted No. 2 Georgetown at the end of February in Madison Square Garden in what was—and still is—the highest-rated college basketball game ever to air on ESPN. Thompson walked onto the Garden court just before the introductions, with his suit jacket closed up tight. When all eyes were on him and as the boos from a capacity crowd cascaded down, Thompson opened his coat with a flourish to reveal that he was, somehow, wearing a reasonable facsimile of the same exact hideous sweater as Carnesecca's. Georgetown's coach smiled broadly and pirouetted obligingly to give photographers a good view. Carnesecca chuckled. Mullin would grudgingly admit 30 years later, "It was a pretty good play." The contest would be forever known as "the sweater game," and the Hoyas won by 16.

Georgetown rolled with similar ease through the Big East tournament, and defeated St. John's again in the title game. The Hoyas and St. John's both received top seeds in the expanded 64-team NCAA tournament. Massimino said that Villanova, which had lost to Carnesecca's team by 15 in the Big East semifinals, was happy just to hear its name called on Selection Sunday.

For his part, Thompson didn't doubt for a moment that Massimino's team belonged in the tournament. The Georgetown coach had already remarked to reporters in February: "Let me tell you something. Some team is going to get Villanova in the NCAA tournament and they're going to think it's going to be an easy game, and they're going to be in for one hell of a surprise."

If Villanova was happy just to be in the tournament, the Wildcats were not so pleased when they took a second look at their bracket and saw that they would, in fact, be playing a true road game in the round of 64. Villanova would face Dayton on its home floor at Dayton Arena. As soon as the pairings were announced, a friend of the Flyers program, who happened to be a New Jersey resident, called the Dayton coaching staff and said he'd taped several Villanova games that season. Coach Dan Donoher and his players spent a good portion of Monday watching those games. Nevertheless, Villanova escaped against future Dayton head coach Anthony Grant and his Flyers 51–49, after UD's Sedric Toney missed a baseline jumper with three seconds remaining.

Even a win against Dayton seemed to do no great favors for the

No. 8 seed Wildcats, who would next face top seed Michigan. When the *Philadelphia Daily News* got a look at the bracket and saw this "true road game followed by No. 1 seed opponent" scenario, it cited Villanova's draw as exhibit A in what its headline called A KILLING FIELD FOR BIG 5. By guard Dwayne McClain's estimation, UM's front line of Roy Tarpley, Richard Rellford, and Butch Wade outweighed Villanova's "by about 20 pounds" per player. After the Wildcats pulled off the 59–55 upset, however, Michigan coach Bill Frieder pointed to something more important than weight. "They played a perfect game," he said of Villanova. Both teams had used a 45-second shot clock that year during the regular season, but this was the last NCAA tournament played without a clock. When the Wildcats secured a 46–43 lead with 4:22 remaining, Massimino signaled to freeze the ball. (The "signal" was often simply the coach yelling, "We've got enough.") Villanova shot 14 of 16 at the line the rest of the way to seal the win. "Thank God the clock was turned off for the tournament," Massimino said after the game. "Down the stretch, our kids did what we do best. We have been through this before. We've held the ball quite a bit."

Massimino's next challenge was an opponent that had already defeated the Wildcats that season and, in particular, one player who had destroyed them to the tune of 30 points and 13 rebounds. Villanova forward Harold Pressley said before the rematch that this player "really stood out in my mind more than Michael Jordan," and Pressley had guarded both stars. To advance in the bracket, Villanova would have to get past Len Bias and Maryland. In January, the Terrapins had defeated Holy Cross, Notre Dame, and Villanova in a six-day span that Maryland fans referred to as "Holy Week."

This time around, the game between the Terps and the Wildcats would be played in Birmingham, Alabama. Pinckney fronted Bias within the Villanova zone in an attempt to deny him the ball and succeeded brilliantly, limiting Maryland's All-American to eight points. When Adrian Branch pulled the Terps to within seven with 5:44 to play, Massimino told his team to hold the ball. "We've won over 95 percent of our games when we stalled at that point," Massimino claimed afterward.

The Wildcats prevailed 46–43 to earn a date against North Carolina in the regional final. For once, it was not a nail-biter. Villanova beat Kenny Smith, Brad Daugherty, and the Tar Heels 56–44 behind what seemed at the time to be incredible 76 percent shooting in the second half. The Wildcats were going to their first Final Four since 1971.

Georgetown and St. John's were headed to Lexington, Kentucky, as well. The Hoyas had run into a bit of difficulty when Ewing got into foul trouble against Georgia Tech in the Elite Eight. Nevertheless, Thompson's team recorded a tough six-point victory against Mark Price, John Salley, and the Yellow Jackets at the Providence Civic Center. As for Carnesecca's men, their closest shave had come in a 68–65 win over center Joe Kleine and Arkansas in the round of 32.

Georgetown and St. John's would face each other for a fourth time in one semifinal at Rupp Arena, while Villanova played Memphis State in the other game. It was the Tigers that were the outliers, a team that was neither Catholic nor from the Big East. The 1985 Final Four was therefore referred to as the "separation of church and Memphis State." Tigers coach Dana Kirk congratulated himself and his team for having "already won the non-Catholic national championship." In the end, neither national semifinal turned out to be much of a contest. Georgetown recorded its third win of the year against St. John's, this time by a 22-point margin. On the other half of the bracket, Villanova won a low-scoring affair, 52–45, over Memphis State. Keith Lee had fouled out for the Tigers with more than 10 minutes remaining, yelling at the officials as he departed, while McClain had needed just nine shots to lead all scorers with 19 points.

It had been 30 years since La Salle played San Francisco for a national title at Kansas City's Municipal Auditorium. Now, two Catholic teams were going to do it again. Or, as Bill Raftery would say to Big East associate commissioner Mike Tranghese that Monday evening, "Hey, Mike, just another Monday night game in the Big East."

The front-page USA Today headline on April 1, 1985, famously read: VILLANOVA VS. A 'GOD.' From the New York Daily News: HOYAS COULD BE

BEST TEAM EVER. The *New York Post*: IT'S DAVID VS GOLIATH. The level of respect being afforded the defending champions was both understandable and somewhat overstated. It was understandable because no less a basketball authority than Carnesecca himself had, after St. John's Final Four loss to Georgetown, compared the Hoyas to "the great teams of San Francisco with Bill Russell, the great Kentucky teams of the past, the UCLA clubs, and, of course, the Indiana team. We tried everything against them." Nevertheless, the "Villanova vs. a 'god'" attitude was perhaps a bit overstated. Georgetown had been in a close game against Georgia Tech just a week earlier, not to mention that Villanova had played three close games against the Hoyas in four tries over the course of the previous two seasons, and the Wildcats had actually come out on top in one of those contests. That win by the Wildcats at the Capital Centre in January 1984 had provided SMU with the tape it used to come within two points of defeating Georgetown in the ensuing NCAA tournament. The Hoyas were a clear favorite in the 1985 national title game. Villanova, however, was an unusual underdog, one that had clearly underperformed during the regular season. And the Wildcats weren't underperforming any longer.

That Monday opened with a shock for Villanova. Al Severance, the former head coach who'd discovered the pure-shooting Wildcats legend Paul Arizin already on campus nearly 40 years before, suffered a heart attack in his hotel room at the Final Four that morning and died. Later that evening, at the team's pregame meal, Massimino told his players that Severance would be on the rim in spirit blocking Georgetown's shots. Villanova had already been playing with a purpose in the postseason on behalf of Jake Nevin. Incredibly, Nevin had begun his tenure as the team's trainer in 1929. He had been confined to a wheelchair after being diagnosed with Lou Gehrig's disease in April 1984. Nevin was a familiar fixture at the end of the Wildcats bench throughout the six games of the 1985 NCAA tournament.

Villanova's longtime trainer watched his team get off to a slow start against Georgetown. The Hoyas built a 20–14 lead in the first 10-plus minutes, leading announcer Billy Packer to warn on the telecast that "you're talking about an 80-point-type game, and an 80-point game Villanova can't win—they have to slow this pace down." Actually, the pace *was* slow, but the fact that neither Packer nor anyone else could tell this was the case was indeed worrisome for Massimino. When Packer issued his warning, the two teams had played a mere 13 possessions of basketball. The problem for the Wildcats wasn't that the tempo was fast; the problem was that Georgetown was doing whatever it wanted on offense and had scored two points on 10 of its first 13 possessions. By the time Massimino had his team spread the floor to run out the clock with 1:55 left in the first half, however, things had settled down from a Villanova perspective.

The Hoyas scored just eight additional points after their initial 13-possession surge, and the Wildcats trailed 28–27. That became a one-point lead when Villanova's Pressley rebounded his own miss in the lane and put it in the basket. On Georgetown guard Wingate's last-second miss from the top of the key, his teammate Reggie Williams took offense when Chuck Everson, the Wildcats' 7-foot reserve, made contact while boxing out for a possible rebound. Williams responded by thrusting both hands with full force at the left side of Everson's head and landing a glancing impact immediately after the horn. In later years, the only question on such a dead-ball violation would be whether it rose to the level of an ejection. In 1985, it was a no-call, a decision blessed by the CBS announcers. One might conclude things were different back then, except for the fact that Massimino was visibly enraged. To the extent that he could sprint, Massimino fairly sprinted into the locker room—with the lead, a raised fist, and a ready-made message about standing up to Georgetown's tactics. Villanova assistant coach Steve Lappas would later call the sequence "huge emotionally."

It was now a standard low-scoring Villanova tournament game, and the outcome turned on a five-possession sequence that started with five minutes remaining. Wingate had just given Georgetown a 54–53 lead on a shot soon to become almost entirely extinct, a 15-foot bank from the left side. After Villanova ran a full minute off the clock on its ensuing possession, Pinckney rose in the lane to attempt a shot, only to have Ewing get his hand on the ball. Pinckney momentarily lost control of the ball, regained possession in midair, and still got a shot up, of sorts, but it missed wildly and went out of bounds. The sequence went into the box score as a Villanova turnover instead of a miss, thus preserving the evening's beautiful field goal percentage.

Thompson at this point attempted to do what Massimino had done so effectively throughout the entire tournament. With less than four minutes left and holding a one-point lead, Georgetown went into a spread offense and tried to run some clock. Instead, the Hoyas gave the ball away after just seven passes. Under pressure along the right sideline, Bill Martin fired the ball directly at Horace Broadnax's ankle, resulting in a ricochet into Dwayne McClain's eager hands. Villanova called time-out with 3:25 remaining and ran its half-court offense for about 45 seconds, with the ball never once going into the paint. Finally, Wildcats guard Harold Jensen drained his crucial 17-footer from the right side. As the basketball saying goes, Jensen appeared to be open for a reason. Other things being equal, Georgetown was apparently content to give that shot to a reserve who averaged less than five points a game. The sophomore nailed it and, in fact, would go 5 for 5 from the field on the evening. The Wildcats drew fouls on each of their next three possessions, made all six free throws, and built a 61–56 lead with 1:15 left in the contest. By then, the outcome was virtually decided, a fact that was not lost on the players for either team. Nova's Gary McLain made eye contact with a reporter, ran to the sideline, and yelled, "We got it, we got it."

Because this would be the last 75 seconds of Division I men's basketball ever played without a shot clock, a five-point lead in the hands of a veteran team was surprisingly safe. When the final horn sounded on Villanova's remarkable and indelible 66–64 victory, Massimino was engulfed instantly in a teeming mass of assistants and other well-wishers. The euphoric horde acted as a tide that brought the coach irresistibly to center court, despite at least one futile motion on his part in the direction of shaking hands with Thompson. The

Georgetown players huddled under one basket. Ed Pinckney stood, shouting joyously, with his arms raised. Soon the nets would be cut down, and one of them would be draped around the neck of Jake Nevin. Billy Packer finally managed to chase down Rollie Massimino and put a microphone in front of him. "Nobody thought we could do it," the coach yelled ecstatically, "but I did!"

When the celebration had ended on the Main Line, the Expansion Crew had graduated, and Massimino had accepted an endorsement deal with Rolaids but had turned down an offer from the New Jersey Nets, the aftermath of Villanova's 1985 national championship would stand out as one of the more curious sequels in the history of NCAA titles. The Wildcats were 23–14 the following season before falling to 15–16 in 1986–87. Reporters sought out the last Catholic program that had dipped into similar straits of mediocrity after winning it all and asked the coach there what he thought of developments at Villanova. "Winning the national championship is easy," said Marquette head coach Hank Raymonds, an assistant to McGuire on the 1977 championship team. "Capitalizing on it is the hard part. People think it just happens. Well, it doesn't."

Capitalizing on a national championship was becoming increasingly difficult at Villanova by 1987. Gary McLain triggered a sensation in March of that year when he claimed that he had both used and sold cocaine during his four years on campus, up to and including being high while attending the ceremony held for the national champions at the White House. His exclusive "as told to" cover story in *Sports Illustrated* stated in its opening sentence: "I was standing in the Rose Garden, wired on cocaine." McLain also implied that the coaching staff had known of these activities during his career, an implication Massimino vehemently denied. The article was timed to coincide with the start of the 1987 NCAA tournament, and, coming on the heels of the tragic death of Len Bias the previous year, it was indeed the talk of the sport that spring.

Beginning in 1988, all teams in the NCAA tournament were informed that they were subject to drug testing. In spite of the turmoil, Massimino managed to take a team featuring Doug West and Mark

Plansky to the 1988 Elite Eight before losing to eventual national runner-up Oklahoma.

Finally, in 1991, Villanova's decision to scale back its participation in the Big 5 caused its own kind of uproar. For 35 years, the Wildcats, Saint Joseph's, La Salle, Penn, and Temple had played each other at the Palestra. Now, Villanova was announcing that, due to Big East commitments on the one hand and NCAA limits on the number of games played on the other, it would have to reduce its Big 5 footprint from four games to two. Additionally, the Wildcats had already said that they would play these games either at their four-year-old on-campus venue (known since 2018 as Finneran Pavilion) or at the Spectrum, but not at the Palestra. Fairly or not, Massimino bore the brunt of local displeasure. As with the McLain fallout, he was infuriated and insisted repeatedly that he was being unfairly maligned. In 1992, when Massimino announced that he was leaving to take over for Jerry Tarkanian at the University of Nevada, Las Vegas, a number of undergraduates at a Villanova assembly broke into the "Na-na-na-na, hey, hey, hey, good-bye" chant—a scant seven years after a national title.

The new coach of the UNLV Runnin' Rebels ran into trouble after just two seasons when reports alleged that his salary had been intentionally underreported by the school to the state of Nevada. Massimino took two years off from basketball and then won 44 percent of his games over the course of seven seasons at Cleveland State. It wasn't until the 21st century that the coach would find contentment in basketball once again, and then it would be at tiny Keiser College in West Palm Beach, Florida. Massimino coached there for 11 seasons starting in 2006, once leading the Seahawks as far as the NAIA Division II title game. The coach passed away in 2017, but not before he celebrated Villanova's 2016 national title alongside the onetime assistant coach he had originally hired in 1987, Jay Wright.

Over the course of 33 years, Massimino and Wright combined would win three national championships for Villanova, with the first coming in 1985, by virtue of what was later called a "perfect game" against Georgetown. In the countless interviews he gave before that game,

Massimino had repeatedly stated that in order to win, his team would have to shoot at least 50 percent while not committing turnovers. What happened instead was that the Wildcats achieved the same result by shooting 79 percent and turning the ball over frequently. Villanova scored 66 points in the game's first 57 possessions and then clutched the ball tightly on possession number 58, after it had been inbounded with two seconds left in the game. It was an outstanding performance against Patrick Ewing and the Georgetown Hoyas, and, of course, the 22-of-28 shooting was even better than outstanding. Whether or not it truly constituted a perfect game has been in the eye of the beholder ever since. The Wildcats also gave the ball away no fewer than 17 times on those same 58 possessions. In other words, Villanova shot 79 percent from the field while recording a 29 percent turnover rate.

Before the game, Massimino had held forth on the cardinal importance of treasuring the basketball against Georgetown's pressing defense. His team plainly fell short on that front, and, as we now know, it turned out it didn't matter. Indeed, on two consecutive possessions with less than six minutes remaining in the first half, the Wildcats were unable to so much as advance the ball to half-court. Nevertheless, Villanova shot its way out of that challenge with a dazzling display of accuracy. As a result, the bottom-line figures for scoring are markedly less stellar than those for shooting. While recording 66 points in 58 tries is exemplary, it's also a level of scoring that would be surpassed on a per-possession basis by Villanova in title games in both 2016 and 2018 and, for that matter, by North Carolina in a losing effort in the former year. None of which, of course, can detract from the totemic stature of that night back in 1985.

Actually, an imperfect game is even better, or at least far more inspirational, than a perfect one. The immaculate shooting and abysmal ball handling displayed by Villanova against a legendary opponent that evening makes for a better parable than any out-of-body experience like true perfection could ever furnish. The win in all its granular glory suggests that perhaps any of us can reach our chosen pinnacles as our actual flawed selves.

14.

Parity in the Big East

I f following up on a national championship is hard for a program, following up on a year where three of your teams make it to the Final Four has proven to be, as yet, impossible for a conference. No league has ever equaled that feat again, nor, for that matter, has any combination of Catholic teams been able to do so. The year 1985 still stands as both a Big East and a Catholic mountaintop.

Not that there weren't valleys at that same time. In the early years of what was by all accounts an extraordinarily successful Big East conference, there were nevertheless questions raised regarding the league's parity. Providence, Seton Hall, and Connecticut were often found at the bottom of the standings. The Pirates, for example, were 10–56 in Big East play over their first five seasons. "One of the concerns about the league's bottom three schools is that they're always the same," Dave Gavitt admitted in January 1985. Rumors began circulating to the effect that Seton Hall in particular was in danger of losing its membership in the Big East. In 1984, the league office had issued a three-year deadline for UConn, Boston College, Villanova, and Seton Hall to replace their current home venues. While the other three programs built Gampel Pavilion, Conte Forum, and Finneran Pavilion, respectively, Seton Hall worked out an agreement with what was then called Byrne Meadow-lands Arena. Still, if the Big East office had to scold its programs at times, it also acted as a protector. Television networks doing business with the league in the mid-1980s found themselves obliged to carry Providence, Seton Hall, and Connecticut games in addition to George-town, Syracuse, and St. John's contests.

These efforts paid off sooner than Gavitt ever could have expected, as both Providence and Seton Hall advanced to Final Fours in the late 1980s. The Friars hired New York Knicks assistant coach Rick Pitino in 1985, thrilling Gavitt both as an ex-Providence coach and as the Big East commissioner. "I think," he said, "the other coaches in the Big East will pay more than a passing glance when they pick up their paper and see who the new Providence coach is." From his perch at Northeastern, Jim Calhoun warned those Big East coaches about what they could expect. "When he was at BU," Calhoun said of Pitino, in referring to Boston University, "our games weren't even like games, they were confrontations." Pitino declared recruiting to be the first order of business, though, ironically, four of his five leading scorers when he reached the 1987 Final Four would be players he'd inherited from Joe Mullaney.

One of those holdovers was Billy Donovan. When Pitino arrived, Donovan had averaged 13 minutes a game over two seasons as a pass-always point guard. He told his new coach he wanted to transfer to a program with a lower profile, one where he could earn more playing time. Pitino advised him to stay put, lose 15 or even 20 pounds, and work on his shot. As a junior, Donovan emerged as a prolific scorer and distributor for a team that was playing at a faster pace and upping the pressure on defense. Other key veterans of the Mullaney era included Ernie "Pop" Lewis, Dave Kipfer, and Steve Wright. The most prominent Pitino addition in the Final Four season would be Indiana transfer Delray Brooks. In 1984, Brooks and Danny Manning had been the only two high school players in the country invited to try out for the Olympic team. Brooks left the Hoosiers in the middle of his sophomore year, however, and, when Notre Dame told him it didn't take transfers, he started looking into Providence. Pitino asked IU about Brooks, and Bob Knight replied, in Pitino's version of the conversation, that "Delray had slow feet, couldn't shoot or dribble, that he was terrible getting over the screen and that he didn't possess great athletic ability." Undeterred, Pitino took Brooks anyway, and the transfer made a smooth transition as the second scorer behind Donovan.

Providence embraced the introduction of the three-point shot in 1986–87, and before the season had even started, Pitino was telling his players at practice to be aware of the line. This awareness made the Friars an outlier nationally. "I don't like the damn rule," said Knight. The openness to three-pointers also made PC the exception to the rule in the Big East. Rollie Massimino termed the new rule "completely ridiculous." Speaking of his own players, Pittsburgh coach Paul Evans said, "I don't want them looking down. I think this rule is disruptive. A player isn't sure whether he's in front of the line or behind it, so he looks down, wasting valuable time." Seton Hall's P. J. Carlesimo perhaps strained credulity when he said in the preseason that none of his players had been able to make a single three-point shot in nearly three weeks of practice. Jim Calhoun, on the eve of his first season at Connecticut, declared, "I think it cheapens the game." Jim Boeheim agreed. "I don't like it," he said. "I watched the Russians play this summer on TV, and everybody was throwing it up. It was boring." Interestingly, the one Big East coach besides Rick Pitino that did give a green light to his players right from the start on three-pointers was John Thompson, albeit not nearly to the same extent as PC's coach.

These two pioneers in the field of perimeter orientation met in the 1987 Elite Eight in Louisville. Top-seeded Georgetown had been expected to make it that far, while the No. 6 seed Friars were a surprise. Providence had needed overtime to escape Austin Peay and then blitzed No. 2 seed Alabama in the Sweet 16 with 14 made three-pointers in a wild 103–82 blowout. Writers, and even Thompson, expected to see more of the same from the Friars in the regional final, but Pitino elected instead to pound the ball into the paint. With his NBA background, he knew that fear of the three-point shot could be just as significant a factor as actual three-point shots. Donovan scored 20, but 16 of his points came at the line as Providence again won easily, 88–73. "We had to extend our defense for the three-point shot," Thompson said. "What happened is that their big men started to score." In the national semifinal at the Superdome in New Orleans, however, Syracuse held PC to just five three-point makes and 40 percent shooting on two-pointers as Boeheim's team recorded a 14-point victory. Pitino had glimpsed the college game's three-point future, but he'd already coached his last contest with the Friars. That July, the 34-year-old was named head coach of the New York Knicks.

One year after Pitino took Providence to the Final Four, Seton Hall played in the NCAA tournament for the first time in the school's history. The Pirates made their debut as a No. 8 seed before losing by 29 to top seed Arizona in the round of 32. Carlesimo returned five of his top eight scorers the following season, and the team started 1988–89 by capturing the title at the Great Alaska Shootout. Two weeks later, the Pirates were ranked in the AP poll for the first time since 1954–55. The Seton Hall roster that season could boast of two Olympians in Andrew Gaze and Ramon Ramos, who had represented Australia and Puerto Rico, respectively, in international competition. Gaze teamed with leading scorer John Morton to form a dangerous perimeter-shooting duo, while the 6-foot-8 Ramos scored inside and defended the rim.

Seton Hall was still undefeated in the first week of January after beating freshman Alonzo Mourning and Georgetown by eight in front of the largest crowd ever to see a game, including NCAA tournaments, at Byrne Arena. Observers marked that night as the moment when the Pirates for the first time came into possession of a true home court at what had previously been a partially filled NBA arena. "This building's become very special to us," Carlesimo said after the victory over the Hoyas. Seton Hall was promptly hammered by 24 at Syracuse in its next game, but the crowds kept coming to the Meadowlands. The Pirates finished second to Georgetown in the Big East race, and entered the 1989 NCAA tournament as a No. 3 seed with a 25–6 record. Had the brackets gone true to form, the Hall would have bowed out against No. 2 seed Indiana in Denver. Instead, Morton, Gaze, and Gerald Greene combined for 48 points, and the Pirates won by 13.

Spectators noticed that Indiana's Bob Knight and P. J. Carlesimo had what appeared to be a lengthy and cordial conversation during the traditional postgame handshake. "I told P. J., 'I think you have a better team than us,'" Knight explained afterward. "They certainly played better tonight." In fact, tournament opponents were finding it difficult to stay close enough to the Pirates to even have a shot at winning in the final minutes. After a 23-point win over UNLV in the regional final, Seton Hall had played its way to the Final Four in Seattle by recording an average margin of victory of almost 15 points.

Georgetown came within one game of joining the Pirates at the Kingdome at the 1989 Final Four. Thompson had won a recruiting battle for Mourning that may have been just as intense as the one for Ewing nearly a decade earlier. Ultimately, the 6-foot-10 star from Chesapeake, Virginia, said no to Syracuse, Maryland, Virginia, and Georgia Tech so that he could say yes to the Hoyas. As a freshman that season, Mourning blocked a remarkable 15 percent of opponents' two-point attempts during his minutes, while supporting the offense as the second-leading scorer behind senior Charles Smith. Thompson's team was ranked No. 2 in the nation in the preseason and never fell below the No. 7 spot in the AP poll. Granted, none of that seemed to matter in the round of 64 against Princeton. The Tigers very nearly became the first No. 16 seed ever to defeat a top seed, but Pete Carril's men went down to defeat 50–49. Georgetown then navigated its way past Notre Dame and NC State before losing to Duke by eight at the Meadow-lands. It was the Blue Devils who advanced to meet a Seton Hall team that was winning tournament games with a minimum of drama.

That trend continued for the Pirates in the national semifinal against Duke. After trailing in the first half by 18, Seton Hall broke loose for 62 points in the closing 20 minutes and won 95–78. Danny Ferry scored 34 in his last game as a Blue Devil, but it wasn't enough to prevent Carlesimo's team from meeting Michigan in the national final. Students in South Orange and alumni across the nation took note the day before the game, when the Wolverines' Mark Hughes told the press in Seattle, "I'm sorry, I don't even know what conference they're in. They're from New York, or Jersey somewhere, right?"

Seton Hall came achingly close to making Michigan eat those words, but in the end the Pirates could not quite do so. UM's Rumeal Robinson, who shot 65 percent at the line during the 1988–89 season, gave his team a one-point lead by converting two free throws on a one-and-one opportunity with three seconds remaining in overtime. Coming out of the ensuing time-out, Ramos fired a baseball pass from under the Wolverines' basket to teammate Daryll Walker at the far end of the court, but Walker's desperation three-point attempt banked off the board and off the front of the rim. Michigan had won 80–79, despite a heroic 35-point performance from John Morton. The evening marked the first time that a national title game had gone to overtime since Loyola Chicago defeated Cincinnati in 1963.

By the time the Big East observed its 10th birthday in May 1989, the league already had eight Final Four appearances and two national titles to its credit. Both championships and seven of the berths in the national semifinals had been recorded by Catholic programs from a league where, as Gavitt put it, money was once tight. Unlike the ACC or the Big Ten, he said, "six of nine schools are Catholic and they pass the basket twice on Sunday. We don't have that kind of money." That was changing even as Gavitt was claiming poverty. The Big East did, in fact, have that kind of money as of the mid-1980s, thanks to the lucrative rights deals negotiated by Gavitt for a conference he had envisioned and, more than any other single figure, created.

That alone would mark a preeminent career, surely, but with Dave Gavitt we are instead confronted with someone closer to the Alexander Hamilton figure of basketball: Final Four coach and athletic director, US Olympic team coach, Big East founder and commissioner, and NCAA men's basketball committee chair. He also played on the last Dartmouth team to win an Ivy title, and when Gavitt stepped down as Big East commissioner in 1990, he became senior executive vice president of the Boston Celtics. Gavitt advanced the sport of college basketball by expanding its footprint geographically, by negotiating its fleeting but vital truces with football ingeniously, and, no less, by debunking myths about the necessity of professional specialization biographically.

The rise of Gavitt's Big East coincided with the moment in the 1980s when college basketball at long last learned to love the shot clock. It had taken far too long, and by the time Villanova won its national title in 1985, the danger for the game was that the NCAA tournament itself, the sport's showcase, was coming to be seen as fostering incentives to hold the ball. Houston had lost the 1983 national final to an NC State team that scored just 54 points, and the next year the Cougars defeated Virginia in a national semifinal by putting 49 points on the board in a contest that went to overtime. Similarly, Massimino's Wildcats won their championship averaging less than 53 points per tournament game after a season in which they had recorded a mean of 71 per contest. By putting a floor underneath how slow a game, even an NCAA tournament game, could get, college basketball's stewards wisely prevented a worrisome trend from becoming a disastrous turn of events.

No sooner had the clock been introduced in the tournament than a coach on the West Coast began experimenting with just how fast basketball could get.

15.

Loyola Marymount
and Time

rom 1975 to 1995, St. John's opened its seasons by hosting an event named in honor of former coach Joe Lapchick. The event was titled the Joe Lapchick Memorial Classic in its early years, and then became known simply as the Lapchick Tournament. The idea was for St. John's to start each year with two easy wins in Queens over inferior opponents. Lou Carnesecca's team ran its record to 26–0 in Lapchick competition when it defeated Loyola Marymount 88–85 on November 29, 1987. What was an unusually challenging Lapchick game for St. John's in fact marked just the second time that Hank Gathers had played for coach Paul Westhead as a member of the LMU program. Bo Kimble, Gathers's teammate and friend from high school, would miss the first six games of that season due to injury, but the word was already out that Loyola loved to run. St. John's earned three technical fouls for interfering with the ball after their own made baskets. When Carnesecca was asked if his team had been intentionally slowing down its Jesuit opponent by doing so, the coach replied implausibly, "I wish I could be that smart. Maybe the Jesuits would think that up. We're just poor little Vincentians."

Despite its location in the Westchester section of Los Angeles,

Loyola Marymount in the late 1980s was Philadelphia through and through. Westhead had come off the bench in the 1961 Final Four for Jack Ramsay at Saint Joseph's. He would later say he sought to model himself in part on Ramsay, who was not only the head basketball coach at St. Joe's but also served as chairman of the education department for the school. When Westhead's playing days were finished, he earned a master's degree in English literature at Villanova and was then hired as an instructor in the English department at the University of Dayton. Only incidentally did Ramsay suggest to UD that perhaps they could use Westhead as a volunteer assistant on the men's basketball team. Westhead was an assistant to Jack McKinney at St. Joe's in 1968–69, and he secured his first college head coaching position at La Salle, where in 1970 he succeeded Tom Gola. In Philadelphia, he was already dabbling with a faster pace, despite the absence of a shot clock. When opponents held the ball, Westhead's Explorers would on occasion attempt to bait the opposing offense into shooting by having just four players actively defend. Westhead called it his "box-and-none" defense. After nine seasons at La Salle, he reunited with McKinney, who by this time was head coach of the LA Lakers.

The new assistant coach's career—and, indeed, life—took an unexpected turn on November 8, 1979, when McKinney was seriously injured while riding his bicycle near his home in Rancho Palos Verdes. Westhead acted as interim head coach of the Lakers starting the next night. "This is my profession," he said, "what I've been programmed for 18 years to do, so coaching is easy. Worrying about the status of a friend is not easy."

Magic Johnson was a rookie and Kareem Abdul-Jabbar was 32 when the Lakers won the 1980 NBA title under interim coach Westhead, defeating Julius Erving and the Philadelphia 76ers in six games. Westhead was then officially named head coach, only to be fired in November 1981 after Johnson told the press, "I can't play here anymore. I want to be traded." The star insisted, however, that the decision to sack Westhead had been made by owner Jerry Buss alone, a razor-thin distinction captured nicely in a *Los Angeles Times* headline: BUSS

MAKES WESTHEAD DISAPPEAR; IT'S MAGIC. Westhead took a turn coaching the pre–Michael Jordan Chicago Bulls, only to be discharged there as well after just one season. By the summer of 1985, he was teaching English at Marymount Palos Verdes College when Loyola Marymount suddenly found itself with a vacant head coaching position. Westhead's onetime St. Joe's teammate Jim Lynam had been hired at LMU that April, but he quit to take a job as an assistant with the Sixers without ever having coached a game for the Lions.

Gathers and Kimble grew up in Philadelphia, and they had teamed with future La Salle star and NBA journeyman Doug Overton on a Dobbins Tech high school team that won the city's Public League championship in 1985. Kimble was leaning toward playing for John Chaney at Temple until Southern California head coach Stan Morrison made a late and ultimately successful push for Gathers. At that point, Kimble elected to follow his friend to LA, and the duo loved USC from the start. When Gathers was told the area around the Southern Cal campus was considered by locals to be distressed, he remarked, "In Philadelphia this would be a suburb." Both players recorded promising seasons with the Trojans as part of a heralded "Four Freshmen" recruiting class, which also included Tom Lewis and Rich Grande. Lewis and Kimble made the Pac-10's all-freshman team for 1986, and if events had taken a different turn it's likely Gathers and Kimble would have played four happy seasons together at USC.

Instead, Morrison was eased out as coach and given a job in the athletic department after the 1985–86 season. The four soon-to-be sophomores asked for a meeting with athletic director Mike McGee. Later reports would state that the players brought with them a short list of suggested replacements for Morrison, including Paul Westhead, UC Irvine's Bill Mulligan, and Pepperdine's Jim Harrick. McGee selected none of the above, and hired George Raveling away from Iowa.

The onetime Villanova star shared a Philadelphia link with Gathers and Kimble, but by the time he was introduced, the local media had already reported that he wasn't the preferred choice of the four players. When asked about this at his introductory press conference, Raveling answered, "You can't let the Indians run the reservation. You've got to be strong, too. Sometimes you have to tell them they have to exit."

Gathers was inclined to still give Raveling a chance, but Kimble wanted out. This time, it would be Gathers following Kimble. The two considered Pepperdine before choosing to play for Westhead at LMU. Kimble said that meeting Westhead for the first time had closed the deal. "We found that feeling we had been looking for in one meeting with Coach Westhead that we hadn't been able to find in two or three meetings with Coach Raveling."

Loyola Marymount's scoring had already jumped by 12 points a game in Westhead's first season. The coach had been continuously experimenting with a faster pace, starting with his days at La Salle, running up through summers coaching in Puerto Rico, and extending to his brief yet spectacular stint running McKinney's "Showtime" run-and-gun principles with the Lakers. By the time Gathers and Kimble were eligible to play in 1987–88, the Philadelphia duo was joining a deep roster that also featured senior Mike Yoest, UCLA transfer Corey Gaines, and sophomore perimeter threat Jeff Fryer. Westhead now had the players he needed, and this would be the season where, for the first time, the coach would commit fully to the fastest possible tempo.

The Lions would run the fast break in assigned lanes on literally every touch and try to force opponents to accelerate by deploying a full-court man-to-man press. Once LMU had the ball, the key, quite simply, was to sprint. "The defense may know what you are doing," Westhead stated in his typewritten notes for the team, "but you continually beat them to the spot." Westhead's undersized team also attacked its offensive glass collectively and audaciously with little or none of the concern for transition defense traditionally exhibited by coaches. "Everyone runs to designated spots every play," Westhead explained, as he pointed to Coach Sonny Allen's tenure at Old Dominion in the 1970s as having inspired many of the concepts LMU was embracing. "It's preordained. We want to minimize the time between possession and shot. It's an assigned fast break operation."

Westhead was willing to concede the occasional easy score in order to draw the opponent into Loyola's preferred style. "I've never seen a basketball player who could resist a 3-on-1 break," the coach observed. "We want you to take the 3-on-1. The shots that will be taken we are more accustomed to taking than you are. We're going to have a better crack at a high-percentage shot than you are." Scoring that season skyrocketed to 110 points per game, a level of production unseen in Division I since the UNLV teams of the 1970s. Westhead joked that his team referred to the 45-second shot clock as "the four to five second clock." Asked why no other D-I program was using the same style, the coach responded, "I guess nobody's as crazy as yours truly."

In February of 1988, Loyola Marymount appeared in the AP poll for the first time in the program's history. Including the three-point loss at St. John's in the Lapchick Tournament, the Lions had opened their season 3–3 without the injured Kimble. Once he joined the rotation, LMU proceeded to win its next 25 games, rolling through the West Coast Athletic Conference undefeated and earning the program its first league title in 27 years. Loyola completed its WCAC sweep by scoring 82 points in the second half of a 142–127 win at home over Pepperdine and then won three close games at the conference tournament to capture the league's automatic bid. While the Lions would be playing in the NCAA tournament for the first time since 1961 (and for just the second time ever), there was still some grumbling among the LMU faithful that the AP poll's No. 16 team was given a No. 10 seed by the men's basketball committee. Loyola was paired in Salt Lake City with a Wyoming team that was itself ranked No. 14 in the country. Westhead's team defeated Fennis Dembo and the Cowboys 119–115. "You start running with them, they outshine you," Dembo reflected in defeat. "They were possessed tonight."

By this time, the Lions had earned alliterative nicknames in the media. Westhead was the Guru of Go, and his players were the Wizards of Westhead. Loyola Marymount's first-ever NCAA tournament win set up a game in the round of 32 against No. 2 seed North Carolina. "I have to admit," Tar Heels coach Dean Smith told the press in Salt Lake, "I wish we were playing Wyoming." Smith noted that a game against

Westhead's system was really a game and a half. "You'd like five days instead of one day to prepare for them. The game could well be in the hundreds. It's a 60-minute game the way they play, the number of possessions you get."

Westhead's style placed a particular burden on official scorers, expected to record every shot attempt, block, and turnover for posterity. "It's been a nightmare," one of Loyola's stat crew members confessed. "We don't always know who had an assist or rebound. A lot of it is guesswork." For the North Carolina game, the official scorer was kept busy counting dunks and layups off of backdoor cuts by the Tar Heels. UNC buried LMU 123–97 and broke Villanova's three-year-old tournament record for field goal percentage in the process. Smith's team converted 49 of its 62 attempts from the field, yielding a 79 percent success rate. Nevertheless, Westhead saw the promise inherent in a 28–4 season that included a 25-game win streak. "We've had a pretty good run," he remarked with some understatement. "Nothing lasts forever."

Yoest and Gaines had just played their last games as Lions, and without them the Loyola Marymount defense took a significant step back in 1988–89. Kimble additionally struggled all season with knee injuries, sitting out 13 games and operating at a reduced level of performance when he did play. The season would therefore be remembered as something of a lost opportunity for LMU.

Even as Westhead's team regressed to a 20–11 record, however, Gathers individually was emerging as one of the best players in the country. As a junior, he led the nation in both scoring (33 points) and rebounding (14 rebounds), a feat equaled in NCAA history only by Wichita State's Xavier McDaniel, four years earlier. Naturally, Gathers's statistical twin-killing was aided and abetted by the Lions' pace. Nevertheless, Gathers did so while shooting 61 percent from the field. The NBA talk that had once seemed improbable for a 6-foot-7 player who functioned as a center in LMU's system now appeared more realistic; perhaps there was a future for Gathers as a 220-pound rebounding workhorse at the next level after all.

Loyola lost to Arkansas 120–101 in the first round of the 1989 NCAA tournament, and Gathers, already 22 years old, elected to stay in school for his senior season. His mother, Lucille, was adamant that she wanted to see her son become the first member of the family to earn a bachelor's degree.

After one season at Southern Cal and two at LMU, Gathers was a career 56 percent shooter at the line. Driven to desperate measures, the natural right-hander announced that as a senior he would try shooting his free throws left-handed.

Westhead's team opened its 1989–90 season with a 102–91 loss at top-ranked UNLV, a respectable showing on the road against Larry Johnson, Anderson Hunt, Stacey Augmon, and Greg Anthony. The game also marked the last loss Loyola Marymount would suffer for over a month. The Lions were 4–1 when they hosted UC Santa Barbara on December 9. Gathers had just shot a free throw and was still standing at the line with 13:56 remaining in the game when he suddenly collapsed. He was attended to by the team doctor, and after a few moments he sat up. Soon, he was walking off the court under his own power with his fists raised, signaling to the crowd that he was fine.

Gathers was taken to Centinela Hospital Medical Center for what were termed precautionary tests. He remained hospitalized for two nights, undergoing both an electrocardiogram and testing on a treadmill. His former coach at USC, Stan Morrison, phoned the notoriously poor foul shooter at the hospital and joked that "some guys will do anything to keep from shooting a free throw." When Gathers was released from the hospital, he was held out of practice and, instead, watched his teammates work out from the sidelines. He told a reporter that he'd nearly broken the hospital's treadmill, adding with customary bravado, "I'm still the strongest man in America." Westhead said all of Gathers's "tests so far are normal, but [doctors] are trying to be extra sure, to cover every base."

By the time Gathers was given an angiogram at Daniel Freeman Marina Hospital nine days after his collapse, doctors were focusing on what appeared to be an irregular heartbeat and reduced blood flow to the heart. When Loyola traveled to its first game since Gathers's episode, he stayed behind in LA. The game at Oregon State was carried by ESPN and promoted as a showdown between the high-scoring Lions and a Beavers team led by Gary Payton and ranked in the top 25. Surprisingly, LMU won 117–113, without Gathers, in a game where Kimble scored 53 points and Payton recorded 48 before fouling out.

Two days after his team's victory in Corvallis, Oregon, Gathers received medical clearance to return to practice. His collapse was termed an "isolated insidious incident," or, as Gathers put it, "I guess what happened to me was just one of those things." As a precaution, he sat out the marquee home date of the season, an ESPN-televised game at Gersten Pavilion against an Oklahoma team ranked No. 7 in the AP poll. The Sooners had averaged 102 points per game in their own right the previous season, and head coach Billy Tubbs hyped the game at LMU by vowing, "First team to 200 wins." OU posted a 136–121 victory, with Gathers watching in uniform from the bench.

As Gathers prepared to return to action at the end of December, he was under instructions to take 240 milligrams daily of the beta-blocker Inderal, a drug whose side effects were said to include lethargy and weakness. A home game against Niagara marked his first basketball in three weeks, and, in the box score of LMU's easy win, Gathers looked fine: 22 points on 10-of-19 shooting to go along with 11 rebounds in 24 minutes. Nevertheless, Westhead felt like his star wasn't at full strength, saying that "at times he was off. I thought he played well, but from past performances that wasn't the Hank you see all the time."

Gathers then scored 20 points and grabbed eight rebounds in a 115–113 loss at Xavier, a night where he was just 7-of-23 from the floor. His team was making its way eastward for what was supposed to be both an easy win and a chance for Gathers, Kimble, and Westhead to see family and friends in Philadelphia. The next game on the schedule was at Saint Joseph's, Westhead's alma mater and also a team that sported a 1–7 record. It would be the first time Westhead had coached in

Philadelphia since Game 6 of the 1980 NBA Finals. "I just wish Hank was at full readiness," Westhead told a reporter before the game.

Loyola barely escaped with a 99–96 win over the Hawks, courtesy of Kimble's 54 points and his running 30-foot three-pointer at the buzzer. Kimble personally scored 27 of LMU's last 31 points in the contest. Gathers, however, managed just 11 points on 5-of-11 shooting, and was "totally spent at halftime," according to Westhead. "It's only fair to say that Hank Gathers is not nearly close to his game." Two nights later, the Lions played at La Salle, a game that provided an opportunity for Gathers and Kimble to catch up with their friends Doug Overton and Lionel Simmons. A product of South Philadelphia High School, "L-Train" Simmons was about to become the Explorers' first consensus first-team All-American since Gola in 1955, not to mention a Wooden Award winner. The 6-foot-7 wing had averaged a 28–11 double-double as a junior, and during his career, La Salle would play in three consecutive NCAA tournaments for the first and last time in program history. The 1985 Philadelphia Public League championship game between Southern and Dobbins Tech had produced an ample supply of talent—with Simmons, Overton, Gathers, and Kimble.

Before a capacity crowd at the Philadelphia Civic Center, LMU defeated La Salle 121–116. Gathers recorded easily his best game since his return, hitting 12 of 20 shots and posting a 27–12 double-double. "I feel three or four times better than I did Thursday night [against Saint Joseph's]," he exulted after the game. One recap speculated that he'd been "rejuvenated by two more days at home" since his listless showing against the Hawks. It's also conceivable, however, that by this point, in early January 1990, Gathers had started cutting down the dosage with his Inderal, or even that he was failing to take it entirely on a game day.

Accounts of the season put together after the fact would depict Gathers in a more or less continuous negotiation with doctors, one where the player sought a lower dosage and the medical professionals scheduled appointments that Gathers did not necessarily keep for follow-up tests. "I knew," he would say weeks later, "if there was any way for me to do well, [the doctors] were going to have to cut back the medication." As these discussions continued, Loyola traveled to Baton Rouge, Louisiana, in early February to play Shaquille O'Neal, Chris Jackson (Mahmoud Abdul-Rauf, as of 1993), Stanley Roberts, and LSU. The Tigers won 148–141 in overtime, as O'Neal fairly rampaged at will against the smaller Lions. The freshman blocked four shots in the first 60 seconds alone, on his way to posting a 20–24–12 points-rebounds-blocks triple-double. Nevertheless, Gathers tallied 48 points, despite giving up at least five inches in height to both O'Neal and Roberts.

Loyola Marymount easily captured the regular-season title in what was now called, as of 1989–90, the West Coast Conference. The conference tournament was scheduled to be held that year on the Lions' home floor, where Westhead's team was bracketed with Gonzaga in the quarterfinals. After LMU won by 37 points, Bulldogs coach Dan Fitzgerald was asked if an early 10–0 run by Loyola had been the game's turning point. "The turning point may have been breakfast," he answered.

Gathers had accounted for 28 of his team's 121 points. "I'm the most doctor-tested man alive," he liked to say. His mother was in town for the tournament, and that Friday, Gathers told a reporter from Channel 2 in Los Angeles, "I feel great. I'm in the best shape of my life. My mom's out here, and I'm looking forward to some good home cooking." Gathers also informed a different reporter that his medication by this point was "almost down to nothing." In the semifinals to be held the following day, Sunday, March 4, 1990, the Lions would face Portland.

The game tipped at 5:00 p.m. Loyola Marymount was already ahead 23–13 in the opening minutes when, on yet another fast break by the Lions, Terrell Lowery delivered the platonic ideal of an alley-oop assist from just across half-court. Gathers was on the receiving end of the pass, and he elevated effortlessly to slam home one of his most thunderous dunks. Even in Westhead's system, plays this spectacular could not happen every minute. This would be what would stand out to the 4,000-plus people who would, inevitably, carry with them for the rest of their lives the memory of having been in Gersten that day: the fact that pandemonium could ever be enveloped and extinguished completely within a matter of seconds by silence.

Trotting back to take his position in the pressing defense, Gathers slapped Lowery's hand in acknowledgment of the assist, and, as he reached midcourt, turned to face Portland's inbound pass. He took two lateral steps to his right. Then he collapsed. Gathers had been unable to make any effort to break his fall, and the impact of a 220-pound man hitting the floor was loud. A spectator later said that even if you hadn't been watching Gathers at that particular moment, everyone heard him fall. Play stopped instantly, and players from both teams, including Lowery and Kimble, instinctively went toward Gathers. He struggled to get up from the floor and was on his hands and knees, attempting to stand. By this time, he was surrounded by medical personnel who were telling him to stay down. Gathers went back down to the floor, on his back, and appeared to lose consciousness. The game clock was stopped with 13:34 remaining in the first half. It was 5:14 p.m.

Gathers's mother and his aunt were both at the game, and they came down out of the stands and stood above the doctors attending to Gathers. One of Portland's players that day was future NBA coach Erik Spoelstra. Decades later, he was still shaken. "The absolute silence in the gym after he fell," he would say, "it's something I'll never forget." After a few minutes, Gathers was lifted onto a stretcher and taken out of the arena as the team physician began cardiopulmonary resuscitation. Lucille Gathers clung to her son's friend, former USC assistant coach David Spencer, who appeared dazed. The public address announcer informed the crowd that the players had gone to their locker rooms for 10 minutes, but 10 minutes became 30. A second announcement was then made that the rest of the game, as well as the evening's second semifinal, which was to have been between San Diego and Pepperdine, would not be played at that time. The crowd filed out silently. Gathers was pronounced dead at Daniel Freeman at 6:55 p.m.

That same evening in Albany, New York, Gathers's friends from

Philadelphia, Doug Overton and Lionel Simmons, were playing for La Salle against Siena in a Metro Atlantic Athletic Conference tournament semifinal. The Explorers had the game put away and led by 16 with 1:20 remaining in the contest when word of Gathers's death reached the sidelines at Knickerbocker Arena. Stunned and distraught, La Salle head coach Speedy Morris reflexively called time-out. As described by a reporter covering the game, Morris then brought his players to the bench and informed them of what he had just learned.

> Junior guard Doug Overton, who seconds earlier had been wildly grinning and waving a "No. 1" finger, suddenly slumped into his chair...
>
> Unsteadily, [Overton] stood up and headed down the corridor that leads to the locker rooms at the Knickerbocker Arena. He was sobbing.
>
> Teammate Lionel Simmons cried in his mother's arms.

The announcers working the game had not yet learned of events at Loyola Marymount, however, and could tell viewers only that "Simmons has suddenly become very emotional, and we don't know why."

WCC commissioner Michael Gilleran announced that night that the rest of the league's tournament had been canceled. "We're just trying to focus on what ought to take precedence," he said, "something more important than winning or losing a ballgame." As the regular-season champions, Loyola Marymount would be awarded the league's automatic bid for the NCAA tournament. The next day, Westhead said his players had not yet made a decision on whether to continue with the season but that he would honor whatever course of action they chose. Kimble was already saying that Gathers would want the team to play in the NCAA tournament, and, indeed, in short order the players confirmed their intention to continue the season. Kimble would further announce that, as a tribute to Gathers, he would shoot his first free throw of each game left-handed.

* * *

A memorial Mass was held at Gersten Pavilion on Tuesday, March 6, at noon, and a member of the Loyola Marymount faculty, the Rev. Tom Higgins, told of once having said to Gathers, "You're the only person I've ever met funnier than I am." Gathers had replied, "Definitely, Father." The harmony of the memorial service, however, soon proved to be in short supply, as questions were raised and fingers were pointed with regard to Gathers's death. On Wednesday of that week, the *Los Angeles Times* anonymously quoted "a cardiologist familiar with the case" who said Gathers had been told to stop playing basketball after the fainting episode in December. "We told Hank that if he wanted to live the best he shouldn't exercise," the cardiologist said. "Hank Gathers was going to play basketball. It didn't matter what some doctor told him." Yet Loyola swiftly revealed the existence of a letter signed by a Los Angeles internist on December 21, 1989, which had released Gathers for "full participation" in seven to 10 days.

On Selection Sunday, the entire Loyola Marymount team was on a flight en route to Philadelphia to attend Gathers's funeral. When word circulated through the plane that the Lions had received a No. 11 seed and would play New Mexico State, Westhead and the players were surprised at how low they were seeded. On the plus side, LMU would be playing in Long Beach, close to home. Any home area advantage would be welcome, for the Aggies were a tough opponent; Neil McCarthy's team was 26–4, with a win over UNLV to its credit. Loyola started the game by outscoring NMSU 11–1, but an overeager Kimble picked up his fourth foul with 4:45 remaining in the first half. Westhead nevertheless left his star in the game, triggering boos of disbelief from Loyola fans and causing one New Mexico State player to tell Kimble his coach must be crazy. Asked about leaving Kimble in the game, the coach would explain, "I firmly believe if you have your best player sitting on the bench, he's of no value."

Kimble never did pick up a fifth foul. When he was fouled in the act of shooting for the first time with 14:46 left in the game, Kimble stepped to the line. The Lions had a 64–50 lead. He bounced the ball six times with his left hand, and then, instead of a left-handed version of a normal free-throw motion, he executed more of a one-handed push shot. Once the ball had found the bottom of the net, the crowd in Long Beach erupted loudly and joyously; Kimble had kept the promise he'd made in Gathers's honor. The second, right-handed, free throw also went in, part of the 33 points Kimble would accumulate in the second half alone and the 45 he would score in the game. In the aftermath of LMU's 111–92 victory, one in which the Aggies committed 24 turnovers, Coach McCarthy said Loyola "went after the ball like a one-eyed dog in a butcher shop." Kimble had also pulled down a career-high 18 rebounds. "You can just call me Baby Hank," he told reporters.

Defending national champion Michigan no longer had top scorer Glen Rice, but the Wolverines still had four of their five leading scorers from the previous year. Steve Fisher's team was the No. 3 seed, and the coach said he hoped the game in the round of 32 against LMU would not be "in the 130 to 140 [point] range. We have to make sure fatigue is not an opponent." In a way, Fisher's hope was realized. Instead of being in the 130 to 140 range, Loyola Marymount's point total was 149 in a 34-point win. As for fatigue, after the game, UM's Terry Mills would describe what he and Loy Vaught had experienced: "[Loyola] kept Loy and myself running up and down the court constantly. It seemed like when we were at half-court, [Jeff] Fryer was shooting a three-pointer."

It was a game in which the NCAA tournament record book was rewritten for decades to come. The previous record for most points in a tournament game was 127, a standard set, appropriately enough, by Paul Westhead's Saint Joseph's team in the 1961 third-place game that went to four overtimes. Fryer set a tournament record by converting 11 three-pointers on his way to 41 points. In addition, Loyola as a team set a tournament record by making 21 shots from beyond the arc.

After scoring 84 points in the second half against Michigan, the Lions put just 22 on the board in the first half of their regional semifinal against Alabama in Oakland. The Crimson Tide took the 45-second clock down under 10 at every opportunity and even passed up precisely the 3-on-1 opportunities that Westhead said no player could resist. Head coach Wimp Sanderson succeeded in forcing LMU out of its preferred style, and, no less, offered a token of respect by slowing Robert Horry and the rest of his major-conference team to a crawl against a No. 11 seed from the WCC. Yet Loyola won the 62–60 rock fight in which it did not shoot well at all, by pounding the offensive glass and forcing Alabama into 24 turnovers.

Loyola Marymount became the first team from its league to reach the Elite Eight since San Francisco did so in 1957. Unfortunately for the Lions, however, their iconic 1989–90 season was fated to both begin and end with a loss to UNLV. For once, LMU gave the ball away about as many times (23) as the opponent (24). When the Runnin' Rebels weren't committing turnovers, they were getting open looks at the rim and converting on 65 percent of their two-point attempts. The result was a 131–101 win for Jerry Tarkanian's team.

Kimble had put 42 points on the board but required 32 shots to so. Still, in this, the final game of his team's historic run, he received not one but two standing ovations from the entire crowd, including fans of the Rebels. The first came when he sank his left-handed free throw. The second occurred when Westhead took his senior out of the game with 1:03 remaining. Westhead said the three wins that got his team this far were "proof" of the unexplainable. The victories had been "examples of the human spirit rising above occasions," he believed. "But we're not angels, and we can't always rise above."

Hank Gathers died due to hypertrophic cardiomyopathy, the same heart disorder that would prove fatal for the Boston Celtics' Reggie Lewis in 1993.

Gathers's family filed a lawsuit, which, in the scheme of things, was perhaps to be expected. What was seen as more surprising was that the suit was announced by the family's attorney, Bruce Fagel, at a crowded news conference just five days after Gathers's death and, more jarringly, three days before the funeral. "People were shocked," a Loyola Marymount official said a year later of the timing. In addition, Gathers was a father, and the child's mother filed her own suit. Tensions also reportedly rose briefly between the Gathers family and Bo Kimble, who was the No. 8 overall pick in the 1990 NBA draft and signed a $7.5 million contract with the Los Angeles Clippers.

When Fagel held another press conference in January 1991 and charged that Paul Westhead was personally responsible for Gathers's death, Westhead, who by this time was coach of the Denver Nuggets, countersued for defamation of character. The headlines that came after the run to the 1990 Elite Eight were no longer particularly uplifting or transcendent. No one was invoking the human spirit anymore.

Time softened these edges, at least in the public's memory of the 1990 tournament run. Loyola Marymount unveiled a statue of Hank Gathers outside Gersten Pavilion in February 2020, on the 30th anniversary of that season. Had the ceremony been held even two or three weeks later, it would have run afoul of the challenges and restrictions attendant to a global pandemic. Timing has always been everything in relation to the legend of LMU.

The records left behind by that season and by that era are in the literal sense incredible, meaning that the numbers are not credible, not to be believed. Yet they are true. Loyola Marymount averaged 122.4 points a game in 1989–90, and, of course, that number was actually lowered when the Lions scored 62 and 101 points in their final two outings. Kimble led the nation in scoring as a senior at 35 a game. The team's feats in individual games were no less remarkable. The 40-minute contest between Loyola and Michigan in the 1990 round of 32 consisted of 106 possessions, approximately twice the amount of basketball that had been furnished by the slowest yet recurrent NCAA tournament slugfests of the mid-1980s. Throughout the era, games against United States International University were the Lions' go-to source for access to the record book. The year after Westhead and Kimble departed, new head coach Jay Hillock and new leading scorer Terrell Lowery would carry on the legacy. Loyola would put up 186 points in a single game against USIU (which would merge with another institution and be known as Alliant International as of 2001).

It's tempting to classify Loyola Marymount's season scoring average of 122.4 as one of the proverbial records that will never be broken. The only team in the 21st century to average more than 100 points was Virginia Military Institute in 2007, a season in which the Keydets' mean figure clocked in at 100.7. Yet points per basketball game is a curious quantity, a performance measure that captures style and preference as much as it does achievement. Westhead's style and preference in 1990 were what has come to be known as "the system," and a team that wants to set scoring records would be well-advised to use the system, or something like it. Kimble, in his 50s, would reportedly seek head coaching jobs at the collegiate level so that he could help teams do just that. Nevertheless, the system remains far more celebrated and chronicled than used. Westhead himself termed it "doomed to fail," and his own coaching record includes its fair share of lows to go along with a trio of highs: the Lakers in 1980, LMU in 1990, and the WNBA title Westhead won as head coach of the Phoenix Mercury in 2007.

The system thrived with two players the caliber of Gathers and Kimble, and with a perimeter shooter as accurate and prolific as Fryer. Perhaps similar talents could be assembled again, and a remarkably entertaining form of the game could emerge anew. The system does possess the virtue of stripping the game to its purest player-centered form. College basketball, with its two head coaches and three officials, presents us with a floor populated by five adults and 10 students. Too often it's the former that interfere and prevail. If nothing else, the system liberated the 10 players.

"When I watch a game on television," Westhead said during that indelible 1989–90 season, "and see a team meandering up the floor on offense, then meandering down on defense, it's only playing half the game. I think you should play the full game. Time is precious."

16.

Gonzaga and Mystery

onzaga made its NCAA tournament debut after 37 years of Division I competition on March 16, 1995. The opportunity came as a shock.

It was supposed to be a rebuilding year for the Jesuits in Spokane after the previous team had recorded arguably the best season in the Bulldogs' history. That 1994 group had won the regular-season title in the West Coast Conference and even defeated Stanford at the NIT. The team also featured four seniors, and, sure enough, Dan Fitzgerald's Zags opened WCC play at 0–6 the following season. Nevertheless, Gonzaga regrouped and won 10 of its last 11 games. The bracket at the 1995 WCC tournament was busted when, shockingly, future NBA great Steve Nash and regular-season champion Santa Clara lost in the quarterfinals on the Broncos' home floor to last-place Loyola Marymount. With an open path, John Rillie and the Bulldogs captured the automatic bid. Rillie scored 96 points in three WCC tournament games, breaking a record previously held by Hank Gathers. The Zags were awarded a No. 14 seed in the NCAA tournament, and bracketed with Maryland in Salt Lake City.

"Never heard of them," the Terrapins' star, Joe Smith, said when asked about Gonzaga University. Smith's teammate Duane Simpkins fared better on the impromptu quiz administered by the press in Salt Lake: "As much as I know about them is that John Stockton played for them." A discussion then ensued on the correct pronunciation of "Gonzaga," a topic the Terps and some members of the press found innocent enough but one that a few Zags regarded as tedious if not patronizing. Fitzgerald in particular appeared fatigued by the "What's a Gonzaga?" brand of coverage. "We now have indoor plumbing in our locker rooms," the coach told a writer that week. Gonzaga lost to Maryland by 24.

Fitzgerald had recruited Stockton and coached him as a freshman at GU in 1980–81 before reassigning himself solely to his duties as athletic director and turning the team over to Jay Hillock for four seasons. Stockton soon became a legend to anyone paying attention. He led what was then called the West Coast Athletic Conference in points, assists, and steals in 1984, and did so while shooting 58 percent from the field. Stockton even made it to the last round of tryouts for that year's Olympic team. While he ultimately wasn't selected by US coach Bob Knight, Stockton could take solace in the fact that he was a 6-foot-1 guard from the WCAC who'd been cut along with the likes of Charles Barkley. When Utah drafted Stockton that summer with the No. 16 pick, one Jazz scout offered the ultimate accolade for point guards from Catholic programs by comparing Stockton to Dick McGuire. In 1985, Fitzgerald returned to the sidelines as head coach while continuing to serve as athletic director. He hired Dan Monson, son of then Oregon coach Don Monson, as an assistant in 1988, and Mark Few joined the program as a graduate assistant the following year.

The program was already on the upswing under Fitzgerald, and the win in the 1994 NIT against Stanford at Maples Pavilion was especially sweet both for Gonzaga and for leading scorer Jeff Brown. Before the 6-foot-9 senior was named West Coast Conference player of the year, he had been a high school junior attending a Stanford summer camp with hopes of being recruited by the Cardinal. Those hopes went unrealized, but after Brown scored 27 in Palo Alto that day for the Bulldogs, Stanford head coach Mike Montgomery conceded, "In retrospect, we probably made a mistake."

Few was recruiting Portland native Matt Santangelo at the time, and the assistant coach was now able to tell the young man, "You can go to Stanford, but we just beat Stanford." Monson would take over as head coach in 1997, inheriting from Fitzgerald the nucleus that would ignite the program's extraordinary run of success. Players like Santangelo, Richie Frahm, Jeremy Eaton, and Axel Dench would one day be celebrated as having been in on the ground floor, but they could also collectively harken back to a little-noticed 15–12 season under Fitzgerald in 1996–97.

Monson led his first team to a regular-season WCC title and one win at the 1998 NIT. Scoring that first season increased significantly as the Bulldogs devoted a third of their shot attempts to tries from behind the three-point line. The following year, it was the defense's turn to improve: Eaton, at 6 foot 11, returned from a redshirt season and teamed with 6-foot-8 Casey Calvary to limit opponents to 44 percent shooting on their two-point attempts. The Zags captured their second consecutive regular-season league title, and this time they breezed through the conference tournament. It marked the first time Gonzaga had ever captured both WCC regular-season and tournament championships in the same season.

The NCAA gave the Bulldogs a No. 10 seed and a pairing in Seattle against Minnesota. Monson was pleased with all of the above. "Our seeding [is] more than fair," he said after the 1999 selection show. "A No. 10 seed means you're a top 40 team in America. Obviously, we think we're a little better than that, but we'll trade that in for where we're playing." The NCAA men's basketball committee had discussed whether putting Gonzaga in Seattle constituted an unfair advantage but decided that a venue five hours away from campus by car conferred no such benefit.

The day before the game, the St. Paul *Pioneer Press* reported that over the course of five years, at least 20 University of Minnesota basketball players, including four members of the 1998–99 team, had had their classwork completed for them by a staff member in the university's academic counseling office. The four current players were suspended, including the team's second-leading scorer, Kevin Clark. The next day, the Bulldogs defeated the Golden Gophers 75–63 on the strength of 26 points and five three-pointers by Frahm. Minnesota then announced that it would engage an outside firm to investigate the allegations leveled against the basketball program.

The Zags would be up against "West Coast basketball royalty" in the round of 32. Stanford was returning all five starters from a lineup that reached the 1998 Final Four. Monson's team made the most of the opportunity. Stanford held a 1–0 lead for 11 seconds in the early going but was never ahead again. The Bulldogs scored a landmark 82–74 victory, one in which the 5-foot-8 Quentin Hall was credited with eight rebounds. GU's upset win triggered euphoria at KeyArena. Frank Burgess, a consensus second-team All-American with the Zags in 1961, had been pacing up and down his section's steps nervously before he was finally able to release that tension joyously. "People always talk about Gonzaga and Spokane like they're the end of the line," yelled Burgess, by then a federal judge. "They know better now."

Gonzaga encountered more difficulties against No. 6 seed Florida in Phoenix than it had experienced against the No. 2 seed Cardinal in Seattle. This was the first Gators team Billy Donovan had taken to the NCAA tournament, and the 33-year-old coach very nearly made the Elite Eight. Despite five steals from Hall, the Bulldogs were down to their last gasp with 15 seconds remaining in the contest when UF inbounded the ball under the Zags' basket with a one-point lead. But the Gators' Brent Wright was called for traveling and, with 4.4 seconds left, Calvary rebounded a Hall miss and put it in the basket for a 73–72 Zags win. Gus Johnson, calling the game for CBS, was ready with an iconic shout: "The slipper still fits!" Gonzaga had equaled Loyola Marymount's run to a regional final from out of the WCC nine years earlier.

Like the Lions, however, the Zags would lose to the eventual national champion one step short of the Final Four. Connecticut limited Santangelo and Frahm to 3-of-20 shooting, but the Bulldogs still somehow fought to within 63–62 on an acrobatic Hall three-pointer with 35 seconds remaining. In an era when the shot clock was also 35 seconds, Gonzaga started fouling. The Huskies made all four free throws and survived 67–62.

Even before tip-off, Dan Monson had already been rumored to be the top candidate for a number of other coaching jobs, leading Calvary to quip, "If he does leave, he better hope he doesn't play us." Four months after the loss to UConn, Monson was introduced as the new head coach to replace Clem Haskins at scandal-wracked Minnesota. Within 48 hours of the Gophers' announcement, Mark Few was named as Monson's successor.

There weren't many features being written in the 1990s about why Catholic schools were so good at college basketball. The genre that had flowered so unmistakably in the 1980s would rise again in 2016 and, especially, 2018. By contrast, in the 1990s, there were zero Final Four appearances recorded by Catholic programs. Naturally, there were some near misses.

The same year Gonzaga made its celebrated run to the regional finals, St. John's reached the Elite Eight in its first season under Mike Jarvis. After stops at Boston University and George Washington, Jarvis had been hired in 1998 to succeed Fran Fraschilla, and the Red Storm were led that first season by Bootsy Thornton, Ron Artest, Erick Barkley, and Lavor Postell. (Artest would become Metta World Peace between 2011 and 2020, and then Metta Sandiford-Artest as of 2020.) St. John's earned a No. 3 seed in the 1999 field of 64 and used a zone defense in the second round to dismantle Bob Knight's penultimate Indiana team by 25. In the Sweet 16 in Knoxville, Tennessee, the Johnnies prevailed 76–62 against No. 2 seed Maryland, before losing by three to Scoonie Penn, Michael Redd, and Ohio State. The program's run to the Elite Eight bookended an identical showing at the beginning of the decade, when a St. John's team led by Malik Sealy did succeed in defeating top seed Ohio State only to fall by 17 to Christian Laettner and eventual champion Duke in a 1991 regional final played at the Pontiac Silverdome. Seton Hall also advanced to the Elite Eight that March, but Terry Dehere, Anthony Avent, and their teammates lost by 12 to undefeated UNLV at the Kingdome in Seattle.

In a glass-half-full view, the 1990s were at least not lacking for Big East representation in the Elite Eight. John Thompson made his final appearance in a regional final in 1996. Allen Iverson was a sophomore averaging 25 a game that year, but Georgetown was no match for Marcus Camby and UMass in what became a 24-point blowout. Coach Pete Gillen would lead Providence as far as the 1997 Elite Eight, where God Shammgod, Jamel Thomas, Derrick Brown, and Austin Croshere played eventual champion Arizona to a 45th minute of basketball before falling 96–92. Yet there was one Big East program for which a regional final represented not a near miss after previous Final Fours or even national championships but rather the furthest point of advance in the team's history.

That program was Boston College, which had reached its first regional final under head coach Bob Cousy way back in 1967. An Eagles team led by John Bagley equaled that showing in 1982, and head coach Tom Davis parlayed the run into a move to Stanford that very spring. After a similarly purposeful tenure served by Gary Williams (four seasons and a move to Ohio State), BC hired Jim O'Brien in 1986. Unlike his two immediate predecessors, O'Brien stuck around a while, and by his eighth season this persistence paid dividends. Bill Curley and Howard Eisley were seniors, and Boston College placed a respectable third in the Big East race. That was sufficient to earn the Eagles one of those challenging No. 9 seeds that tends to presage a first-weekend exit in the NCAA tournament. Instead, BC shocked top seed and defending national champion North Carolina 75–72 in the 1994 round of 32, a feat termed in real time "without question the most significant basketball game in the history of BC." A desperation three-point attempt by UNC's Rasheed Wallace was off the mark, and for good measure the Eagles went on to defeat Indiana before No. 3 seed Florida brought the run to an end.

After 11 seasons, O'Brien ultimately did follow the precedent set by Williams and departed for Ohio State in 1997. O'Brien's successor was Al Skinner, who may have had the best Boston College team of all. Opinions will differ, but the categories in play are fairly straightforward. Where the 1994 team was a third-place Big East finisher that outperformed expectations in the postseason, Skinner's 2001 group was both a regular-season and conference tournament champion that ran up against a three-point upset in the round of 32. The No. 3 seed that Troy Bell and his teammates earned that year marks the best placement a BC team has ever been awarded in a bracket, but USC traveled 3,000 miles to end the Eagles' season 74–71 at Nassau Coliseum.

By the time Boston College was eliminated from the 2001 bracket, Gonzaga was appearing in its third consecutive Sweet 16. Few had inherited from Monson a nucleus that included Frahm, Santangelo, and Calvary, and the Bulldogs had earned the unusual distinction of making their first-ever appearance in the AP poll as a preseason selection for the 1999–2000 top 25. However, the warm feelings from the pollsters didn't last. A 5–5 month of December 1999, including neutral-floor losses to Cincinnati, Temple, Cal, Oregon, and Colorado, knocked the Zags out of the polls for good that season. No matter. In both the 2000 and 2001 tournaments, Gonzaga reached the regional semifinals as a double-digit seed, losing first to Purdue and then to Michigan State. The Bulldogs had cemented their status as both perpetual underdogs and as tournament wizards. When Selection Sunday 2002 arrived, however, the "underdog" portion of the image appeared to be out-of-date.

The "founding" generation of players was now gone, replaced by Washington transfer Dan Dickau, as well as Zach Gourde, Cory Violette, Blake Stepp, and freshman Ronny Turiaf. Dickau was a consensus first-team All-American, Turiaf (from France) heralded the program's commitment to recruiting internationally, and Gonzaga was 29–3 and ranked No. 6 in the nation. Expecting a seed to match, the Bulldogs hosted 1,200 fans in a hotel ballroom to watch the selection show. Unfortunately for the Zags, hosting a public event in anticipation of a WCC program receiving a great seed at a time when the rating percentage index still reigned supreme was incautious. When the bracket was revealed, Few and the players in the front row learned they had, in fact, been seeded No. 6. "The wind got sucked out of the whole place," athletic director Mike Roth admitted. "I think it stunned everybody in here, including myself." The stunned reactions were just getting started: Wyoming beat Gonzaga 73–66 in Albuquerque, despite 26 points from Dickau. The Cowboys formed a wall around the basket and blocked no fewer than 12 GU shots. Dickau required fully 24 attempts to get his points in the final game of his college career.

Not only was such a result off-script based on Gonzaga's last three tournaments, fans of the Bulldogs were bereft because they'd so eagerly awaited a shot at the Arizona Wildcats in the round of 32. As chance would have it, that opportunity came the following year, when Dickau was long gone and the Zags had fallen back to a No. 9 seed. Meanwhile, the 26–3 Wildcats were seeded on the top line in the West and expected to reach the Final Four. The result was a two-overtime classic, one in which Arizona escaped 96–95 after Stepp's attempt at a game-winning bank shot bounced off the rim and into the hands of UA's Luke Walton. Stepp's missed leaner from the left block in the 50th minute was immortalized in one of the better college basketball photos of all time. John W. McDonough's spectacular double-page spread in *Sports Illustrated* documented the reaction of every player on the floor, most of the GU bench, and several dozen transfixed spectators in Salt Lake City. The Bulldogs were out, but, even as they were being photographed and eliminated, the good news for aficionados of Jesuit hoops in March 2003 was that another program was still in the hunt.

After longtime assistant Hank Raymonds served for six seasons as Al McGuire's successor at Marquette, another McGuire assistant, Rick Majerus, had taken the helm in Milwaukee. Majerus stayed for three years before taking a job as an assistant with the Milwaukee Bucks, at which time Bob Dukiet had assumed control at MU. A pattern was being established, it seemed: Dukiet coached for three years, Kevin O'Neill for five, then Mike Deane for five more. The post-McGuire era at that point encompassed 22 seasons and two appearances in the Sweet 16 (1979 and 1994). No less an observer than O'Neill himself had reviewed this sequence and remarked: "Al McGuire was the best thing and the worst thing to happen to Marquette University. He was the best for the university because he brought a national championship here, but he was the worst thing for the coaches who had to follow him."

In 1999, Marquette hired Tom Crean. Fresh from his role as Tom Izzo's assistant at Michigan State, the 33-year-old Crean in his first season put a 15–14 NIT team on the floor while scoring a far more momentous triumph off it. Dwyane Wade was lightly recruited out of Chicago initially, due to his size and performance. Even when those metrics improved markedly in his last two seasons at Richards High School in Oak Lawn, academic concerns limited his list of suitors. But Crean was willing to take a chance on him. So, too, was DePaul, and the Blue Demons enlisted the help of DePaul alum Quentin Richardson in recruiting Wade. In the end, however, Wade chose Marquette and signed along with his Chicagoland friend Odartey Blankson.

Unlike his classmate, Wade had to sit out his freshman year as a partial qualifier. When he made his debut as a sophomore in 2001–02, Wade quickly emerged as the leading scorer on a team where Travis Diener was a freshman. The Golden Eagles reached their first NCAA tournament of the Crean era that season, and Wade cemented his status not only as a featured scorer but as a tenacious all-around player. At a listed height of 6 foot 4 Wade led MU in blocked shots in both seasons that he played under Crean. He also ranked among the top 60 players in the nation in steal rate both as a sophomore and as a junior.

Entering Wade's junior season, Marquette was ranked in the top 20 in the preseason for the first time in two decades. The Golden Eagles proceeded to capture an outright Conference USA title in early March 2003, at a time when the league still featured the likes of Louisville, Cincinnati, and John Calipari–era Memphis. All of the above teams made the 2003 NCAA tournament, but the collegiate portion of the D-Wade legend was almost extinguished in the round of 32. No. 3 seed Marquette blew a 10-point halftime lead, and Missouri took Crean's men to overtime before freshman Steve Novak nailed three three-pointers in the extra session to deliver a 101–92 victory. After squandering another lead (up 11 with five minutes left) yet recording a three-point win against No. 2 seed Pittsburgh, MU was confronted with No. 1 seed Kentucky in Minneapolis. Tubby Smith's Wildcats were 34–3 and ranked No. 1 in the nation. They had posted a 16–0 record in an SEC that featured five other NCAA tournament teams besides UK. Yet they were more or less destroyed 83–69 by Dwyane Wade personally. In one of the greatest individual performances in regional finals history, Wade recorded a 29–11–11 points-assists-rebounds triple-double that, characteristically, also included four blocks.

Marquette's first Final Four since 1977 ended quickly and brutally with a 94–61 loss to Kansas in New Orleans, but Wade's explosion against Kentucky had shown the NBA everything it needed to see. He was selected with the No. 5 pick in an extraordinarily talented 2003 draft, which also included LeBron James, Carmelo Anthony, and Chris Bosh.

With Wade setting a shining example, these years were a time of plenty for individual talent at Catholic programs. Joining Wade on the All-American first team in 2003 was Xavier's David West, a three-time Atlantic 10 player of the year who'd averaged a 17–10 double-double during four seasons that spanned the Skip Prosser and Thad Matta eras. West's senior year brought in its wake a top-10 ranking and a No. 3 seed for the Musketeers, only to end against defending national champion Maryland in the 2003 round of 32. The following year, Providence's Ryan Gomes also earned first-team All-American honors as a 6-foot-7 junior who led the Friars to their highest AP ranking since the Dave Gavitt era. Among all the noteworthy individual seasons recorded at Catholic programs from 2003 to 2005, however, the one Wooden Award winner was Jameer Nelson at Saint Joseph's in 2004.

During Nelson's career, the Hawks made three NCAA tournaments in four seasons for the first time since Mike Bantom was playing for Jack McKinney in the early 1970s. Nelson was a scoring point guard who had debuted by averaging nearly seven assists as a skilled 6-foot-0 freshman. Head coach Phil Martelli then brought in Delonte West, and St. Joe's improved each season as the two future NBA players matured. By 2003–04, the Hawks were ranked No. 17 in the preseason, a status Martelli's team more than justified by proceeding to win its first 27 games. On the other hand, the first loss was nothing if not emphatic. St. Joe's had just been named No. 1 in the AP poll for the first time all season when the team lost to Xavier by 20 in the first game of the 2004 Atlantic 10 tournament. What would the men's basketball committee do with a 27–1 team coming off a 20-point loss to an unranked opponent?

The answer to this question turned out to be that the committee would give that team the No. 1 seed in the East region. St. Joe's was the last No. 1 seed to be named on the selection show, after Stanford, Kentucky, and Duke had already been revealed. CBS's Billy Packer famously took issue with the committee's decision, saying, "I don't agree with St. Joe's being a No. 1 team." Naming first one and then several alternative recipients for that last No. 1 seed, Packer continued: "I think that without question Oklahoma State deserved to be in that No. 1 seed position...I don't believe St. Joe's can go and beat Oklahoma State. I don't think that they can go and beat a club like Texas and a club like Pitt and a club like Connecticut."

At that very moment in Philadelphia, Martelli, his players, and a throng of supporters had gathered in Alumni Memorial Fieldhouse to watch as the brackets were announced. No sooner had Packer finished than Martelli yelled out to the crowd, "Being perfectly blunt, Billy Packer can kiss my ass." When the selection show had ended, Martelli did a spot on ESPN and was asked to respond to an ESPN.com poll in which 88 percent of respondents agreed with Packer that St. Joe's would not reach the Final Four. "You know what?" Martelli replied. "You know what the problem is? Most of the people in Philadelphia don't know how to use a computer, so they couldn't vote."

The seeding suspense wasn't restricted to St. Joe's that evening. Gonzaga was riding a 21-game win streak, and Few's Bulldogs were 27–2 overall after running the table in WCC play for the first time in school history. The Zags wondered whether they would receive a lower seed than expected yet again, but this time, as they watched the show at Few's house, they breathed a sigh of relief. Gonzaga was given a No. 2 seed and would play its first two games in Seattle. Unfortunately for GU, the first two games were the only two games: Few's team was rocked 91–72 in the round of 32 by No. 10 seed Nevada. Nick Fazekas and the Wolf Pack were already ahead by 20 in the game's first 15 minutes, and Stepp and Violette had their careers ended then and there. Turiaf, who had watched all but four minutes of the first half sitting with two fouls, would be back for one more season.

Saint Joseph's fared better than Gonzaga, surviving consecutive tough games against Texas Tech and Chris Paul and Wake Forest to face Oklahoma State in the regional final at the Meadowlands. The two teams entered the game with a combined record of 60–4. All season long, the Hawks had buried opponents with a perimeter-oriented attack that both attempted and converted a high number of three-pointers while taking outstanding care of the ball. On this day, however, three-point specialist Pat Carroll was 3-of-11 from beyond the arc and, meanwhile, St. Joe's was being gashed on the interior by OSU's Joey Graham and Tony Allen. The Hawks' usual superiority in turnovers was therefore more crucial than ever, and this time that advantage meant the game went down to the wire. In fact, the last 83 seconds of basketball unfolded without interruption even by a foul, much less a time-out.

Carroll drained his third three-pointer from the top of the key with 29.9 seconds left, to give the Hawks a two-point lead. John Lucas answered fearlessly for the Cowboys with his own three from the left side with 6.9 seconds on the clock. Finally, Nelson brought the ball down the floor and got an open look, but it was a step-back jumper from 18 feet. The shot was well short, and Oklahoma State advanced to the Final Four with a 64–62 victory. Jameer Nelson's Wooden Award–winning season ushered him into the 2004 NBA draft, where he would be selected with the No. 20 pick. The next time a national player of the year candidate came from a Jesuit program, it would be Gonzaga's turn.

Adam Morrison was a freshman on that 2003–04 Gonzaga team that earned by far the highest seed in program history to that time. He had played his high school ball just a few miles from the GU campus at Mead, and legend had it that when Mark Few scouted him for the first time, the coach wasn't impressed. Morrison had an odd and not terribly athletic gait and appeared to be a gunner if not a chucker.

Few was restating these objections to his assistant coach, Leon Rice, over the phone at halftime when Rice sensibly asked how many points Morrison had scored so far. The answer was 30, and Few stayed for the second half. Still, at the beginning of Morrison's first year at GU, he'd been merely one of "the three freshmen, Sean Mallon, Adam Morrison, and Derek Raivio," in the local press's season preview. He turned out to be a mild surprise that season for Few as a scorer off the bench, one who averaged less than 21 minutes but was second only to Turiaf in terms of points per 40 minutes.

He became a starter as a sophomore and excelled in sheer points per game. At this stage of his career, however, it was telling that Morrison was occasionally praised as an outstanding "midrange" scorer. This was a tacit euphemism for someone who was not yet a consistent three-point threat, and in 2004–05, the one season that Morrison and Turiaf played together as starters ended with the No. 3 seed Bulldogs falling by two points in the round of 32 to Texas Tech in Tucson. Morrison was 1 of 6 from beyond the arc in that game and required 22 shots to record his game-high 25 points. Yet he would emerge as a much more complete threat on offense the next year, in his junior season, and the change would be unmistakable as early as the 2005 Maui Invitational in November. Gonzaga recorded a memorable 109–106 win over Michigan State in three overtimes at the Lahaina Civic Center, a game in which Morrison scored 43 points. Less than two weeks later, he recorded the same number of points, this time in a 40-minute 99–95 loss at Washington.

Morrison's combination of voluminous yet accurate shooting along with hair recurrently described as "floppy" meant that there would be comparisons to Pete Maravich. The Zags were winning games and, indeed, the program would again earn a No. 3 seed in the 2006 NCAA tournament, but at this moment in time Gonzaga was not stopping anyone on defense. Morrison himself sported an IF IT WASN'T FOR OFFENSE, I'D PLAY DEFENSE T-shirt. While the Bulldogs defense had been very good as recently as 2004, this was no longer the case. Instead, the Zags now won with an outstanding offense alone, and it did make for entertaining games. In the second half of a win at Loyola Marymount, Morrison went on a personal rampage during which he put up 37 points and knocked down eight three-pointers. He was vying with Duke's J. J. Redick for the national scoring lead and for various player of the year honors. In the end, Redick would win both the Wooden and Naismith awards, while the two players would share the Oscar Robertson Trophy, bestowed by the US Basketball Writers Association. The USBWA's award ceremony was a bit awkward that year, in fact, because only one trophy had been ordered.

Morrison and Redick had both been eliminated from the 2006 NCAA tournament by the time they negotiated with each other for possession of a single trophy. Indeed, both ended their tournament runs and college careers on the same night, and both players were seen crying. Top seed Duke was shut down by Tyrus Thomas and the defense of LSU. Then, in Oakland, Gonzaga blew a nine-point lead with less than four minutes remaining against UCLA. The Bulldogs were still clinging to a one-point advantage when they inbounded the ball under the Bruins' basket with 19.7 seconds left. UCLA's Jordan Farmar then stripped the Zags' J. P. Batista, took three quick dribbles, and fed Luc Richard Mbah a Moute for the go-ahead score. Raivio received the ensuing inbounds pass and rushed the ball upcourt, only to have it tapped into a tie-up that went UCLA's way on the alternating possession arrow.

This is when Morrison wept, but there were still 2.6 seconds left. The Bruins' Arron Afflalo made only the second of two free throws, and GU's David Pendergraft then ran the baseline and was able to deliver a nice baseball pass, but Batista missed what would have been a tough game-tying shot at the buzzer. Morrison was selected with the No. 3 pick in the draft that summer, only to be branded as a pro bust in short order. There wasn't anything categorically far-fetched about spending a lottery pick on a 6-foot-8 scorer who'd converted 43 percent of his threes at a high volume while also drawing fouls and making shots inside the arc. Nevertheless, it fell to Morrison to serve as one more reminder that American-style sports drafts can be humbling for the people doing the drafting.

Gonzaga soon returned to its good defensive ways, but the Bulldogs were being typecast in these years as West Coast Conference lions that annually turned into NCAA tournament lambs. The perception was born of the fact that after Coach Monson and Frahm, Santangelo, and Calvary had so brazenly stormed to the 1999 Elite Eight, Coach Few and his players were unable to duplicate that feat over the next 15 years. Sweet 16s also grew scarce, with the agonizing 2006 UCLA game being the program's only advance to the second weekend between 2002 and 2009. Then again, Gonzaga was, remarkably, in the NCAA tournament every March without fail.

While appearing in the NCAA tournament every year marked an extraordinary turn of long-term events for GU, doing so for any program exposes its fans to single-elimination heartbreak. It was Gonzaga, for example, that drew the short end of the stick and was bracketed to play Stephen Curry and Davidson in the 2008 round of 64. The Wildcats went all the way to the Elite Eight, while for a second year in a row the Bulldogs went home after 40 minutes. A 2009 team featuring Josh Heytvelt, Jeremy Pargo, Austin Daye, and Matt Bouldin then grabbed a No. 4 seed only to run into eventual champion North Carolina in the regional semifinal. Over the ensuing three seasons, rotations featuring Robert Sacre and Elias Harris won 79 games and continued the NCAA tournament streak.

The last of those three seasons, however, also marked something of a breakthrough by the Zags' Lasallian rivals at Saint Mary's. In 2012, Matthew Dellavedova and the Gaels captured both the WCC regular-season and tournament titles. For the first time since 1997, Gonzaga didn't hang either banner in Spokane. Was one to two NCAA tournament wins annually both an achievement and a ceiling?

On March 4, 2013, Gonzaga was named the No. 1 team in the AP poll for the first time in the program's history. Elias Harris, Kelly Olynyk, Kevin Pangos, Gary Bell, and Mike Hart were 29–2 and had just run the table in WCC play. The Bulldogs would roll through the conference tournament and earn their first-ever No. 1 seed in the NCAA field.

Then No. 16 seed Southern played the Zags into the 40th minute before losing by just six, and Few's team was eliminated 76–70 in the round of 32 by Fred VanVleet and Wichita State. The Shockers made a season-high 14 three-pointers in Salt Lake City, five of which came during a string of eight straight scoring possessions in the game's final seven minutes. The loss marked the fourth straight year Gonzaga was sent home in the second round.

VanVleet would be scoring in double figures for an NBA world champion by 2019, making WSU one unusual No. 9 seed. Just the same, the close call against the No. 16 seed in the first game followed by defeat in the second cemented the skepticism that Gonzaga would face nationally going forward. Absent a deep run in the NCAA tournament at some point, that skepticism would continue, no matter how glittering the Bulldogs' regular-season record might be. The presumption that there had to be something ersatz about any achievements the Zags recorded prior to mid-March was hardly universal, but it was unmistakably persistent. And that presumption had to make what transpired in the 2015 and, especially, 2017 NCAA tournaments all the sweeter for the Bulldogs.

Gonzaga reached the Elite Eight in 2015, and it was recognized even by players born in the 1990s, much less by Few, as a boundary that had been crossed. As Pangos put it, "Now if people ask about the Elite Eight team, it's like, 'Which one?'" By this time, the rotation featured Kentucky transfer Kyle Wiltjer, Pangos, Byron Wesley, Bell, and a pair of big bodies in the paint, Przemek Karnowski and Domantas Sabonis. The run ended in the regional final against eventual champion Duke, but an even better outcome was still to come for the Bulldogs. The following year was dedicated to rebuilding, which, in Gonzaga terms, now meant sharing the regular-season WCC title with Saint Mary's, winning the automatic bid, and advancing to the Sweet 16.

To be sure, the rebuilding didn't necessarily result in a team recognized from the start of the next season as a national championship contender. In the 2016–17 preseason, the Zags were ranked No. 14, no better than in a normal year and worse, actually, than the previous preseason. But the ranking turned out to underestimate this particular roster: Karnowski, Zach Collins, Nigel Williams-Goss, Jordan Mathews, Johnathan Williams, Josh Perkins, Killian Tillie, and Silas Melson.

In a sequence similar to that charted by Saint Joseph's 13 years earlier, Gonzaga went out and won its first 29 games. Mark Few had statistically the best defense in the program's history, one that forced misses in the paint while also denying three-point opportunities. On offense, these Bulldogs made their two-pointers and took care of the ball. The Zags remained undefeated until the final day of the regular season when they lost at home, of all places, to BYU by eight. Shaking off defeat, Gonzaga won the WCC tournament and, again like St. Joe's in 2004, earned a No. 1 seed.

Any bad first-weekend spirits left over from being a top seed in Salt Lake City in 2013 were avoided in a 20-point win out of the gate. Those memories came back with a vengeance, however, in what was nearly a catastrophic collapse against Northwestern. Once down by 22, the Wildcats rallied to within five, a margin that would have been three in the final five minutes had officials not missed Zach Collins reaching up through the cylinder to block Dererk Pardon's shot at the rim. No call was made, except for the technical given to NU head coach Chris Collins when he ran screaming onto the court demanding a basket interference call. Gonzaga survived, 79–73. A Mathews three-pointer in the final minute of the regional semifinal then allowed the Bulldogs to defeat West Virginia by three in San Jose before, anticlimactically, the Zags reached their historic first-ever Final Four via an easy victory in an all-Jesuit Elite Eight showdown against No. 11 seed Xavier.

Few's team again made things interesting by allowing an opponent to rally in the second half, this time in a national semifinal played in Glendale, Arizona, against South Carolina. When the Gamecocks' 16–0 run was finished, Frank Martin's team possessed a two-point lead in the final eight minutes. Again, Gonzaga survived. Holding on to a three-point advantage in the final seconds, Few elected to have his team foul rather than allow a potential game-tying shot by Sindarius Thornwell. With 3.5 seconds on the clock, Thornwell intentionally missed the second free throw, but the Zags' Killian Tillie grabbed the rebound and made his foul shots to secure a spot in the finals against North Carolina.

The national championship that year was decided between equals, both in terms of ability and, no less, size. The Bulldogs weren't used to seeing opponents that could match them in both length and heft, and the Tar Heels scored the night's last eight points to win 71–65. UNC's front line limited the Zags to just 12 two-point makes out of 40 attempts. As Few put it, "They disrupted us, climbed up into us, and kind of drove our offense outside the normal area." Finally, Gonzaga was hampered when Nigel Williams-Goss, after scoring to put the Bulldogs up by two, reinjured an ankle he had already twisted against South Carolina. The 37–2 season ended as the most successful one in the program's history, but also one that left the Bulldogs wanting more.

Gonzaga earned another No. 1 seed in 2019, with Rui Hachimura and San Jose State transfer Brandon Clarke, and then lost by six to eventual runner-up Texas Tech in the regional final in Anaheim. When basketball was suspended by the coronavirus in March 2020, the Bulldogs had pocketed both the WCC regular-season and tournament titles at 31–2 and were on course for still another top seed.

That there is no precedent for the trajectory Gonzaga basketball has charted starting roughly in the mid-1990s commands near-universal assent. Even Butler's appearance in two consecutive national title games, while no less extraordinary in terms of sheer probability, doesn't feel quite commensurate in terms of sustained flouting of what are supposed to be college basketball's laws of gravity.

Marquette under McGuire, Georgetown under Thompson, and Connecticut under Jim Calhoun all made dramatic and more or less enduring transformations as programs compared to what they had been previous to those coaches. Yet to more fully replicate the Gonzaga miracle, the three programs in question would have to be still independent, still in the ECAC Southern division, and still in the Yankee Conference, respectively. Part of what's so distinctive about the spectacle in Spokane is that the Bulldogs have been members of the WCC, under the league's changing names, since 1979, when Dan Fitzgerald led the program's move into the conference from the Big Sky. Numerous programs, from Creighton and Xavier to Texas Christian and Baylor, have helped themselves through upward mobility in conference affiliation. The Bulldogs have not, and Few himself has estimated the number of recruits he's lost over his career due specifically to the Zags' conference.

The origin story from the 1990s of how Mike Roth, as athletic director, and the school's president at the time, the Rev. Robert Spitzer, expended abundant effort and scarce dollars on the building of a previously obscure basketball program is itself an inspirational parable. Unfortunately for other programs, it's less clear that the origin story can be reenacted as a blueprint. Spitzer surely came closer to the true nature of his own labors and those of Roth, Monson, and, later, Few, when he said 20 years after the fact: "Did I think all of this would really happen? I had my doubts, but I did think there was a charm that differentiated our team from other teams, almost a higher sense and higher spirit. We were lucky too."

Gonzaga's methods are easier to duplicate than its success. Features have been written variously purporting to have traced the rise to Few, to Monson, and to Fitzgerald. Assistant coach and heir apparent Tommy Lloyd is an unparalleled recruiter of international talent, yet, even for Lloyd, the world is large and the Bulldogs' roster size is fixed. For all the success the program has carved out for itself in securing talent from abroad, the best player in Gonzaga history was a Spokane native. John Stockton's career at GU long predated the program's rise to greatness.

Ultimately, when confronted with the question of how exactly Gonzaga did become Gonzaga, we're left with mystery and paradox. These familiar quantities in the Catholic faith have been shown to great effect for decades by a coach who's the son of a Presbyterian minister. As Roth puts it, "This literally has never been done in college athletics before. It's one thing to catch lightning in a bottle. It's another thing to keep it going for 21 straight years." One might call it a miracle.

17.

Wright and Villanova

ollie Massimino announced on April 1, 1992, that he was leaving Villanova, and he further stated that he would be accompanied on his move to UNLV by all his assistant coaches: Tom Massimino, John Olive, and Jay Wright. Tom Massimino and Wright did follow their head coach to Vegas, but Olive struck out on his own that very week. He accepted the position as head coach at Loyola Marymount, beating out five other finalists including UC Santa Barbara assistant Ben Howland.

Villanova replaced Massimino with Steve Lappas, who had served as an assistant on the Wildcats staff before becoming head coach at Manhattan in 1988. Kerry Kittles was a freshman on the new coach's first Villanova team in 1992–93, and by the time the 6-foot-5 scoring guard was entering his junior year the feeling in Philadelphia was that the good times, finally, were back. The team's bottom-line numbers in the mid-1990s were indeed impressive: 75–25 overall, with three consecutive top-four seeds in the NCAA tournament. But while Kittles would earn first-team All-American honors as a senior and depart as the program's all-time leading scorer, the period is remembered primarily for three consecutive early exits from the postseason.

Wright was meanwhile plying his trade at Hofstra. He had arrived on Long Island in 1994, and his eye was instantly drawn to a recruit in his backyard, relatively speaking: Speedy Claxton at Christ the King in Middle Village. At 5 foot 11, Claxton was largely ignored by the prestige programs, but Wright recruited the guard intensively and even sent him handwritten notes. Impressed, Claxton committed to Hofstra before his senior season. Wright, with his sharp eye and early legwork, had signed a player who would be a first-round pick in the 2000 NBA draft. The Flying Dutchmen prospered accordingly: Hofstra made its first NCAA tournament appearance in 23 years in 2000.

The following season, even without Claxton, Wright's team was again in contention for the automatic bid from the America East when ESPN arrived to carry the conference tournament's title game. The network had a Flying Dutchmen logo cued up and ready to go minutes before tip-off, at which time a school official rushed into the production truck and informed ESPN staff that the school now preferred to be referred to as the Pride.

The Hofstra Pride defeated Delaware, and Wright returned to the NCAA tournament for a second consecutive year. UCLA promptly dismissed the Pride 61–48 at Greensboro Coliseum on the tournament's first day, a Thursday. The following Wednesday, Wright was at Rutgers interviewing for the head coaching job there. Tennessee also wanted to talk to Wright, who went so far as to tell one friend confidentially that he was heading to Rutgers. But two days later, Lappas and the Villanova administration came to an agreement on a parting of ways. Villanova had actually signed Lappas to a contract extension in July 2000, but by March 2001 the coach had compiled a 38–26 record over the previous two seasons while missing the NCAA tournament both years. As seen in Dana O'Neil's excellent history of the Wright-era Wildcats, *Long Shots*, the fast exit made by Lappas appeared to be accelerated by Villanova's realization that Wright was about to be hired by Rutgers. By Sunday, athletic director Vince Nicastro was meeting with Wright in what the *Philadelphia Inquirer* termed "an undisclosed location in southern New Jersey." Nicastro offered Wright the job on the spot, and the new coach was introduced at a press conference on Tuesday.

Not everyone in Philadelphia was pleased with the flurry of human resources activity the Villanova administration had carried out over the course of a single weekend. "You can't say 'loyalty' like Shazam," observed Temple head coach John Chaney. "You have to be selfish if you're a coach. You can't trust presidents and athletic directors. You look at Steve Lappas—he graduates his players, he wins, and that's not enough."

For his part, Wright didn't sound overly concerned at the press conference. He promised to carry on a tradition of great Villanova coaches, mentioning Al Severance, Jack Kraft, Massimino, and Lappas by name. "My wife and I had resigned ourselves to the fact that we would have to coach somewhere, but never back home," the Bucks County native said. "We never even considered this...I'm thrilled. I'm overwhelmed." All new coaches hit the ground running on the recruiting circuit, but Wright did so and succeeded. He signed Randy Foye, Allan Ray, Curtis Sumpter, and Jason Fraser that first season. Kyle Lowry committed the following year.

When Wright's first recruiting class played together as juniors in 2004–05, Villanova earned a No. 5 seed in what was the Wildcats' first NCAA tournament appearance in six years. Despite the program's long absence, Wright's 22–7 team that season may have been even stronger than its seed indicated. Six of Villanova's seven losses that year had come by a combined total of just 17 points. In any event, the Wildcats lent support to the theory that they had been underseeded by reaching their first Sweet 16 since 1988. To make it that far, Wright's team had defeated a talented group of Florida sophomores that included Joakim Noah, Corey Brewer, and Al Horford, marking the last NCAA tournament loss those players would ever suffer.

The reward for beating the Gators was a game in the Carrier Dome against top seed North Carolina. Villanova would play the Tar Heels without second-leading scorer Sumpter after the junior tore a knee ligament in the first half against Florida. Wright drew the obvious historical parallel: "In this game, we're probably perceived as being as much of an underdog as we were when Villanova defeated Georgetown in that final game." The Wildcats very nearly followed that script by playing a four-guard lineup in the absence of Sumpter. With 2:11 left to play and North Carolina up by eight, UNC's Raymond Felton fouled out for the first time in his college career and, even in Coach Roy Williams's phrasing, the Tar Heels seemed to "panic" as a result. The Wildcats had pulled to within 66–63 in the closing seconds when Allan Ray drove into the lane, drew contact from Rashad McCants, and heard a whistle just as he launched a shot that was good. Ray and the entire Villanova team rejoiced and started making the "count it" signal with the clock stopped at 9.0 seconds, but the call was traveling on Ray. North Carolina would survive 67–66. To Bill Raftery, who was working the regional semifinal for CBS, the traveling violation whistled on Ray was "the right call." To one Philadelphia tabloid, however, the sequence appeared in a somewhat different light: IT'S ALL OVA: DISPUTED WALK CALL GETS HEELS OFF THE HOOK.

To Wright, the game may have reinforced the idea that the four-guard look deserved further study. Over a decade later, he would speak of playing UNC without Sumpter and say that "in that game we could see how [the Tar Heels] were huge, and we saw how it spread them out, how they had to chase us, how it opened up lanes to the basket."

Curtis Sumpter reinjured the same knee in practice that October and missed the entire 2005–06 season. The four-guard lineup was no longer an intriguing idea for Villanova; it was a necessity. Kyle Lowry would replace Sumpter in the starting lineup.

In one reading, the rest is small-ball history: Villanova shared the Big East regular-season title with Connecticut at 14–2, earned a No. 1 seed in the 2006 NCAA tournament, and went all the way to the Elite Eight before losing by 13 to eventual champion Florida. True enough, and this picture can perhaps be enhanced further still with just a bit of additional background. One of the biggest changes from one season to the next for the Wildcats was simply that they stopped losing so many one-possession games. Another difference was that, ironically, the 6-foot-1 Lowry was a far less prolific contributor of both three-point makes and attempts in 2005–06 than the 6-foot-8 Sumpter had been the previous season.

Even so, the offensive and defensive assignments forced on opponents by having Lowry on the floor along with Foye, Ray, and Mike Nardi did indeed make Villanova different. Foye, a first-team All-American, was the tallest of the guards, at 6 foot 4, and the foursome customarily took the floor with the 6-foot-8 Will Sheridan. It had to be interesting for Wright to note that with that kind of lineup, even in the Big East, the Wildcats' defensive rebounding held up just fine. As a team, Villanova really did devote a larger share of shot attempts to three-point tries, even though Lowry individually did not. Wright was exploring interesting territory on offense, as were coaches like John Beilein at West Virginia and Mike Brey at Notre Dame. In Brey's case, the scheming would soon benefit his power forward Luke Harangody, named 2008 Big East player of the year.

Whether by schematic exploration, savvy recruiting, or some combination of the two, John Thompson III was achieving noteworthy results of his own at Georgetown around this same time. Thompson had succeeded his father's successor, Craig Esherick, in 2004, and the Hoyas reached the 2006 Sweet 16 in the coach's second season. The next year, a nucleus featuring Jeff Green, Roy Hibbert, and DaJuan Summers was doing something offenses aren't supposed to be able to do. In effect, Georgetown had one of the best offenses in the nation in terms of adjusted efficiency, despite the fact that this same offense was turning the ball over at a higher than average rate.

There have been teams that have shot more accurately than the Hoyas did that season, and other teams have rebounded a higher percentage of their own misses. But few if any offenses have ever done both things as well. Georgetown averaged right at a point and a half on possessions where it didn't commit a turnover in Big East play, a figure not approached by any major-conference offense since then. The Hoyas rode that strength to the 2007 Final Four, where they lost

67–60 to Greg Oden, Mike Conley, and Ohio State. Georgetown was the first Catholic program to reach a Final Four since Dwyane Wade and Marquette had done so in 2003. The Jesuits were about to make way for the Augustinians on that honor roll.

By the end of the decade, Wright had welcomed what was, in effect, his second generation of talent into the Villanova program in the form of Scottie Reynolds, Dante Cunningham, Corey Fisher, and Corey Stokes. Villanova was still putting versatile players on the floor who tended to top out at about 6 foot 8, but it was becoming clear that labels like "four-guard offense" could be in the eye of the beholder. The Wildcats were no longer particularly perimeter-oriented, for example, and this state of affairs would persist for the next five years. Wright's 2008–09 team didn't attract much notice during an exceptional Big East season in which three of the conference's other teams would be awarded No. 1 seeds in the 2009 NCAA tournament. Conversely, Villanova grabbed a No. 3 seed and easily won games against American and No. 6 seed UCLA at Philadelphia's Wachovia Center (renamed the Wells Fargo Center the following year). The team at last garnered some attention, however, when it traveled to Boston for the semifinals and dismantled Kyle Singler and No. 2 seed Duke 77–54. The Wildcats had proceeded as far as they could go without running into one of those top-seeded league rivals. Pittsburgh awaited Wright's team next.

In what turned out to be a preview of the future, Villanova's 2009 Elite Eight game came down to a length-of-the-floor inbounds play in the final seconds. While the play was run from the same set the Wildcats would use against North Carolina in the 2016 national title game and achieved the same result, the sequence unfolded much differently. Levance Fields had tied the game at 75 for the Panthers with 5.5 seconds remaining. Villanova's play was set up for the ball to be inbounded to Scottie Reynolds, just as it would be inbounded to Ryan Arcidiacono in a similar situation seven years later. This time, however, Pitt was overplaying Reynolds. Instead, Villanova's Reggie Redding delivered a pass farther up the floor to Dante Cunningham, who was, in effect, boxing out Sam Young to receive the ball. The ball came in high, and Cunningham jumped to get it, delivering a nice touch pass in midair that hit the streaking Reynolds in stride. Reynolds drove around DeJuan Blair and into Gilbert Brown in the lane. Brown didn't want to foul, and Reynolds converted the floater to seal the win with 0.5 seconds left. Villanova had reached the Final Four for the first time since the 1985 championship season.

While the Wildcats eventually lost by 14 to North Carolina in Detroit, Wright and his program appeared to have climbed the mountaintop. Kentucky and the Sixers both made inquiries regarding Wright's availability that off-season, but the Nova coach elected to stay put. Villanova won 20 of its first 21 games in 2009–10 and rose to No. 2 in the AP poll. In early February 2010, Reynolds was putting together a senior season that would end with him being named a first-team All-American. Villanova's freshmen that season included Maalik Wayns, Dominic Cheek, and Mouphtaou Yarou. To this day, that group constitutes what is statistically the highest-rated recruiting class Villanova has signed in the modern era.

The signs could hardly have been more positive. Yet from that point in February 2010 until the dissolution of the "old" Big East in March 2013, Villanova would post a 58–52 mark. Included in that run would be a 13–19 season in 2011–12. It was the darkest stretch of Wright's tenure, and it was more troubling than it would have been if this were a newly hired coach struggling through a rebuilding year or two. In the case of a coach who was a decade into his run and who had put together a series of outstanding recruiting classes, it appeared that perhaps the program had lost its way.

Villanova assistant coach Billy Lange rejoined the staff in 2011 after seven years at the Naval Academy, giving him a fresh perspective on what he saw. Lange would later reflect on this period and tell Dana O'Neil that the highest-rated recruiting class ever seemed to be part of the problem. "Every coach in the Big East would have taken those players," he said. "But they weren't coming to Villanova for the same reason Coach wanted them to come." Or, as Wright himself would say: "We had some guys who were juniors and seniors and not happy about it. They thought they'd be out early."

The Wildcats did manage to return to the NCAA tournament in 2013 as a No. 9 seed. On paper, it wasn't a particularly efficient team, especially not in terms of shooting accuracy. But Wright again had a nucleus returning the following season that he felt could improve: James Bell, JayVaughn Pinkston, Darrun Hilliard, and two freshmen, Ryan Arcidiacono and Daniel Ochefu. The Big East would be different that next season, reduced to a 10-member league with seven Catholic holdovers from the "old" conference and three new members: Butler, Xavier, and Creighton.

One of those new Big East members would give the league both its player of the year for 2014 and the Wooden Award winner that year, Doug McDermott. While his father, Greg McDermott, was coaching at Iowa State, Doug had played for the same team, at Ames High School, that featured future North Carolina and NBA star Harrison Barnes. Doug McDermott had committed to Northern Iowa, but he changed his mind and played at Creighton when his father was hired there as head coach. The son had not been highly rated as a high school recruit, an error that became apparent early in his freshman year. For decades, high-volume individual scoring outside the paint had often entailed a certain forbearance on the part of coaches. Such scoring frequently came at the cost of a relatively low percentage of made shots by the player in question. However, with the 6-foot-8 McDermott and the new breed of high-volume plus high-efficiency stars like Weber State's Damian Lillard and Lehigh's C. J. McCollum, coaches were able to have their cake and eat it too.

McDermott personally exemplified one of the two traits animating the reconfigured Big East of 2013–14, and with him in the rotation, his team exemplified both. On the one hand, the Big East had responded to Syracuse, Pittsburgh, and Notre Dame jumping straight to the ACC by adding basketball programs recently elevated by spectacular individuals. In the case of Butler, this individual was of course former head coach Brad Stevens, even though he himself was gone by the time the Bulldogs started playing in the Big East. But with Creighton, that program elevator was the younger McDermott. The Bluejays also checked a second box, of course, as a Jesuit program with an illustrious history that included the likes of Kyle Korver and Paul Silas, not to mention the team's leading scorer in 1956, future baseball Hall of Famer Bob Gibson. Where once the Big East had roamed as far as Miami at football's behest, now the league founded in Providence, Rhode Island, with an eye toward threading together the East Coast's major media markets, was happy to land in Nebraska in the pursuit of Catholicity and basketball, not necessarily in that order.

The first regular-season title in the newly reconfigured Big East was won by Villanova in 2014. Whatever strange malaise had afflicted the Wildcats for the better part of four seasons was, it seemed, long gone. Wright's offense charted a remarkable transformation from one year to the next, one that was all the more striking because many of the players were the same in both seasons. Yarou had completed his eligibility after the 2012–13 season, but, otherwise, Villanova still rose and fell on the efforts of figures like Bell, Pinkston, Hilliard, and Arcidiacono, who were now joined by freshman reserves Josh Hart and Kris Jenkins. The starters' shots were now, for the first time, going in the basket, and observers that season could be forgiven for being struck by individual achievements that would later appear to also be, in no small part, systemic results. Hilliard, for example, set analytically inclined hearts racing that year. Here, surely, was another Doug McDermott, albeit at a much lower volume.

While Creighton set the standard where offense was concerned in the first season of the "new" Big East, Villanova wasn't far behind, and Wright was achieving these results while preserving the very good defense from the previous year. Wright's team rolled through the 2013–14 regular season with a 28–3 record and appeared to be in contention for the program's first NCAA tournament No. 1 seed in eight years. Then Big East No. 8 seed Seton Hall floored Villanova 64–63 in the conference tournament quarterfinals on a step-back buzzer-beater from 20 feet by Sterling Gibbs. "We're not going to overreact," Wright said after the game. "I know it's a big story and it's crushing to us not to be able to keep playing in this tournament, but it happened. We'll deal with it and get it right." Instead of a top seed, Villanova was given a spot on the No. 2 line in Buffalo, where, in the round of 32, they faced a No. 7 seed that had required overtime just to defeat Saint Joseph's in the first round. Nevertheless, Shabazz Napier and eventual national champion Connecticut easily disposed of Villanova 77–65.

Nine players had appeared in Villanova's loss to UConn, and just two had been seniors: James Bell, a starter, and Tony Chennault, coming off the bench. Wright brought back everyone else the following year and the regular-season results were little short of spectacular. Certainly, no team in the program's modern era had ever lost fewer games. The Wildcats arrived at the 2015 Big East tournament at 29–2 and, despite a close call in the semifinals against Kris Dunn and Providence, captured the automatic NCAA bid.

A decade earlier, Wright had turned heads with a four-guard lineup. Now, the nomenclature had shifted slightly. The key stylistic term had long since become "bigs," by which it was meant a player who didn't shoot three-pointers, just as much as it denoted an individual who was actually large. That season, Wright occasionally had two bigs on the floor, in the form of the 6-foot-11 Ochefu and the 6-foot-7 Pinkston. More often, however, one of those players would be replaced by the 6-foot-6 Jenkins. Either way, the results were unmistakable. In a season that featured a striking concentration of great teams nationally, Villanova's offense was right there statistically with the likes of Frank Kaminsky and Wisconsin, Jahlil Okafor and Duke, and even undefeated Kentucky itself. Receiving a No. 1 seed in 2015 was a bit like going in the top five of the 2003 NBA draft, an achievement to cherish. The Wildcats were indeed awarded one of those top seeds, along with the Blue Devils, the Badgers, and UK. It wouldn't go as well for Villanova as it would for the other three, however.

The men's basketball committee sent the Wildcats to Pittsburgh, where in the second round they would encounter the winner of a game between North Carolina State and LSU. As Wright and his staff scouted the game, they discussed the Tigers in depth as Coach Johnny Jones's team held a comfortable lead for the balance of the contest. "Then we started saying, 'Whoa, let's start looking at NC State here, pay attention,'" Wright would relate after the first round.

The Wolfpack definitely had Villanova's attention after the next 40 minutes of basketball. NC State defeated the Wildcats 71–68 in a game where the 33–2 top seed never led after the intermission. For a second consecutive year, a Villanova offense that had excelled at making two-pointers during the season was utterly unable to do so against a lower seed in the round of 32. It felt like a repeat of the program's tournament struggles in the mid-1990s, only with two additional charges added to the bill of indictment. Once again, the Wildcats were the team that always had a beautiful regular-season record yet always folded in the tournament's first weekend. Now, it was further said the Wildcats relied too much on three-pointers while compiling those misleading regular-season records against a suspect and diluted Big East. The game even spawned the "piccolo girl" meme after a member of Villanova's band was shown on camera weeping while playing her instrument in the aftermath.

"I know we have to answer to the fact that we did not get to the second weekend again," Wright said that evening. "We have to own that, but it's not going to define us within our program."

Not getting to the second weekend had also been the knock on Notre Dame for over a decade, but the Fighting Irish were in the process of shedding that label in unsteady yet ultimately spectacular fashion. At first, Mike Brey's team had seemed intent in preserving its reputation for March struggles. The Irish barely got by No. 14 seed Northeastern in the 2015 NCAA tournament and needed overtime to put away Butler. Once Notre Dame reached its first Sweet 16 in 12 years, however, the team beat Wichita State by 11 and played undefeated Kentucky into the final seconds of a classic regional final. Jerian Grant and his teammates had taken low-turnover basketball to new heights all season, and the Irish gave the ball away just once in the second half against UK. Andrew Harrison had to convert two free throws with six seconds remaining to secure a 68–66 win for Kentucky.

The Villanova freshman class going into the 2015–16 season included Jalen Brunson, Mikal Bridges, and Donte DiVincenzo. The fact that Brunson blended in that year as a fourth option on offense along-side Hart, Jenkins, and Arcidiacono belied the fact that the freshman actually represented something of a departure for Wright's program. For one thing, Brunson was a McDonald's All-American who rated out as the highest-ranked recruit to commit to the school since Wright's highly decorated yet ultimately disappointing freshman class of 2009–10. The other novel feature about Brunson was that he was a starter at Villanova as a freshman.

On paper, the Wildcats were a 2015 NCAA tournament No. 1 seed that had returned seven of its top nine scorers and added a national top-20 recruit. In reality, pollsters were wary of placing much faith in this program. Villanova was ranked No. 11 in the preseason, a diffident verdict that appeared richly deserved when Wright's team was blown off a neutral floor in Hawaii by Buddy Hield and Oklahoma in December. The Sooners won by 23, and 12 days later Virginia didn't have any particular problems defeating the Wildcats 86–75 in Charlottesville. Villanova dropped to No. 17 in the rankings, but, as Wright's team regained its balance and was in the process of running off what would be its third consecutive 16–2 Big East record, the pollsters changed their tune. The Wildcats ascended to No. 1 in early February, a status that was earned partly by default. There was no equivalent to the undefeated Kentucky team from the previous season and, surprisingly, the top ranking marked a first in the history of the Villanova program.

A late-season road loss to an excellent Xavier team knocked the Wildcats from the top spot, and, for the second time in three years, Villanova lost a one-possession game to Seton Hall in the Big East tournament. This time, the defeat came in the championship game, giving Isaiah Whitehead, Angel Delgado, and the Pirates the program's first Big East tournament title in 23 years. The Wildcats would enter the 2016 NCAA field of 68 playing close to home, at the Barclays Center in Brooklyn, as a No. 2 seed.

Iowa would be the biggest obstacle between Villanova and the second weekend. Wright's team entered the contest having failed to reach the Sweet 16 in each of its last five attempts, with three of those tries having come with a No. 1 or No. 2 seed attached. Before this game, Coach Wright acknowledged the pressure. Referring to his current players and to a Final Four run seven years earlier, he said: "They still know about 2009 and they want that. If we don't do something in the next few years, the recruits are going to forget about '09." Villanova opened a 25-point lead by halftime and beat the Hawkeyes by 19. An old curse had been smashed, but the next two games would prove even more enlightening.

At the 2016 Sweet 16 in Louisville, Villanova finally proved that the glittering advanced statistics it kept piling up on offense in the Big East really could translate into production against a quality opponent in the NCAA tournament. The unlucky victim was No. 3 seed Miami. In what was actually a game as slow-paced as an average regular-season contest for Virginia, the Wildcats rang up 92 points. "They're just an incredible offensive team," Hurricanes coach Jim Larrañaga marveled. "We were playing at a high level [in the ACC], but nobody shot the three and stretched our defense like these guys did. They only took 15 threes. It seemed like they took 30 and made 25 of them."

The scoring sprees and aesthetically pleasing possessions came to an abrupt halt, however, against No. 1 seed Kansas in the regional final. Jenkins sat for more than eight minutes in the second half with four fouls, and his team converted just four three-pointers in 40 minutes. Yet Villanova survived the 64–59 battle. The Jayhawks were experiencing perimeter struggles of their own, and Bridges was credited with five steals that went toward the Wildcats' total of 11.

When Villanova smashed Oklahoma by 44 points at the Final Four in Houston, the game represented both a payback for the December loss and a gesture toward Villanova's hallowed 1985 championship.

In terms of converting shots into points, Hart, Jenkins, and their teammates actually outperformed what their predecessors did against Georgetown 31 years earlier. Of course, the 2016 team had the benefit of a three-point line. For the record, shooting 24 of 31 on your two-pointers and 11 of 18 beyond the arc translates into a higher effective field goal percentage than the 22-of-28 performance the 1985 team recorded back when everything was a two-pointer. In other words, Villanova as a program had afforded its fans the luxury of considering which of their Final Four teams three decades apart posted the more historically extraordinary shooting performance.

The national championship game against North Carolina is destined to live forever on YouTube because of how it ended, but it was an outstanding contest for the previous 39-plus minutes as well. Wearing home uniforms as the higher seed, the Tar Heels started slowly, then roared back with a 25–13 stretch, only to have but a five-point lead to show for it at halftime. Villanova answered in kind by building what at the time seemed a decisive 10-point advantage with 5:29 remaining. Phil Booth had come off the bench for the Wildcats and was well on his way to a team-high 20 points on the night. UNC closed to within one on two occasions but was unable to draw even, and the Heels were down to their last gasp when Hart's two free throws pushed the lead back out to three with 13 seconds left.

Coming out of the time-out, North Carolina's Isaiah Hicks was screening to free up Marcus Paige, even though, with a three-point lead, Daniel Ochefu was ignoring Hicks entirely and simply staying out top to deny Joel Berry's pass to Paige. But when Paige received the bounce pass, Ochefu slipped and fell near the right hash mark. Temporarily open, Paige took two dribbles toward the arc and, with Ryan Arcidiacono running at him, launched a double-clutching 24-footer that rattled home. Paige's three-pointer with 4.7 seconds left was plainly one of the most memorable shots of national championship game history, and it was about to be superseded.

Before Villanova inbounded the ball out of the ensuing time-out, Ochefu grabbed a mop from the youngster whose one job was to wield said implement. The 6-foot-11 junior then set to work on the floor. Ochefu knew where he had hit the court, and he was well aware that his responsibility was to set a screen for Arcidiacono at this same spot in a matter of seconds. The Wildcats ran the same basic set that had worked with 5.5 seconds against Pittsburgh in the 2009 regional final. Kris Jenkins inbounded to Arcidiacono, who dribbled toward Ochefu's screen on the left side of the floor at midcourt, then switched to his right hand. Jenkins was trailing Arcidiacono by 10 feet all the way down the floor, and at midcourt, with his hands already up to receive a pass, he started calling, "Arch, Arch, Arch." His teammate turned to his right at the far side of the Final Four logo and flipped the ball back to him. With a tie score, the Tar Heels were showing by their very positions that they were more fearful of a length-of-the-floor Scottie Reynolds play. When Jenkins rose up to shoot his three-pointer from NBA range, there was no opposing player near him. At the last moment, Hicks closed on Jenkins and contested the shot just as the ball was being released.

The clock read "0.8" when the ball left Jenkins's hand, and the game was nominally over when the horn sounded and the shot was just reaching its apex. After another half second or so, the shot fell, the game was decided, the championship was won, and history was written. Jenkins's feat was a buzzer-beater in the truest sense of the term. The ball was released, then the horn sounded, and then the shot fell. Release, horn, swish. A few scattered purists would point out that a miss by Jenkins would have meant overtime rather than defeat. Perhaps someday there will be a national championship buzzer-beater that not only decides the outcome but changes a sure loser into a winner. When that occurs, the shot will take its place alongside the close of the 2016 title game as college basketball at its peak.

In the aftermath of "The Shot," some observers asked why an excellent shooter like Jenkins was virtually unguarded for the last 4.7 seconds of the game. It turns out that this state of affairs occurred more or less by design. The Tar Heels elected to station Brice Johnson directly under the basket to guard against both a length-of-the-floor dribble and a full-court pass. "Kris made a heck of a play," Heels coach Williams said afterward. "Brice was guarding him. Kris was taking it out. Brice was all deep. Make sure they didn't throw anything long."

In winning six NCAA tournament games, the Wildcats had scored a total of 501 points in just 385 possessions. The ghosts of UConn and NC State in the previous two tournaments had been hard to shake, but once that spell was broken the Villanova offense, even with the Kansas game thrown in, put on a show that will be very difficult for future teams to top.

Then again, to set those standards, a team has to make it that far. In 2016–17, the Wildcats would learn the hard way that their run of bad outcomes in the second round had merely been interrupted and not solved altogether. Even as Josh Hart was named a first-team All-American, as Jay Wright won a fourth consecutive outright Big East title, and as Villanova earned another No. 1 seed, the team was again sent home the first weekend. The giant slayer this time was Wisconsin. Nigel Hayes made a deft one-on-one move off the dribble from the right side against Mikal Bridges, drove under the basket, and laid the ball in with his left hand to break a tie with 11.4 seconds left. It was the difference, as the Badgers prevailed 65–62. The loss was a reminder of how tournament outcomes determine how a team talks about itself. When Villanova was 32–3 and a No. 1 seed, it was a chip off the old block. When it was 32–4 and heading home, depth was a concern, the injury to Phil Booth that year was a tough break, and so, too, was the fact that Omari Spellman had been ruled ineligible as a freshman.

Wright had to bid farewell to Hart, Jenkins, and Darryl Reynolds after losing to the Badgers, but Booth was healthy the next season, Spellman was eligible, Brunson and Bridges returned, and DiVincenzo and onetime Fordham transfer Eric Paschall became starters. The names, along with that of one Jay Wright, are worth remembering for students of offense. What Villanova had done on that side of the ball in the 2016 NCAA tournament, it would more or less do for the entirety of the 2017–18 season. In Big East play, the Wildcats converted better than 60 percent of their two-point tries for a second consecutive season, and now they were doing so by driving their turnover rate down to levels close to the sport's performance horizon.

Yet Villanova, at 14–4 in conference play, didn't even win the Big East. That honor instead went to Xavier, which compiled a 15–3 record. Chris Mack's team had an excellent offense in its own right, one led by Trevon Bluiett and J. P. Macura. The Musketeers earned a No. 1 seed in the 2018 NCAA tournament, a first even for a program with a long history of excellence in March. Starting in the mid-1980s, Pete Gillen took Xavier to six consecutive NCAA tournaments and reached the 1990 Sweet 16 with a team featuring Tyrone Hill. Skip Prosser took the reins in 1994, and coached the likes of James Posey, David West, and Lionel Chalmers, kindly passing the last two along to his successor, Thad Matta. From the time Matta arrived in 2001, down through the tenure of Sean Miller, and all the way to Mack's Big East champions in 2018, the Musketeers advanced to three regional finals and seven Sweet 16s. The 2017–18 team carried on this tradition with a conference title, to go along with wins over Wisconsin, Baylor, and, most crucially, crosstown rival Cincinnati.

By chance, Xavier had company that season in the "historic year from a Midwestern Jesuit program" category. Even if the 2018 NCAA tournament had never taken place, it would be fair to call the 28–5 season put together by Loyola Chicago up to that point the program's best effort in decades. After George Ireland stepped down as head coach in the 1970s, the team endured some challenging years. Porter Moser was hired in 2011 after serving as an assistant under Rick Majerus at Saint Louis. The tough years continued early in Moser's tenure, but by the time 2017–18 rolled around the coach had put many of his desired pieces in place. He had a veritable Jalen Brunson clone and 2018 Missouri Valley Conference player of the year in 6-foot-1 scoring point guard Clayton Custer, an Iowa State transfer. Ben Richardson, a 6-foot-3 senior, was Custer's high school teammate and Loyola's defensive stopper. Marques Townes was Moser's versatile wing, Donte Ingram and Cameron Krutwig were workhorses on the defensive glass, and Ingram was a perimeter threat as well. All of the above combined to earn the Ramblers a No. 11 seed in the NCAA tournament, and the rest is history.

Team chaplain Sister Jean Dolores Schmidt won instant fame when Loyola prevailed in a series of exceedingly close games. The cast of last-possession heroes changed with each passing contest for the Ramblers: Ingram hit the game-winner against Miami in the round of 64, Custer did the same to Tennessee in the next round, and Townes salted the game away with a three-pointer against Nevada in the Sweet 16. As chance would have it, Loyola's 16-point victory in the Elite Eight over No. 9 seed Kansas State in Atlanta provided a departure from this suspenseful pattern. The Ramblers became just the fourth No. 11 seed in history to reach the Final Four, following in the footsteps of LSU (1986), George Mason (2006), and Virginia Commonwealth (2011).

Michigan would defeat Loyola by 12 in San Antonio, but it was a glorious return to the Final Four by the program 55 years after Jerry Harkness, Les Hunter, John Egan, Vic Rouse, and Ron Miller brought home a national championship. Harkness himself, at age 77, was on hand in Atlanta to witness the miracle and join the celebration. "It's back," he said, "it's back. It's beautiful that they went before I went into a hole in the ground."

Villanova didn't add a Big East regular-season title to its résumé in 2018, but the program did produce its first-ever Wooden Award winner, in the person of Jalen Brunson. As a 6-foot-3 junior, Brunson posted the best numbers of his already outstanding career for assist rate, turnover rate, and three-point makes and accuracy. Nevertheless, some of Brunson's toughest competition for individual honors came from teammates that were also posting personal bests. It was the Darrun Hilliard effect all over again. Wright's players really were that good, and they were also plying their talents in a system that captured their performances to maximum effect.

As the second seed in the 2018 Big East tournament, Villanova defeated Providence in overtime in the title game to capture its second consecutive automatic NCAA bid and its third in four years. When the Wildcats received their No. 1 seed in the tournament, they proceeded to record the most dominant six-game run since North Carolina's title in 2009. Defeating Radford, Alabama, West Virginia, Texas Tech, Kansas, and Michigan in sequence, the Wildcats won every game by at least 11 points. At the Final Four in San Antonio, Villanova made 18 three-pointers in a 16-point victory over the No. 1 seed Jayhawks. Then, in the title game against the Wolverines, Donte DiVincenzo personally ran amok and made five shots from beyond the arc on his way to 31 points as the Wildcats won 79–62. Those will be the portions of the run that are remembered, and rightfully so. It's also true that Villanova played excellent defense both against the Wolverines and against the Red Raiders in the regional final. The national champions that year were a complete team.

The 2018 Wildcats additionally marked a sea change in at least two respects. During its six-game run to a title, Villanova attempted more shots from beyond the arc than the team did inside it. Wright also played the entire tournament, as indeed he did the whole season, with no one taller than 6 foot 8 on the floor. While these two mile markers surely reflect what is commonly called "the three-point revolution," the example of point guard Brunson repeatedly posting up his defender in the paint during his junior year suggests an additional conclusion. The common denominator between Brunson doing his best Patrick Ewing impression and the 6-foot-8 Spellman spotting up in the corner or even handling the ball up top was that in both instances the Wildcats were forcing individual defenders into situations that made them uncomfortable. This kind of versatility helped make Villanova offenses remarkably accurate, and the Wildcats both reflected and contributed toward a trend in which stars are expected to make their shots. Wooden Award winners Jalen Brunson, Zion Williamson of Duke, and Obi Toppin of Dayton lead one to wonder how many future recipients of the same award will make less than 60 percent of their two-pointers. Villanova helped to drive that shift.

Winning two national titles in three seasons put Wright and Villanova in very select company historically. That level of success invites slavish imitation, but it was, and still is, unclear that there is any one aspect of what worked for the Wildcats that can be translated directly into two titles in three years. Villanova never led Division I in the share of attempts launched as three-pointers, for example, or in how few two-point jumpers it tried. Wright's rotations tended to be experienced, but there were always plenty of older rosters to be found. The most that can be said of Wright is that he brought all of the above together and that it worked beautifully. With luck, the future will belong not to those who try to copy him point by point but to those who are just as creative and independent as he was during that miraculous stretch of basketball.

The story of Catholic college basketball in the NCAA tournament era both begins and, so far, ends with Villanova. The Wildcats reached the first-ever NCAA national semifinals in 1939 and won a national title 79 years later. Overall, the program has appeared in six Final Fours and won three national titles. Even leaving aside the 1971 tournament run that was later vacated, the Wildcats' body of work still stands unsurpassed. No other Catholic program has won three NCAA titles, and only Georgetown has also reached five (official) national semifinals.

Villanova is often referred to as unusual, if not singular, within the Catholic basketball tradition, both for the school's affiliation (Augustinian as opposed to Jesuit, Lasallian, Vincentian, etc.) and for its location (pastoral or suburban as opposed to urban). Historically speaking, the Wildcats are also unique within that same tradition in terms of their success. The lion's share of that credit goes to Jay Wright, a coach who paid tribute to his predecessors by name in his first press conference. His successor will have even greater cause to do the same.

Epilogue

Identities

hen James Naismith was traveling via ocean liner to the 1936 Olympics in Berlin, he wrote a letter to his wife back home in Kansas and described the following scene:

> Last night we had a cabaret in the dining room and an Episcopal minister made a joke about the Catholics and there were plenty of them there, then to straighten things out he said that if he were not an Episcopal, he would be a Catholic, then all the other denominations booed him. I have not seen him on deck or in the lounge since. I guess he hunted a hole to hide in. I am keeping quiet. I may be uninteresting, but do not make that kind of fool of myself.

By the 1930s, Naismith was, at last, achieving a modest yet growing degree of renown as the inventor of basketball. Granted, his was a narrowly circumscribed fame. Sports don't often have solitary inventor figures and, more mundanely, Naismith himself, now in his 70s, was eking out a rather precarious living by this time. The National Association of Basketball Coaches in effect took up a collection among the membership in order to fund Naismith's trip to Germany. Catholic colleges and universities in particular should have given generously to that collection.

If there were no game of basketball, Catholic colleges and universities would have been deprived of one of their defining characteristics in the public imagination. As Frank Deford phrased it in the aftermath of the peak moment furnished by the 1985 Final Four, "For many Americans, college basketball is the outward and visible sign of Catholicism in the United States." It is perhaps the ritual of basketball itself, more than any particular success within the sport, that binds this one faith to this one game. The defining quality of Catholic basketball programs is not that they necessarily prevail but, instead, that they persist—as a familiar, distinct, and cohesive body of the sport's disciples. When speaking of Catholicism in the United States, college basketball is an identity as much as it is a prowess.

This connection between the game and the Church is more often criticized than doubted. Particularly in the 1980s when, for a brief moment, it seemed that Catholic programs were not only ascendant but on the cusp of becoming hegemonic, it was asked what good were wins if in the process the Church lost its soul through its presence at the highest—and, on occasion, most tawdry—levels of the sport. It was an appropriate question fated to be diminished in salience on the court by a total Catholic absence from Final Fours throughout the 1990s and to be superseded off it by far weightier and more sinister revelations. From Georgetown University profiting in 1838 through the sale of 272 enslaved men, women, and children to the mephitic sexual abuse scandals that would engulf the church as a whole in the 21st century, Catholicism and its American institutions of higher learning have graver sins for which to atone, surely, than what in the 1980s was termed "big-time college basketball."

The NCAA itself is funded in large part by passion for a 68-team single-elimination tournament. For Catholic programs in this event, the famine of the 1990s was as aberrant in terms of success as was the feast of the 1980s. The overall trend across nearly a century instead speaks to a level of success in between the two extremes: Catholic programs constitute 12 percent of Division I institutions. Since the inception of the NCAA tournament in 1939, those same Catholic programs have accounted for 12 percent of the teams that have played in national semifinals while winning 12 percent of the national titles. The second two numbers jump or dip year to year as time goes by and as a 2018 (two Catholic Final Four teams and a national champion) is succeeded by a 2019 (the 49th Catholic no-show in 81 rounds of national semifinals up to that time). Nevertheless, the overarching tendency is relatively clear. In purely instrumental terms, Catholic teams on the whole may be characterized more aptly as good or very good rather than as dominant or elite.

The Catholic affinity for college basketball, however, has always been more than a purely instrumental bond. The "Jesuit All-American" teams of the 1950s merit our notice not for being superior to plain old All-Americans but because someone thought to put such a list together at all. (Though, to be sure, the Jesuit honorees could hold their own, including as they did the likes of Dick Boushka, John O'Brien, Ken Sears, and, eventually, Bill Russell, K. C. Jones, and Tom Heinsohn.) The National Catholic Invitational Tournaments of that same era are of interest less for their champions than for their very existence—and, indeed, for a legacy transmitted down through, of all people, Duke athletic director Kevin White.

In the early 1980s, when White was athletic director at Loras College, a Catholic school in Iowa, he once paid a visit to Marquette. As he was touring the athletic facilities in Milwaukee, he happened across the trophy that Tex Winter and his MU team had won at the 1952 NCIT. Intrigued, White started asking questions about this event from decades ago that he had never heard of before.

By 1984, Loras was hosting an annual National Catholic Basketball Tournament. In White's thinking, the new event was a perfect fit for a financially challenged athletic department that had two primary assets, basketball and Catholicism. During its 17-year run, the NCBT became the nation's largest regular-season basketball tournament for small colleges. Saint Louis legend Ed Macauley was a frequent attendee, as were Ray Meyer, Al McGuire, and Hank Raymonds. By virtue of being held in Dubuque, Iowa, in the winter, the tournament also became a regular stop for presidential candidates who were campaigning for the Iowa caucuses. The Catholic basketball being played at the NCBT wasn't necessarily or uniformly excellent. It was, instead, Catholic basketball, differentiated by history, culture, and, above all, identity more than by performance.

Higher education in the United States was originally synonymous with religious affiliation, and in the 21st century, Catholic programs loom large among a dwindling and ecumenical band of hardy survivors that preserve that spiritual ambition. Often in name and always in mission, the Catholic programs are part of an aspirational breed apart—in theory if not always in practice. To be sure, the breed apart includes other faiths and other universities, including those, like Southern Methodist and Texas Christian, that wear their missions in their very names.

Explanations for why Catholic teams "are so good at" college basketball tend to founder on this same reef, one that makes no distinctions between differing institutional types. In practice, Catholic teams have no monopoly over the qualities that are ritually said to have favored Catholic teams. The program that made the best basketball use of a location in one of the nation's great cities, for example, would appear to have been UCLA. The oft-cited "low barriers to participation" in the sport, by which is meant lower than football in terms of roster size and necessary equipment, are equally low for all programs, be they public or private, secular or religiously affiliated. "Concentrating on" basketball at the expense of football is a durable tendency displayed by Kansas and Duke in addition to an administrative classification carried by most Catholic institutions other than Notre Dame and Boston College. Finally, if the fortunes of San Francisco in the 1950s and Loyola Chicago in the 1960s rose in proportion to their access to elite Black players, the same dynamic was exhibited to equal or greater effect by Cincinnati and by the Bruins. If there is a specifically Catholic secret sauce for basketball success, it remains elusive.

Even when wins are plentiful, Catholic teams can speak in the familiar language of the underdog. Villanova and Gonzaga combined to appear in three consecutive national title games as either No. 1 or No. 2 seeds from 2016 to 2018, yet both programs tell backstories that paint themselves as scrappy outsiders thriving in part through shrewd recruiting. For the Wildcats, the parable centers on a dip in team performance around 2012 despite the presence of highly rated recruits. From that point forward, the story goes, Villanova learned to prize character along with, or even before, talent. For the Bulldogs, the tale revolves around being driven to scour the globe for talent because the legacy blue-chip programs from the major conferences had a lock on one-and-done-level players domestically.

To be sure, such self-portrayals are incomplete. (Villanova's recruits have been pretty highly rated coming out of high school, even after 2012. Gonzaga signed a homegrown one-and-done in the person of Zach Collins.) Nevertheless, the way these elite programs choose to view themselves points toward an enduring feature of Catholic college basketball. Teams from the "parish" tradition tend to see themselves as operating at one remove from the blue bloods of the "plains" tradition. While San Francisco became the first undefeated team ever to win an NCAA title, the Dons played in a fledgling conference and had to survive a preliminary-round game in the NCAA tournament to capture their first national championship. Georgetown in the Patrick Ewing era is still the closest thing Catholic basketball has ever had to a true New York Yankees–type behemoth in perceptual terms. Yet even the Hoyas' preeminence proved to be relatively short-lived compared to multidecade expectations carried by the most consistent blue-chip programs.

Teams from the "parish" tradition stand out, even in their lean years, simply because they are always identifiably Catholic. When Syracuse was criticized in the 1980s for allowing a car dealer who was an athletic booster to sit with the team at games, the school's athletic director, Jake Crouthamel, responded by saying, "Some schools have priests on the bench." Some schools do, and it's a distinguishing feature. Where else do you see priests celebrating dunks?

All religiously affiliated programs aspire to lofty goals, at least in mission. The goals often remain unattained, but they persist, just as basketball holds the potential for transcendent moments even as reality often confronts us instead with dull games. Within this population of religiously affiliated institutions, the Catholic programs are a breed apart by virtue of their numbers, by their shared and instantly recognized identity, and, not least, by their legacy of indelible moments.

From George Mikan changing the game and Bob Cousy dribbling behind his back, to Tom Gola overwhelming opponents and Bill Russell dominating the sport as no one ever had before, Catholic college basketball was already a recognized feature of the national sports landscape by the mid-20th century. Loyola Chicago mounted one of the greatest comebacks in Final Four history to defeat a two-time defending national champion in a title game that came down to the last second of overtime. Marquette captured the last national championship ever won by an independent program. Georgetown appeared in three national championship contests in four years and was denied a second title only because Villanova played what was called a "perfect game." Loyola Marymount set scoring records that stand to this day. Gonzaga charted a path from obscurity to durable excellence that has been matched by few, if any, programs historically. Villanova won two championships in three years, and Ryan Arcidiacono and Kris Jenkins teamed to produce one of the greatest and most iconic buzzer-beaters in the sport's annals.

The Catholic affinity for college basketball is more prominent in some eras than in others, yet it is always present as a recognizable, if prosaic, aspect of one of the West's ancient faiths. The affinity is one remarkable and more or less continuous thread throughout college basketball's history, one that spans many storied teams and holds the promise of wonders yet unseen.

Acknowledgments

Writing a book about the Catholic affinity for men's college basketball was Deirdre Mullane's idea. That alone makes her the ideal agent. Thank you, Deirdre. Sean Desmond bought the proposal that Deirdre and I put together, giving me one of the three best days of my professional life. Thank you, Sean.

Numerous current and former coaches, several former players, and at least one internationally famous team chaplain all made time in their schedules to talk to me about Catholic college basketball. In particular, I wish to acknowledge and thank Charlie Besser, Bo Ellis, Dan Gavitt, Jerry Harkness, Jim Larrañaga, Leon Rice, Sister Jean Dolores Schmidt, Bill Stein, Mike Tranghese, and Kevin White.

Bill Behrens at Loyola Chicago ran interference for Sister Jean and continued to assist me when I had to reschedule due to a canceled flight. The new appointment landed me in the midst of a Loyola- if not Chicago-wide Sister Jean 100th birthday Mardi Gras. Fortuitous indeed. Thanks, Bill.

Jesse Washington kindly helped me along with my work on Georgetown and John Thompson. Steve Politi was prompt, gracious, and informative when I popped up asking questions almost 20 years after the fact about his remarkable February 2001 encounter with Walter Dukes.

My friend and onetime *Basketball Prospectus* colleague Ken Pomeroy is, among other superlatives, the world's leading authority on old college basketball rule books. He was most helpful in getting beyond what the newspapers were saying the rule changes were in the 1950s and discovering what modifications were actually made in that decade.

The copy editing provided in the manuscript stage by Elizabeth Johnson and Carolyn Kurek was both outstanding and greatly appreciated.

Where Google, yours truly, and everyone else had failed, the diligent researchers at the Houston Public Library succeeded in answering my question about an often cited but previously undated residence hall fire in 1959 at Texas Southern University.

Until chaining myself to a laptop for months on end to research 125 years of college basketball, I somehow lived life ignorant of the fact that my fifth-grade basketball coach at Butler School was a third-team All-American. He even played for a college all-star team against the Harlem Globetrotters in Madison Square Garden. A belated tip of the cap to you, Coach Ridley, for being orders of magnitude cooler than my feeble 10-year-old perception could register. In this same vein, I had no idea that the father of my mom's friend Sisty was a referee for the game at the Garden in the 1952 Olympic Trials between Kansas and La Salle. Small world.

The staff at the Sangamon Valley Collection at the Lincoln Library in Springfield, Illinois, jumped to attention on behalf of Bob Gasaway's son when my dad took me up to the third floor one day in December 2019. I needed access to early- and mid-20th-century periodicals that the internet doesn't have, and the staff members were exceedingly helpful.

My wife, Nicole, has supported me in every way, not least in encouraging me to quit my "normal" job and take a shot at sports despite the fact that at the time we had two children under the age of six.

She's the reason there was a basketball writing career, period. Our son Rob was a tireless advocate for a different title for this work. He will name the next such effort if he comes up with another idea as good as "Holy Shot!" Our son Will supplied characteristically instinctive and sagacious responses to my searching compositional questions at the dinner table.

While I was completing this book, cancer claimed my mother's life. My mother was a constant and discerning reader and the first person ever to tell me that I was a good writer. Pointedly and, in retrospect, correctly, she did not tell me this on my first try. I will always cherish the moment when she did. I was fortunate and proud to spend my adult life encountering countless people far less interested in one of Jerri's sons than they were in asking, "How's your mom?" My mom is at peace, thanks, and I'm blessed to have been her son.

A Note on Sources

This book was based primarily on personal interviews, research of contemporaneous accounts in newspapers and periodicals (and, for later years, articles posted online), and published sources. The following works were particularly helpful. I especially wish to recognize John McNamara, author of the brilliant and informative book *The Capital of Basketball*. McNamara was killed along with four colleagues on June 28, 2018, when a gunman opened fire inside the newsroom at the *Capital Gazette*, near Annapolis, Maryland.

Applin, Albert. "From Muscular Christianity to the Market Place: The History of Men's and Boys' Basketball in the United States, 1891–1957." Ph.D. diss., University of Massachusetts, 1982.

Bayne, Bijan C. *Elgin Baylor: The Man Who Changed Basketball*. Lanham, MD: Rowan & Littlefield, 2015.

Carlson, Chad. *Making March Madness: The Early Years of the NCAA, NIT, and College Basketball Championships, 1922–1951.* Fayetteville: University of Arkansas Press, 2017.

Davis, Seth. *Wooden: A Coach's Life*. New York: Times Books, 2014.

Fisher, James T. *Communion of Immigrants: A History of Catholics in America*. New York: Oxford University Press, 2000.

Gleason, Philip. *Contending with Modernity: Catholic Higher Education in the Twentieth Century*. New York: Oxford University Press, 1995.

Goudsouzian, Aram. *King of the Court: Bill Russell and the Basketball Revolution.* Berkeley: University of California Press, 2010.

Grzybowski, David. *Mr. All-Around: The Life of Tom Gola.* Philadelphia: Temple University Press, 2019.

Harkness, Jerry. *Connections: A Memoir.* Ramsey, MN: Smith, 2018.

Henderson, Russell J. "The 1963 Mississippi State University Basketball Controversy and the Repeal of the Unwritten Law: 'Something More than the Game Will be Lost.'" *Journal of Southern History,* Vol. 63, No. 4 (Nov., 1997), pp. 827–54.

Isaacs, Neil D. *All the Moves: A History of College Basketball.* Philadelphia: Lippincott, 1975.

Johnson, James W. *The Dandy Dons: Bill Russell, K.C. Jones, Phil Woolpert, and One of College Basketball's Greatest and Most Innovative Teams.* Lincoln, NE: Bison, 2009.

Lenehan, Michael. *Ramblers: Loyola Chicago 1963, the Team That Changed the Color of College Basketball.* Evanston, IL: Midway, 2013.

MacMullan, Jackie, Rafe Bartholomew, and Dan Klores. *Basketball: A Love Story.* New York: Crown, 2018.

Mahoney, Kathleen A. *Catholic Higher Education in Protestant America: The Jesuits and Harvard in the Age of the University.* Baltimore: Johns Hopkins University Press, 2003.

McGreevy, John T. *Parish Boundaries: The Catholic Encounter with Race in the Twentieth-Century Urban North.* Chicago: University of Chicago Press, 1996.

McNamara, John. *The Capital of Basketball: A History of DC Area High School Hoops.* Washington, DC: Georgetown University Press, 2019.

Moran, Joseph Declan. *You Can Call Me Al: The Colorful Journey of College Basketball's Original Flower Child, Al McGuire.* Madison, WI: Prairie Oak Press, 1999.

Neary, Timothy B. *Crossing Parish Boundaries: Race, Sports, and Catholic Youth in Chicago, 1914–54.* Chicago: University of Chicago Press, 2016.

O'Neil, Dana. *Long Shots: Jay Wright, Villanova, and College Basketball's Most Unlikely Champion.* Chicago: Triumph Books, 2017.

Pomerantz, Gary M. *The Last Pass: Cousy, Russell, the Celtics, and What Matters in the End.* New York: Penguin, 2018.

Putney, Clifford: *Muscular Christianity: Manhood and Sports in Protestant America, 1880–1920.* Cambridge, MA: Harvard University Press, 2001.

Rains, Rob. *James Naismith: The Man Who Invented Basketball.* Philadelphia: Temple University Press, 2009.

Schumacher, Michael. *Mr. Basketball: George Mikan, the Minneapolis Lakers, and the Birth of the NBA.* New York: Bloomsbury, 2007.

Shapiro, Leonard. *Big Man on Campus: John Thompson and the Georgetown Hoyas.* New York: John Macrae, 1991.

Vargas, Ramon A. *Fight, Grin & Squarely Play the Game: The 1945 Loyola New Orleans Basketball Championship and Legacy.* Charleston, SC: History Press, 2013.

Withers, Bud. *Glory Hounds: How a Small Northwestern School Reshaped College Basketball and Itself.* Bud Withers, 2016.

Index

Index

Index

Index

About the Author

John Gasaway analyzes college basketball for ESPN.com. He has taught basketball analytics in the master's of sports management program at Columbia University, and holds a PhD from the Institute of Communications Research at the University of Illinois at Urbana-Champaign.

31901067639817